Otey's Journal

being

the account by

James Hervey Otey, A.B., M.A.*, D.D., L.L.D.

First Bishop of the Tennessee Diocese

of the Protestant Episcopal Church

of his travels in the Summer of 1851

in

England, Scotland, Ireland and Wales

Edited with notes

by

Edwin Thomas Greninger, A.B., M.A., PhD.

in memoriam

Gem Kate Taylor Greninger
B.S., M.A., D. Ed.
1919 — 1994

PREFACE

Several years ago a colleague at East Tennessee State University recommended **Pen and Sword** which contained Randal W. McGavock's diary of his travels during 1815 in Europe and Africa. She said my annual travel letter reminded her of Randal's writings. An editorial footnote in the book revealed that Henry Maney, another Nashvillian who was also in Europe that year, had written an account of his rambles overseas. These two engendered the germ of an article on Tennesseans abroad. Further stimulation came on learning that Bishop James Hervey Otey, a member of McGavock's party, frequently kept a diary and that the one for 1851 is at the University of the South in Sewanee, Tennessee. The holding turned out to be small pocket diary, an expanded account of its notes in a journal, and a letter to his wife from Great Malvern, England.

The more of the journal I read while preparing the article which ultimately appeared as "Tennesseans Abroad in 1851-1852" in the **Tennessee Historical Quarterly**, July 1990, the stronger grew the conviction that the journal ought to be published, an idea shared by my wife, Gem Kate. After the University of the South granted permission to publish it, the long, slow and enjoyable process began of learning more about the topics and people James Hervey Otey mentioned in the journal. Many times his forthright opinions and remarks on and about the English reminded me of the comments by the late Nelson Rightmyer, B.A., B.D., M.A., D. Ed., an Episcopalian priest and fellow historian, especially when with great delight he attempted to convince a Lutheran that the Episcopal Church is **The Church**. Otey's candidness gives his writing some of its appeal. He scoffed at some of the ways the service was conducted and was sensitive to perceived slights by Anglican clergy.

Without the help of friends this account may not have been printed. Such a confession could be regarded as a very loose paraphrase of the remark Bishop Otey made in Latin to his friend A. Cleveland Coxe on p. 154. The need for friends and outside help certainly applies here. First and foremost is Anne Armour, Archivist at the Du Pont Library, University of the South. She made the publication possible by granting permission to publish the journal. Thomas Edward Camp, Librarian of the School of Theology, University of the South, answered my cries for help by supplying materials more frequently found in an Episcopal seminary on the Anglican Church and its offshoots.

Beth Hogan of the Sherrod Library, East Tennessee State University, put me in touch with a researcher in New York. Mildred Kozsuch, who is retired from the Sherrod Library, allowed me to use her private collection of books on English cathedrals. Other colleagues from East Tennessee offered helpful suggestions and encouragement: Frank Williams, a former chairman of the History Department; Colin Baxter, a native Englishman, and member of the History Department; and W. Douglas Burgess, Jr. who provided translations of some of the Latin and deciphered a few of Otey's puzzling scribbles.

In the final stages of preparation Katherine Honour gave the manuscript the intensive treatment reserved for honors papers and theses. While seeking answers to some of her prodding questions I discovered material that previously had eluded me.

Last but not least, despite Gem Kate's desire to remain obscurely in the background, her patience and support must be acknowledged even though at times she insisted that were Bishop Otey alive, she would sue him for alienation of affection.

INTRODUCTION

In the spring of 1852 the Reverend James Hervey Otey, D. D., the first bishop of Protestant Episcopal diocese of Tennessee, joined a group of Tennesseans from the central section of the state in a trip to Europe. Three of them were literarily productive. Only one of the accounts was intentional. Randal McGavock, a graduate of Harvard Law School, later a one-term mayor of Nashville, and a Confederate lieutenant colonel who was killed in 1863 sent a series of letters, signed A TENNESSEAN [sic], to the Nashville **Union**. In 1854 these reappeared in book form as **A Tennessean Abroad, Letters from Europe, Africa, and Asia**.[1] More than a century later the diary which was the basis for the letters was printed along with his earlier and later diaries in **Pen and Sword, the Life and Journals of Randal McGavock, Colonel C.S.A.**

Despite the appearance of the McGavock letters, the honor of being the first Tennessean to publish a book of travels goes to Henry Maney who did not leave Nashville until July, and whose itinerary for two or three months interlaced with that of various members of the original group. Maney's account appeared as a series after he became editor of the Nashville **Gazette** in February 1853. Early in 1854 they were collected and published as **Memories Over the Waters or Stray Thoughts on a Long Stroll**.[2]

Bishop Otey, a long time diary keeper, continued the practice and quickly became so caught up in his experiences that he soon expanded the daily jottings in a pocket sized diary into a larger 5x7 book for the benefit of his family. For some reason following Otey's death no effort was made to publish the journal or the letters from Malvern describing his experiences at Dr. James Wilson's hydropath establishment, Graefenburg House. Instead his papers were donated to the University of North Carolina which ultimately shared some of them with the University of the South, Sewanee, Tennessee. These are in the Jessie Ball DuPont Library. The 1851 journals are among them.

This long account began on 12 May when he left Liverpool for London and ended twelve weeks later on his arrival in Paris. Probably better than any of his other writings the diaries reveal Otey's weaknesses and strengths while bringing out his forceful character. Although church

[1] Randal McGavock, **A Tennessean Abroad, Letters from Europe, Africa, and Asia**—NY: 1854 [Hereinafter **Abroad**]; **Pen and Sword, the Life and Journals of Randal McGavock, Colonel C.S.A.**, Herschel Gower and Jack Allen editors. (Nashville, TN: 1959) [Hereinafter **Pen**].
[2] Henry Maney, **Memories Over The Waters or Stray Thoughts on a Long Stroll** (Nashville, TN:1854) [Hereinafter **Memories**].

affairs have a prominent place in the account, he did not go primarily as a churchman but in hopes of achieving a cure for his water brash or heartburn which often left him weak and nauseous. Except for his involvement with the Third Jubilee celebrating the 150th year of the Society for the Propagation of the Gospel in Foreign Parts (SPG), he was an observer and commented forthrightly on what he saw. His visits to a number of churches and cathedrals did not set him apart from other tourists. Many Americans who have toured Europe have returned wondering if cathedrals and museums are the only attractions. In making his comments the Bishop shows his collegiate background in belles lettres.

Few ordinary travellers have the contacts with as many well known people as James Hervey Otey had. Some of these were the result of the Third Jubilee. At one of its ceremonies Prince Albert granted him the privilege of speaking briefly to the assemblage. Later he responded to a toast by the Lord Mayor of London at a banquet in Mansion House, the mayor's official residence. He had breakfast with the bishop of London and weeks later dined with the family of a Scottish bishop. He also met some of the thinkers and shapers of the Anglican church, people involved in the controversies rising out of the Oxford Movement such as Samuel Wilburforce, bishop of Oxford, and Edward Pusey. Not all of Otey's relationships with the Anglicans went according to his liking. Even though the bishop was addressed as "Milord" in accordance with English custom, a practice that pleased him, Randal McGavock noted,[3] the evident snobbery of the British bishops upset the Tennessean. Reluctantly, he realized that the English prelates ranked him with the Scottish, Irish, and colonial bishops like the diocesan of Bombay. When Otey thought he was snubbed, he accused the English of being the most insufferable of any people under the sun — a rather positive statement for a man who had not previously been out of the United States.

One of the priceless gems in the journal is his astonishment at finding the aged duke of Wellington kneeling beside him at communion. Another occurred in the Scottish highlands where he shared a conveyance with Marie Amelie, widow of the deposed French king Louis Philippe and some of her family. He asked her son-in-law, Prince Augustus of Saxe-Coburg-Gotha, to put out a cigar which the prince did. The day before while visiting Fingal's Cave on Staffa, one of the Inner Hebrides, the bishop led the tourists in singing "Old One Hundred."

The diary is replete with historical and literary references. If his children and grandchildren looked up the people and events mentioned, they

[3] **Pen,** p. 191.

would have acquired a wide knowledge of English and Scottish history. Two tragic figures, Mary Queen of Scots and Bonnie Prince Charlie, fascinated Otey. Without a doubt his interest in Scottish affairs had been stimulated by the novels of Sir Walter Scott whose home he visited. He also talked with the sister of the poet Robert Burns at her home and went to Shakespeare's Strafford-upon-Avon, another station on a literary pilgrimage.

Bishop Otey hid little from these pages for they also tell of his anguish, morbidity, and melancholy. Frequently this was connected with thoughts of one of his three dead children. Once, however, it was sparked by a daguerreotype that he took to be of a living daughter, Mary. He became so ill he had to leave the American section at the Crystal Palace. Another occasion was on 9 June. He was lonely after some or his travelling companions moved on from Malvern where he had gone to cure his waterbrash. Music from a church organ added to his unhappy state of mind.

There are certain harmonies which invariably revive recollections of my dearly beloved and deceased children. Their images rise before my mind in the vivedness of a living reality, and the thought that I can see them no more, almost destracts me. I ask myself the question, can any state or enjoyment of future happiness compensate for the anguish of heart & soul which I have felt under my bereavements? Thou O God! Alone knowest and canst alone, make up of the fullness for our losses in this miserable world.

All in all, the pages of the journal reveal a strong personality, a man who could not be forgotten and who was not given to half way measures. The unknown artist who painted the portrait of Bishop Otey which hangs in a collection of distinguished alumni of the University of North Carolina caught the spirit of this complex man. One viewer saw in the painting the "reincarnation of a neolithic druid" and was impressed by the subject's "wizard-like character."[4] Perhaps those who accompany the bishop via this journal may find themselves coming under his spell as did his Victorian companions.

---

[4] These remarks by Dr. Arthur E. Bye appear in **The Chronicles of the Sesquecentennial,** edited by Louis R. Wilson (Chapel Hill:1947), pp.49 and 54.

State of the Anglican Church

In 1851 in Church of England was in the throes of troubled times. Over the past few years the church had been rocked by events that had shaken its complacency, and in that very year other occurrences ultimately helped bring about a reappraisal of some of its positions and attitudes. With some of the issues Otey was a bemused and curious observer, in others he took a stand.

Perhaps the most significant was the Oxford Movement which started in 1833 with a sermon by John Keble at Oxford University, hence the name. It was a reaction to Rationalism and secular Liberalism. These were perceived as threats against religion and the Church of England in particular because critics began demanding that it be worthy of the money given it. John Henry Newman and Edward Pusey were among the movement's initial leaders. They were scholars who looked to the past to find direction for the future. As a result emphasis was placed on the Apostolic Succession through which at ordination priests become direct heirs of the Apostles with the laying on of hands. This being a fundamental doctrine of the Roman church, some of the Anglican clergy now insisted that their church was the **via media** between Rome and Protestantism, thus furthering the concept of One Holy Catholic Church. To gain support for their ideas, the members of the movement issued tracts and hence were known as Tractarians. By 1845 Newman was convinced he would be happier as a member of the church at Rome. He joined, became a priest and ultimately a cardinal. Others followed including Henry Manning, a future cardinal, along with Archdeacon Robert Wilburforce who had been Manning's brother-in-law and was the brother of Samuel Wilburforce, bishop of Oxford.

Most of the Tractarians remained within the Church of England along with Pusey who was prohibited for two years from preaching because he stated from the pulpit that those who viewed the Eucharist (communion) as a commemorative sacrifice were consistent with the teaching of the English Church. Despite opposition the movement implanted some High Church ideas. More ritual was performed along with a widened observance of church seasons and holy days such as Christmas, Lent and Good Friday.

A similar development occurred within the Protestant Episcopal Church. At the beginning of the nineteenth century priests generally wore a long surplice without a cassock or stole. Before the clergy entered the pulpit, the surplice was replaced with a preaching robe having bands whereas at communion the surplice was worn. Slowly the surplice was omitted and altars were often bare of candles, flowers and crosses. Gradually as a result of the Oxford movement, communion was celebrated more frequently, often weekly. Candles, flowers and crosses reappeared, even robed choirs of men and boys along with stoles and surplices on the clergy.

In addition to the liturgical changes wrought by the movement it cost the Protestant Episcopal Church a bishop and several priests who became Roman Catholics. Otey was involved with one defection and troubled by another. As acting diocesan of Mississippi, he had to depose Pierce Connelly, rector in Natchez, who according to the bishop was the type "the garniture of Rome would attract." Despite this assessment, Connelly's action was heavily influenced by his wife who also took a vow of perpetual chastity so that Pierce could enter the priesthood. Subsequently she founded an order of nuns and died a Roman. Meanwhile her husband with their three children returned to the Episcopal Church and its clerical roll. For thirty years he served as rector of the American Episcopal Church in Florence, Italy. Otey was greatly saddened in 1852 with the defection of Levi Silliman Ives (1797-1867), bishop of North Carolina, a former Presbyterian. His earlier introduction of Anglo-Catholic practices and the establishment of a religious order at Valle Crucis, North Carolina appears to have triggered the final decision. Later Bishop Otey assured members of his diocese that their church was not being "Romanized" as most of those "who have apostatized" originally were from other communions. "They went out from us but they were not of us; for if they had been of us, they would no doubt have continued with us; but they went out that they might be made manifest that they were not one of us."[5] Furthermore he saw no evidence that Rome's beguiling influence was at work in the diocese of Tennessee.

In England the Tractarians were so intent in altering man's spiritual outlook that changes in the law were of minor importance. As long as state did not bother the church, they were not going to worry about worldly affairs such as competition and laissez-faire until these intruded into religion which happened in the G. C. Gorham controversy. Governmental interference in this affair was crucial in H. E. Manning's decision to go to Rome and perhaps in that of Robert Wilburforce.

[5] **Journal of Proceedings of the Twenty-fifth Annual Convention of the Clergy and Laity of the Protestant Church in the Diocese of Tennessee** (1853), p. 8. Since 1789 about fifty clergy have left the Protestant Episcopal ranks for Rome with more than half of these being initially from other Protestant communions. The most were in the years 1849 and 1852 when there were five. Next largest was four in 1855. One of those who left was James Roosevelt Bayley who was the first Roman Catholic bishop of Newark and later archbishop of Baltimore. Another was Edgar Wadhams who became the first bishop of Ogdensburg (NY). George W. Doane, son of George W. Doane, bishop of New Jersey, was another who made the move. (Raymond W. Albright, **A History of the Protestant Episcopal Church** [New York; 1964], pp. 242-43.)

The state became involved when Gorham appealed a decision by an ecclesiastical court. He had been given a political appointment to a living in the diocese of Exeter. The bishop refused to install the appointee as a consequence of views expressed in thirty-eight hours of intense examination, mainly on baptismal regeneration. The answer infuriated Bishop H. Phillpotts. Gorham did not accept the Anglican belief that man is washed and sanctified by the Holy Ghost and made an everlasting heir of salvation through baptism. After being rejected by the bishop, Gorham brought an unsuccessful suit in a church court whereupon he turned to the Judicial Committee of the Privy Council. The decision in 1850 by this body attributed a doctrine to Gorham which he did not hold and declared it not contrary to the doctrine of the Anglican Church. A storm of protest arose with a spate of books and pamphlets appearing. For Manning the decision was the last straw and it drew attention to the limitations of the Privy Council as an ecclesiastical court of appeal. Ultimately the archbishop of Canterbury installed Gorham.

As the controversy was still very much an issue, Otey was drawn into at least one discussion. Two decades later in America the dispute contributed to the split in the Protestant Episcopal Church that led to the formation of the Reformed Protestant Episcopal Church in 1873. The latter's Declaration of Principles denied in the fifth paragraph of the Forth Article "that Regeneration is inseperably connected with Baptism."[6]

For a long time the Church of England was loathe to confront the problem of declining membership. Finally in 1851 it did on "census" Sunday, 30 March, about six weeks before the Tennesseans landed in England. An official count was made of church attendance, Parliament approved because no question would be asked about church preference. No longer would the Non-Conformists fear that many non-church goers would respond to the question with "Church of England." The results found in the census were supported by a report released in 1854 of a survey conducted in 1851 by Horace Mann. Out of a population of nearly 18 million approximately five and a quarter million did not attend any church, 3,773,474 were members of the Church of England, and 3,487,558 were Non Conformists. Mann concluded that the rest were indifferent church goers. Apparently these figures came as a surprise to those who assumed that the English were a nation of church-goers.

Some people attributed the poor attendance to an insufficient number of churches. In 1824 Parliament learned that over 4 million souls had no place to worship. For example Manchester, a city of 187,000 had only

[6] "Gorham Case," **Oxford Dictionary of the Christian Church**. 2nd ed. (NY, 1974). "Reformed Episcopalians," **The New Schaff-Herzog Encyclopedia of Religious Knowledge** (Grand Rapids, MI).

22,468 church seats and Birmingham had 16,000 plus for a population of a hundred thousand. To remedy this the Anglican church began erecting new buildings and encouraging individuals to support the projects. Most of the donations were in Southern England from people who wanted more churches in their areas. As a result of private benefactors Brighton had five new chapels and Leeds one which was built through the efforts of W. B. Pusey. In response to this effort the charge was heard that the facilities were not properly utilized. During the afternoon and evening 66 percent of the seats were not filled. Otey, who twice had difficulty getting a seat, would not agree. He would have sided, however, with those who urged pew holders to open them.

Bishops such as that of London, Charles Bromfield, recognized during his tenure (1828-1857) the need for new churches and built over 200 thereby adding more pew space. Not only were more churches needed but also dioceses, and so two were formed raising the number to twenty-nine, Ripon (1836) and Manchester (1847). When others were sought, opposition in Parliament came from those who were against adding more bishops to the House of Lords. To meet the need churchmen resorted to suffragan bishops, an idea previously proposed. Later new bishoprics were created, steps were taken to equalize the sees and salary schedule was set. Thus all bishops with the exception of London, Winchester and Durham were paid the same.[7] Today with the exception again of the same three prelates eligibility for the other twenty-four seats in the House of Lords is determined by date of consecration. As Otey learned during the festival service of the Third Jubilee of the Society for the Propagation of the Gospel in Foreign Parts, this precedence determined a bishop's place in the procession.

Lack of trained clergy was another factor influencing the decline in church attendance. True the men were nearly all university graduates, but their preparation was in the classics rather than theology. Most of the clerics had had a few theology courses which were not compulsory, taught by instructors who made no attempt to liven the lectures. Prior to 1850 about half of the university graduates entered the ministry because it provided a living. After that date the percentage slowly fell as other economic opportunities appeared including a professional civil service. Those without influence often were forced to accept low paying curateships which apparently averaged £80 a year. Those with influence, like the Reverend Law whom Otey met at Dr. Wilson's hydrotherapy clinic in Malvern, often held several livings from which they reaped the finances

[7] According to **Whitaker's Almanac** (1989) present salaries of the English bishops are: Canterbury £31,870; York £27,820; London £25,870; Durham £22,745; Winchester £18,830; The others £16,915.

while another did the work. Law was a nephew of a bishop of Bath and Wells, G. H. Law, and a brother of Lord Ellenborough, a governor general of India.. Because the clergyman was a younger son of a baron, he was addressed as the Honorable Reverend Law. The curate system as it worked certainly did not help the morale of the poorly paid cleric whose wage was about the same as a skilled craftsman. Otey pointed this out in connection with three Anglican churchmen he met at Malvern.

An argument can be made that perhaps some of the remedies might have appeared sooner if the ancient assembly, convocation, had been active in each of England's two clerical provinces. These assemblies consisting of two houses, one for the bishops and other for "inferior" clergy, existed prior to 1717. They were prorogued that year by Royal Writ when the lower house of the Southern Province vetoed on attempt to censure the writings of Bishop Benjamin Hoadley.[8] That the assemblies had not met since was source of complaint Otey discovered. Exclusion of the laity was another. Within a year of the Tennessean's visit, in 1852 the convocation in the archdiocese of Canterbury was called into session whereas that of York did not meet until 1861. As neither had the desired third house, pressure continued until it was added in 1885. Today the convocations have become the General Synod. Thanks to Bishop William White of Pennsylvania the role of the laity in the general governance of the Protestant Episcopal Church has never been an issue because he insisted that the constitution give them a voice.

Many English non-church goers justified their absence by claiming not only that most of the clergy in the established church were not interested in the poor but that "selfish secularity" motivated these men. What might be regarded as a corollary justification came from both the rich and the poor. Each felt uncomfortable in the presence of the other even in the house of worship, an admission that evoked attempts to abolish pew rents. Mann argued that the perception of the church could be changed through the adoption of an aggressive missionary campaign which used the services of both clergy and laity as the Wesleyans were doing. The Non-conformists, however, were having difficulty winning the lower classes.

A number of the Anglican clergy defended their inactivity with a misconception as Bishop Wilburforce admitted. For too long the ministry was resigned to the idea that the cities were lost to the Church of England and that any effort was futile. This was not so. Although members of the Anglican communion were in a minority in a few sections of London

---

[8] Benjamin Hoadley (1676-1771) maintained that Christ had not delegated authority to ecclesiastics. (**New Columbia Encyclopedia**, 4th ed., 1975 [Hereinafter **NCE**]).

such as the Tower Hamlets east of the Tower, throughout most of the city the majority of the citizens had a loose attachment to the established church. Horace Mann concluded in his study that many of the five million not included leaned toward that church.[9]

The sense of defeatism characteristic of some of the Anglican clergy did not apply to Otey, an American. In his remarks in St. Martin's Hall on 17 June to Friends of the Society for the Propagation of the Gospel in Foreign Parts, he proudly informed the audience that when he went to Tennessee in 1827, no Protestant Episcopal church existed in the state, now there were twenty-one clergy.

While Otey was in England, some Protestants were still agitated over the so-called Papal Aggression. In 1850 Pope Pius IX, having decided the time was right for the restoration in England of Roman Catholic hierarchy, sent Nicholas Wiseman to be the cardinal archbishop of Westminister with twelve suffragan sees. In 1851 Parliament responded with an act that levied a fine of £100 on any Roman Catholic who used the title of bishop.* Although the Ecclesiastical Titles Act was never enforced, the law was part of the reawakened suspicions and fears of the avowed intentions of the Church at Rome to "convert" the English. The reaction led to signs painted on walls declaring: **No Popery! No Wafer Gods!** which Otey mentioned on 15 June. As would be expected, he supported the bishop and clergy of the diocese of Oxford in their November 1850 protest against the establishment of the Roman hierarchy. Their statement declared the Church of England the true and apostolic church and the missionaries of the Roman Catholic Church schismatic and intrusive. On 7 July 1851 Otey wrote the bishop of Oxford that he was in hearty concurrence with the protest and that he represented William R. Whittingham, bishop of Maryland; Carlton Chase, bishop of New Hamp-

[9] That argument appears to be valid today according to the 1986/87 edition of the **Statesman's Yearbook**. Although the Church of England's 1.7 million Easter and 1.7 million Christmas communicants does not compare favorably with the 7 million plus Roman Catholics or Non-conformists, of the 346,389 marriages in England and Wales 34 per cent were performed in the Church of England in 1985 and 30 per cent of the children born in England were baptized in that church.

A few of these arguments are heard today in the United States. According to a Gallup poll 44 per cent or 78 million American adults consider themselves unchurched, meaning they belong to no church or go only on holidays or for weddings and funerals. This figure is up from 41 per cent of 61 million ten years ago. "We do also nothing for the truly unchurched," exclaimed Reverend Alvin Illig, director of the Paulist National Catholic Evangelization Association. Most of the effort "is spent on maintaining the faith of the active." Paul Benjamin, director of the National Church Growth Association, a Protestant group, said "There's a tendency in the church to go along with business as usual. What most people want is a congregation that has warmth and a biblical emphasis." *Johnson City Press*, Sunday, 7 August 1990.

*The premier Roman Catholic noble, Henry Charles Howard (1791-1856), 13th duke of Norfolk (1842) supported the bill. With the appointment of an archbishop (cardinal) the duke's immense patronage power was greatly weakened. In reaction to the loss he flirted with the Anglican Church but prior to his death was reconciled to the church of his fathers. His son, Henry G.F. Howard (1815-60), the 14th duke resigned his seat in the House of Commons in protest of the bill which he ardently opposed. (**Dictionary of National Biography** hereinafter **DNB**).

shire; George Upjohn, bishop of Indiana; and William Green, bishop of Mississippi.

As the Tennessean expected to be in England during the celebration of the Third Jubilee, the same four American bishops authorized him to speak for them. On 26 May he wrote the archbishop of Canterbury, John Bird Summer, that he expected to attend the jubilee celebration because he had an absorbing interest in the society even though the diocese of Tennessee "never derived any direct assistance from the venerable Society." He knew from experience the hard work of the missionary and if there is any group of laborers in the cause of Christ and the Church it is the missionaries. Otey could write thus because in a sense he had been a missionary when he established the Franklin parish. Furthermore he had been a missionary bishop even though this was not part of the formal charge at the consecration nor had he been so designated in some of the territories temporarily under his jurisdiction.

A few segments of the jubilee celebration did not please Otey. he regarded the intoned service at the Cathedral of St. Paul on 15 June as child's play. "It is objectionable from its wearisome monotony and indistinctness." Then the next day at the actual celebration: "the services began—intoned 'again'—losing it seems too very much of their impressiveness and effect." On 22 June when he preached at St. Mark's Church, St. John's Wood on behalf of the society, his performance left him unhappy. He felt "the length of the service prolonged by the manner in which it was conducted—partly **intoned**" hurried him.

Otey was reacting to changes partly stimulated by the Oxford Movement. He wanted the rubrics to stay as is. "It is only in new places where the church and her ritual are unknown that there can ordinarily occur the necessity or expediency of changing in any degree that beautiful order in which we have hither to worshiped with so much comfort, pleasure and profit to our souls.[10]" In addition he was opposed to crosses and communion tables that looked like altars. To him altars meant Christ sacrificed again in Holy Communion. For this reason he refused to consecrate the Church of St. Andrew, Riverside, Memphis until the offending items were removed. While this was part of his own belief, undoubtedly it was influenced by the knowledge that many Tennesseans thought the Episcopal church was too close to Rome.

[10] **Journal of the Proceedings of the Thirtieth Annual Convention of Clergy and Laity of the Protestant Episcopal Church in the Diocese of Tennessee** (1858) pp. 34-41.

Episcopal Church of Scotland

In Scotland the counterpart of the Church of England was Presbyterian rather than Episcopalian. Once the Church of Scotland had bishops; but as a result of the country's troubles in the 17th and early part of the 18th centuries, the Crown came to regard the adherents of the Presbyterian church as more trustworthy than the tumultuous supporters of the older Episcopal establishment. Undoubtedly Otey was aware of some of the history of Scotland prior to his whirlwind tour of the country north of the River Tweed. Now the knowledge was reinforced by personal contacts with authorities of that Episcopal Church and by visits to many of the country's historic sites. This combination makes the Scotch portion of the journal almost a separate chapter and possibly even more interesting than the English one. Obviously, Otey was captivated by this experience.

The American was definitely conscious of the debt his Episcopal church owed to that of Scotland. Without the existence of the latter the younger American body might have had to wait two or three more years before it had bishops. In 1784 Samuel Seabury who sought consecration as bishop of Connecticut and Rhode Island reluctantly turned to the Scottish bishops. Prelates of the Church of England had been unable to perform the rites because Seabury, as an American, could not take the required oath of loyalty to the Crown. As the Episcopal Church of Scotland was now more or less a pariah, a loyalty oath was not required of its clergy. All the Scottish bishops wanted was the assurance that his credentials were in order. Unlike the English, the Scots cared not whether the legislatures of the two states approved. Unlike William Pitt the British prime minister, they were not troubled by the fear that the new American government might regard the consecration of a bishop as British meddling in American church affairs. Pitt's anxiety was understandable. A constitution forbidding the establishment of a national church in America had not yet been drafted.

Unable to secure the essential approval of the British government, Seabury approached the Nonjuring bishops of Scotland. (They had not taken the oath of loyalty.) On 14 November 1784 they consecrated him in a chapel at the home of Robert Kilgour, bishop of Aberdeen and Primus of Scotland. The other two were John Skinner, coadjutor of Aberdeen; and Arthur Petrie, the bishop of Ross and Moray. When Otey and Alexander Coxe (future bishop of Western New York) visited Aberdeen, the house was occupied by Skinner's son who was now the bishop.[11]

[11] Raymond W. Albright, **A History of the Protestant Episcopal Church** (NY: 1974) p. 144.

Seabury's difficulties paved the way for the change. Two years later Parliament removed the oath requirement for Americans but not for Anglicans as Otey noted at an ordination in St. Paul's on Sunday 15 June. First the ordinands, both deacons and priests, took the Oath of Supremacy and allegiance to the queen, "whereupon the ordination proceeded in all respects as with us." After the government changed its stance, the archbishop of Canterbury informed the American church that only three bishops would be consecrated, enough to assure Apostolic Succession. He also stated that none so consecrated would be allowed to officiate in any part of the British realm. This was a long standing disability which until 1864 applied to clergy ordained by Scottish bishops. With the way now clear for the preferred consecration by Anglican prelates, William White of Pennsylvania and Samuel Provoost of New York were consecrated in Lambeth Palace on 4 February 1787 by the archbishop of Canterbury, John Moore; the bishop of Peterborough, John Hinchcliffe; and the bishop of Bath and Wells, Charles Moss. Three years later James Madison of Virginia became the third American consecrated at Lambeth. Hinchcliffe's role in the 1787 consecration was in Otey's mind on his visit to Peterborough Cathedral.

Just as the Oath of Supremacy was an outgrowth of the Reformation so ultimately was the change in the structure of the Church of Scotland. It had the traditional hierarchy of priest, bishops, and archbishops. With the initial triumph of Presbyterianism bishoprics were temporarily abolished only to be reestablished twice. After the Presbyterians drew up the National Covenant in 1638 defending the Protestant religion (Presbyterianism), attacks on the Episcopal Church were renewed. Scots in the south signed the document but few did in the north. The ensuing reaction caused the Glascow Assembly to depose the bishops and assess fines against all those who refused to sign. After the Stuart Restoration in 1660 Episcopacy was restored with the Coventers now the persecuted. The issue was finally settled as a result of the Glorious Revolution of 1688 and its aftermath. The Lowland Scots generally supported William and Mary while the Episcopalian North favored James II, his son and grandson. Because the Highland Scots would not take the oath to William and Mary, their church was disestablished even though numerically larger than the Presbyterian. The Highlanders suffered after 1715 for supporting the Old Pretender and again in 1745 for choosing "Bonnie Prince Charlie" rather than the Hanoverians. Restrictions were placed upon their church because they stubbornly refused to pray for the Georges. In some parishes when the priest attempted to pray for the king, mumbling, coughing and other noises made the prayer inaudible.[12]

Church buildings were destroyed and limitations were placed on the size of a religious gathering. If more than four met to worship, they could be jailed as happened to several laity and clergy. To circumvent the restriction, four would meet in one room and four in another. As a result priests often conducted several services each Sunday. Seabury learned of these restrictions while a medical student in Edinburgh prior to his ordination in 1783. The prohibitions also explain why his consecration was in an upper room rather than a church. Here is where the local congregation worshiped. The celebrated Scottish historian, Agnes M. Mackenzie regards this consecration performed off a back street in Aberdeen as the most important event in the history of the Episcopal Church of Scotland during the period of its quiet and unspectacular persecution.[13] That the harassment had been effective is evident. By 1792 when the Penal Acts were repealed, the church no longer numbered two-thirds of the people as a century earlier: instead four bishops and forty clergy served the shrunken body. Small though it was the Episcopal Church of Scotland influenced the prayerbook adopted by the Protestant Episcopal Church in America at the triennial General Convention of 1795. The wording of the Oblation and of the Invocation were taken from the Scottish Prayerbook, thereby fulfilling Seabury's promise to the Scottish bishops. Actually the two items had been copied from the Anglican Prayerbook of 1549.[14] Because copies of the prayerbook were scarce as late as 1851, most having been destroyed, portions of the ritual, especially the Prayer of Consecration of the communion elements and the prayer of the church were printed and known as "wee books." Probably these were the "pamphlets containing the Scottish Ep. Com: Service" Bishop Skinner gave Otey and Coxe when they visited the younger Skinner in Aberdeen.

During the nineteenth century the Scottish church began recouping some of its losses with an increase in membership and new parishes. Nevertheless it was poor. In the earlier part of the century the annual stipend of some priests was £20 with a few as low as £10 while bishops received about £180. Thirty years later priests averaged about £100. At

[12] In May 1946 this writer witnessed a similar demonstration in Garmisch-Partenkirken when attending a reading of Goethe's **Faust**. During the indtroduction the speaker drew comparisons between the theme and events under Hitler. Whenever the expositor ventured into that sensitive area, a fit of coughing suddenly seized members of the audience. The coughs disappeared when he shifted to other ideas only to reoccur with the return of the touchy subject.

[13] Agnes Mure Mackenzie, C.B.E., M.A., D. Litt., **The Kingdom of Scotland**, (Edinburgh and London, Reprinted 1948) p. 305.

[14] Albright, **History of the P. E. Ch.**, 140. Marion Lochhead claims their origins are in the rites of Orthodox Church (**Episcopal Scotland in the Nineteenth Century** [London, 1966] See it's index under Liturgy and Prayerbook).

the end of the nineteenth century the salary of the incumbent at Kirkwall was £169, at Lerwick £173 with others ranging up to £610, this was greater than the £543 paid the bishop of Argyle whereas the bishop of Moray received £1,054.[15] As a result of the low salaries the bishops frequently continued holding the parish they served before their elevation even when it was in another diocese. Consequently diocesan visits were as infrequent as every three years when the confirming was done.

Otey could understand this duality for he was still rector of the parish in Franklin and later in Memphis because, like many of the Scottish bishops he supervised only a few parishes. Some years his salary was less than $500 on which he did far more travelling than any of his Scottish counterparts as his assignment at times included more territory than the state of Tennessee.[16]

Surely Otey never expected in the course of his discussions with the Scottish prelates that ten years later he too would face the issue of whether to pray for the president of the United States. During the Civil War Otey refused to break with the Protestant Episcopal Church. He maintained that despite the political break the unity of the Protestant Episcopal Church was not shattered. Thus the diocese of Tennessee was not a member of the Protestant Episcopal Church in the Confederate States of America. Because the diocese did not secede from from the older ecclesiastical body while Tennessee was one of the Confederate States the clergy were uncertain what they should do when the prayer included the president of the United States. Otey's solution: use his favorite, the prayer in the Ante Communion. It did not mention the president.[17]

[15] Lochhead, **Episcopal Scotland**, pp. 215-16. In 1993 the church consists of seven dioceses of 341 churches with a total of 57,194 members served by 209 clergy. The bishops now receive a standard stipend of £16,110. **Whitaker's Almanac** (1993), p. 420.

[16] Moultrie Guerry, **Men Who Made Sewanee For Makers of Sewanee Today** (Sewanee, TN: 1944), p. 8.

[17] After the Civil War Richard Wilmer, bishop of Alabama asked his clergy not to pray "for the president and all in civil authority" because only military authority existed in Alabama. General George H. Thomas suspended the bishop and the clergy. President Andrew Johnson revoked the order and helped preserve the separation of church and state (Albright, **A History of the P.E. Ch.**, p. 254).

The Great Exhibition

One of the first things Otey and his companions did as tourists on arriving in London was visit the Great Exhibition of the works of Industry of All Nations which Queen Victoria opened on May Day 1851 The exhibition was intended to show "the point of development at which the whole of mankind has arrived" and be a starting point for "further exertions." As Great Britain was then the workshop of the world, this exhibition was an excellent opportunity for Britain to proclaim the advantages of Free Trade. One building, the Crystal Palace, held it all in an iron and glass structure 1,848 ft. in length, 408 ft. in width, and 66 ft. in height. Work began on 30 July 1850 with the first iron column raised by 26 September. Seventeen weeks later nearly a million square feet of glass lay between 3,300 columns and 2,300 girders. This was possible because interchangeable identical parts were used. No column, girder, or gutter was different from the others. Before the building was open to the public, squads of soldiers jumped, rolled on the floors, made noise like a crowd to test the structure's durability.

The unique design won architect Joseph Paxton a knighthood because it made beloved Prince Albert's dream a success. Victoria was so proud of it that she made several visits, as did numerous other people. During the 140 weekdays it was open from May through mid October 6,063,986 people viewed the exhibition. Many were foreigners, but most were British who took advantage of the excursion rates offered by the railways. Daily attendance averaged 60,000 with 110,000 being the largest. No alcoholic beverages were sold. Water was free. Soda water, lemonade, and ginger beer were available from concessions operated by Schweppes. The firm estimated it sold a million Bath buns, 32,000 quarts of cream, 33 tons of ham and 113 tons of meat. One of the successful novelties was the "retiring rooms and lavatories." Profits were £180,000.

There were over 13,000 exhibitors with one half of the area taken by the host country and its colonies. Lyon Playfair, a young scientist, arranged the displays according to type: raw material, machinery manufactures, and fine arts. Machinery drew crowds as did the electric telegraph which Victoria used to send messages to the citizens of Manchester and Edinburgh. A poem by an unknown author summed up the displays.

> Harvest tool and husbandry,
> Loom and wheel and enginery,
> Secrets of the sullen mine,
> Steel and golds, and coal and wine...

All of beauty, all of use
That our fair planet can produce[18]
Except for the Russian exhibit all the displays were in place by opening day. As far as Randal McGavock and A. Cleveland Coxe were concerned the United States might as well not have sent anything. The former voiced his disappointment in his diary, "A larger space was appropriated to the U. S. than any other nation, expecting that she would do
her best, and the consequence is that nearly all is vacant."[19] Coxe in
Impressions of England classified the large amount of empty space a
desert. He blamed the government for not having America adequately
represented.[20] Otey, however, apparently as a result of his distraction created by what he thought was the daguerreotype of his daughter Mary,
made no comment on the merits of his country's showing. Emotions
forced him to leave without thoroughly examining the American section.

Events after the close of the "World's Fair" as Otey called it, left no
doubt about the efficacy of the design. The palace was torn down and
removed to suburban Sydenham where it served as a theater, concert hall,
and convention center until 1936 when fire destroyed it.

Hydropath

Although Bishop Otey went to England seeking a cure for waterbrash,
he spent nearly as much time in London as he did in Great Malvern, site
of Dr. James Wilson's treatment center at Graefenburg House. The establishment was named for the Austrian village where Vincent Priessnitz
(1799-1851) developed the hydropath procedures followed by Wilson.
The ancient Egyptians, Chinese, and Greeks were aware of water's medi-
cinal value and its relaxing effect on the body. Even John Wesley, better
known for his impact on Christianity, wrote a treatise advocating use of
water to cure ills, **Primitive Physicks or an easy and natural method
of curing most diseases.** As a prevention for apoplexy Wesley recommended "use the cold bath and drink water only" and for rheumatism,
"use the cold bath, with rubbing and sweating." His remedies were based
on common usage.[21] Priessnitz, who had no medical training, developed
his hydropathic treatment after observing animals use water to cure

[18] Quoted in Asa Briggs, **Victorian People, A Reassessment of Persons and Themes 1851-67** (Chicago:
1970) p. 38.
[19] **Pen**, p. 195.
[20] A. Cleveland Coxe, **Impressions of England or Sketches of English Scenery and Society** (Philadelphia:
1863, 5th. ed.), pp. 67-68.
[21] Quoted in J.H. Kellogg, **Rational Hydrotheraphy, a Manual of Physiological and Therapeutic Effects
of Hydriatic Procedures and Techniques of Application in the Treatment of Disease** (Battle Creek, Mich.:
1923, 6th, ed.), pp. 24-25.

wounds. He used water compresses to heal himself when run over by a cart. As he also cured his neighbors through the use of water, his fame spread. When the Austrian government sanctioned his work, he attracted followers including Wilson. Gradually the Austrian extended his procedure by using wet and dry packs to induce sweating followed by a bath plus a douche. He insisted that his treatment was not curing disease, but man. To accomplish his purpose poisonous drugs, intoxicating liquors, and adulterated food were eschewed in favor of water—between ten and twenty glasses a day—fresh air and exercise. Meals consisted of brown bread, butter, milk and water for breakfast and evening, meat and vegetables at midday. As a result of the prohibition of alcohol when Otey returned to London for the SPG Jubilee, he drank nothing alcoholic either for the toast or out of the loving cup, a special ceremony at the Lord Mayor's banquet. He merely raised the glass and the flagon to his lips.

In 1842 Dr. Wilson set up his practice in Great Malvern, a spa already known for water treatments. The bishop probably went there because Wilson's fame had been promoted by Sir E. Bulwer Lytton's **Confessions of a Water Patient** which appeared as a pamphlet in 1847.[22]

What the baths did not accomplish, bathing reputedly did in Aberdeen, where the bishop had his first swim in an ocean. Aside from a notation that the water was very cold and felt good, nothing in the journal attributes his state of well being to that swim. Years later, Coxe recalled that Otey frequently remarked during their travels in Scotland how much better he felt since the swim at Aberdeen. To this Coxe quipped, "Not the first time our Episcopate has been recruited from Aberdeenshire," a reference to Seabury's consecration. When the symptoms reappeared in 1852, Otey tried two spas in the mountains of western Virginia, now West Virginia, White Sulpher Springs and Sweet Springs. Again the waters provided temporary relief. Whenever the bishop was under tension as in the Summer of 1852, he became sick and nauseous.

Slavery

During the European sojourn Otey was defensive about one issue, slavery. Twice he was questioned by people who could not comprehend why Americans continued the practice. Efforts to convince questioners that they misunderstood Southern slavery were unsuccessful. In writing about the incidents he accused newspapers of spreading misinformation

[22] Robin Price, "Hydropathy in England 1840-1870," **Medical History**, Vol. 25 (July 1981), pp. 269-80.

and ill-informed travelers of misrepresenting the situation. On another occasion he was upset at seeing a black with a seat in St. Paul's while whites were without one. Otey was still simmering over being denied a seat until the usher learned the visitor was a bishop. He had no intention of denying the man the right to worship or become a Christian. In fact St. John, Ashwood where he and two of his children are buried, was built in 1840-41 for the Polk family and their slaves. At the outbreak of the Civil War his attitude was ambivalent. He favored leaving the Union to maintain slavery, but as has been shown he was opposed to dividing the Protestant Episcopal Church.

Two blacks were part of Otey's group of tourists. Mary was the servant of Mrs. Felicia Eakins. The other was Frank Parrish, a mulatto who was the servant of Edwin H. Ewing, a Nashville lawyer and former congressman. Whether Frank was a slave is not clear, for on returning to Nashville he was a barber at the Nashville Inn and in 1859 operated a shop in the St. Cloud Hotel where he loved to show his souvenirs of the Holy Land. On his way there in Egypt he was wounded with his own gun in an attack by local villagers on the boat carrying four of the original group from Alexandria to Cairo. An Egyptian had knocked the weapon from Parrish's hand with a big stick.[23]

Unfortunately the bishop's servants did not share his views on slavery as he learned in October 1862 when he returned to his home in Memphis, Tennessee after being gone for nearly six months. The absconding slaves ransacked his furniture before departing.[24]

The Writing

Glasses rarely are needed in deciphering the manuscript as the handwriting ordinarily is not cramped and with little scribbling; nevertheless portions of the original present difficulties for the reader. If the writer's family had trouble determining some words, they could always ask at a later date. Because the editor did not have this privilege, the insertion of a bracketed question mark [?] shows the latter's uncertainty. Undoubtedly in most instances the conjecture is correct.

Several factors account for the difficulties with the text. Some are attributable to the age of the manuscript. In the nearly a century and a half since the writing the ink has faded on some pages far more than on

[23] **Pen**, pp. 288-90.
[24] Ellen Davies-Rodgers, "Otey Family" in **The Romance of the Episcopal Church in West Tennessee 1832-1964**, (Memphis, n.d.) pp. 203-13.

others. The uneven quality of the ink mixture accounts for much of the fading. (In those days people usually made their own ink). Moisture has also had an effect on some pages along the outer edge.

Penmanship created a number of problems. Many of his capital letters were confusing---could it be an "I," a "J," or a "T?" Did the word begin with a small or capital "c?" Was it an "m" or an "n?". The double "ss" produced a lot of pondering because it was written old style with the first "s"being a vertical stroke extending both above and below the line of writing while the second "s" was attached to the first so that the combination occasionally was mistaken for a "p" or an "f" particularly when Otey wrote hurriedly. One of the more memorable examples where the writing produced confusion occurred in the effort to determine the name of an individual mentioned in connection with a statue in York Minister. Despite repeated reexaminations the name was always Sir George Smith., but none of the authorities consulted provided anything which showed that such a person had been "the chief agency in restoring peace between England and America in 1783." The riddle was solved by a response from the cathedral, it was Sir George Saville. A second and third look was often necessary for words following an ampersand because the symbol generally was attached to the next letter. In spite of all efforts some words, phrases and occasionally whole lines are unreadable. Where this is the case, (illegible) appears.

Because Otey had so much to tell and so little space, he resorted to dashes which separated ideas and sequences. Although at times this style gives the impression of having been written in haste, in other situations it heightens the impact such as the description of the various nationalities present in the Crystal Palace. Strike-overs are rare showing that the bishop was a man who knew what he intended to write before he did. The brief notations in the small pocket-sized diary guided his remarks. These notations were useful because the journal entries were not always made that day as is obvious in his recording of the remarks delivered before the Friends of the Venerable Society for the Propagation of the Gospel in Foreign Parts where later additions were made and so announced. Further evidence of this is the phrase "this day." Careful reading tends to indicate that the passage was written on another day. One of the times when the remarks were current are those written at Reading the day before he left England for France... "now I am seated here at Reading in my chambers at the hotel." Two days earlier he mentions having brought the journal up to date.

The writer of the journal is careful of his facts and open in the revelation of his pride and prejudices. His flair with words, his use of foreign phraseology, allusions to the classics and writers both ancient and contemporary—all definitely influenced by a belles lettres background—make this enjoyable and informative reading. James Hervey Otey, like all of us, is a person whom at one moment we want to praise and the next to damn.

The Bishop's Background

James Hervey Otey was born near Liberty, now Bedford, Virginia on 27 January 1800, the next to youngest of Issac and Elizabeth Mathews Otey's twelve children. Years later he changed the spelling of his middle name to Hervey after reading Meditations by James Hervey[25], an English devotional writer. Young James did not intend being a farmer and/or politician like his father who served in the Virginia House of Burgess for thirty years, nor was he interested in soldiering like his grandfather John, a colonel in the Revolution. Instead the young man entered the college at Chapel Hill, North Carolina in 1817 and graduated three years later with honors in Belles Lettres. On 13 October 1821 he was united in marriage with Eliza Pannell of Petersburg, Virginia, a union that produced nine children:

Virginia Maury born 1822 in Franklin, Tennessee, married Benjamin Blake Minor in 1842, had eight children and died at Richmond in 1900; Paul Hooker, MD, born 1825 in Warrenton, North Carolina, married Mary A. Bowles in 1847, one child, and died of yellow fever in Memphis, 1878;[26] Henrietta Coleman born 1826 in Franklin, Tennessee, married in 1846 the Reverend Charles Tomes who died in 1857, bore seven children and died in 1897; Reginald Heber born 1829 in Franklin, Tennessee, and died 1830; Sara McGavock born 1830 in Franklin, Tennessee, and died 1847 of brain fever; Mary Fogg born 1832 in Franklin, Tennessee married Daniel Chevilette Govan in 1853, had six children and died in 1897 of a brain concussion as a result of being thrown from an electric car; Eliza (Doona) R. born 1836 in Columbia, Tennessee, married Richard King Compton 1866, bore four daughters, and died in 1908; Frances J. born 1838 in Columbia, Tennessee, died 1848 of scarlet fever; William Mercer, born 1842 in Columbia, Tennessee, married 1) Pattie Compton in 1864 (died the following year in child birth), 2) Geraldine Gager in 1876, fathered six children and died in 1908.

---

[25] James Hervey (1714-58) was a clergyman, devotional writer and friend of John Wesley while at Lincoln College, Oxford. His **Mediations and Contemplations** written from 1745 through 1747 were filled with truisms and were very popular. By 1791 twenty-five editions have been issued. (**DNB**).

[26] See p. 164.

James and Eliza spent their honeymoon moving to Franklin, Tennessee where the groom organized Harpeth Academy. One of his students was Mathew F. Maury who gained fame with his charts of ocean currents which sailors use to shorten sailing time. In the fall of 1851 when Otey was in Berlin, he visited the celebrated explorer Baron Alexander von Humboldt who praised Maury's work.

The stay in Franklin was short as James received an offer from a private school in Warrenton, North Carolina. The move east changed his life. Despite Tobie Matthew,[27] archbishop of York from 1606 to 1628, having been an ancestor of Eliza Mathews, the future bishop grew up in a family somewhat indifferent to religion. Thus he was not prepared to lead in prayers, as expected in his new work. To help him a friend, probably the local rector William M. Green, gave him a prayer book. Its use led to the study of theology and to baptism by the Reverend Green. On 10 October 1825 Bishop John S. Ravencroft ordained him a deacon and then a priest on 7 June 1827. Returning to Franklin he organized the first Protestant Episcopal parish in Tennessee on 25 August 1827. In 1835 he accepted a call to Columbia, Tennessee.

With the formation of other parishes and the appearance of priests a new diocese was formed with the aid of Bishop Ravenscroft. On 27 June 1833 James Hervey Otey was elected bishop. Six months later on 14 January 1834 in Philadelphia, William White, bishop of Pennsylvania and others consecrated him a bishop making Otey thirteenth in succession.

For more than a decade his responsibilities extended from Kentucky and Missouri on the north and on the south from the eastern shores of Florida to the Pacific, the latter region being known as Indian Territory. From 1834 to 1859 he spent a considerable amount of time travelling by horse, coach, rail and steamboat through the diocese of Tennessee and the areas still without a bishop. His episcopal visits ranged from Florida to present day Oklahoma. Affairs in Mississippi consumed a lot of his time during the interim between the resignation of Leonidas Polk in 1840 and the consecration of William Mercer Green in 1850.[28]

For years Otey and his diocese were beneficiaries through missionary appropriations from older churches and dioceses. Without financial support like this James Otey would not have been able to go to Europe as friends raised money for the trip. Although later he was opposed to newer congregations appealing to those outside the diocese for financial

[27] The archbishop spelled his name Matthew whereas his American descendants changed the spelling to Matthews and also Mathews. See p. 159.
[28] See: Donald Smith Armentrout, **James Hervey Otey, First Episcopal of Tennessee**, (Published by the Episcopal Diocese of Tennessee, 1984); and "J.H. Otey," **Dictionary of American Biography**. (Hereinafter **DAB.**)

help with a building program such as the parish at Loudon, Tennessee proposed doing, the bishop favored the diocese helping a missionary in Texas.[29]

Bishop Otey remained a firm believer in education. As early as 1832 he urged the diocese to adopt a resolution favoring the establishment of "Classical and Theological Seminary"within its bounds whenever funds were available. The first educational institution, however, was the Columbia Female Institute in which Leonidas Polk had a significant part in the founding. Later while Otey was in Europe, the rector, the Reverend Franklin G. Smith, a married man, became enamored of one of his students. On the bishop's return Smith confessed the dalliance all the while insisting nothing had transpired; nevertheless he was relieved of his duties. This led to a closing of the school which reopened that October under William Hardin and operated until the Civil War. The reaction of many of the townsfolk to the dismissal hurt Otey, brought about about a renewal of his water brash, and prompted the acceptance of the offer to move to Memphis which had been extended while the bishop was in the city on his way home from Europe.[30]

Bishop Otey continued pressing for a school to train future priests and in July 1857 chaired the meeting at Lookout Mountain, Tennessee which started the drive that raised nearly $500,000 by the outbreak of the Civil War. Six months earlier on 10 October 1860 Bishop Otey, as chancellor or chairman of the board, presided at the groundbreaking. At the war's end the new bishop, Charles Todd Quintard (1824-1898), rebuilt on the ruins of the school now known as The University of the South at Sewanee, Tennessee.

Events Before the Journal Began

Exactly who promoted the trip to Europe is unclear. Mrs Felicia Grundy Eakins seems to have been one of the promoters. She was a daughter of the late Senator Felix Grundy, widow of William Eakins who died in 1847 leaving her wealthy, and a maternal aunt of Randal McGavock. Felicia persuaded her nephew to make the trip and on 25 January 1851 she and Bishop Otey conferred on the voyage. How the bishop became involved is unclear although the "go-between" could have been Charles Tomes, rector of Christ Protestant Episcopal Church,

[29] Otey, Diary, 31 March 1852. This is in the manuscript collection, University of North Carolina.
[30] From the day after Otey's return to Columbia at the end of March 1852 the problems of the Institute constitute one of the main themes of his diary for the year.

Nashville, a man whom Otey ordained in 1844. On 7 January 1851 the bishop wrote the rector that **deus volt** God willing, he would go to Europe. Later that day violent vomiting sent him to bed.

More than a month later, 21 February, Otey began arranging his papers, an act he regarded as prudent in view of the anticipated trip abroad. The next day he wrote his will and the following day confirmed his daughter, Elizabeth Ripley. Early in March he received a letter from Charles P. McIlvaine, bishop of Ohio, with an introduction to Charles R. Sumner, bishop of Winchester. Shortly afterward Otey wrote his annual report for the diocesan convention which would begin the third Wednesday of May in Memphis. Meanwhile on 5 March he heard through the Reverend Tomes that the packetboat **Waterloo** was scheduled to sail from New York on 11 April. Eight days after getting the news he left Columbia, Tennessee for Nashville accompanied by his wife even though their youngest child, Mercer, was ill but not with a life threatening sickness. On 18 March he boarded a boat in Nashville and reached Washington on the 31st. Here he called on the secretary of the Navy, William Graham who hailed from North Carolina; Daniel Webster, secretary of State; and President Milliard Fillmore. From the national capital He headed toward Richmond for a visit with his oldest child, Virginia Otey Minor, and her husband, B. B. Before leaving for New York which he reached on 7 April, he baptised a granddaughter.

By the 10th the other twelve members of the party had arrived and on the 12th all departed for Liverpool. The group consisted of Edwin H. Ewing (1809-1902), a Nashville lawyer, member of the Tennessee General Assembly 1841-42, and of the U. S. House of Representatives 1845-47; Frank Parrish, Ewing's mulatto servant and a Nashville barber; Benjamin Litton, another Nashville attorney; William Wales of Nashville; James B. Price (1832-1892) of Lebanon, Tennessee, son of Colonel and Mrs. M. A. Price. (His mother was a niece of Sir Edward Barry); James D. Maney (1830-   ) an older brother of Henry Maney, author of **Memories Over the Waters**. Although Henry went to Europe later in the Summer, their paths did not cross. Mrs Felicia Eakins and her seven year old daughter, Willie; Felicia's servant Mary Jane; and Maria Bass, a cousin of Randal McGavock (1826-1863). He was a graduate of Harvard Law in 1848, and after the travels was mayor of Nashville for a year, became a colonel in the Confederate Army and was killed at the battle of Raymond, Mississippi. Joseph D. Hamilton of Nashville was the other member.

A few days after they were out at sea a severe gale suddenly sprang up, destroyed some sails and threw the ship on its beam. When this happened: "Ewing said he was prepared for the worst, Bishop Otey trusted in the saving power of Providence, Hamilton and Wales pulled at the ropes for life and death. Mr. Litton bid farewell to his wife and children. Aunt Felicia gave up the ghost and our servants rolled in their bunks."[31]

The voyage ended on 8 May when the **Waterloo** arrived in Liverpool and the passengers disembarked.

---

[31] The material on Otey's activities prior to sailing came from his 1851 diary whereas the names of the group and the reaction to the storm are from **Pen and Sword**, pp. 171, 179 and 182.

The Journal
(Chapter 1)

May 12, 1851. Monday at a quarter to 12 left Liverpool by Railway for Manchester.[1] Passed at first, up an inclined plane, thro' a very long and dark tunnel. The total immersion of one in darkness, if I may say so, from the bright light of the mid-day sun, & for so long a time, was exceedingly unpleasant. After clearing the tunnel we very soon descended an inclined plane with velocity & though a deep chasm, as it appeared, walls of stone & solid rock rising on either side and presently found ourselves in the open country. For the first time, we beheld anything like a rural scene or prospect in England. Manufactories with their tower-like chimnies were pouring forth dark volumnes of smoke and beclouding the atmosphere around as far as the eye could reach. I have not seen a clear sunset, or a bright sunrise since I have been in England. Many persons express surprise that the air is always so full of vapor in this country. How can it be well otherwise, when vast numbers of furnaces with which the whole country is studded, are continually adding their contributions to darken the land, & shroud the heavens in gloom. What these various manufactories are producing we had no means of knowing could not venture on a probable conjecture. The car stopped at no place longer than minute or two and the passengers enroute are not crowded together as with us in large cars accommodating 50 or 100 hundred persons, from whom inquiries maybe made while proceding, but our party alone occupied only one apartment, in the cars, which are partioned off after the manner of stage coaches with us. The lands on both sides of the road, are in a high state of cultivation—every foot of ground appears to be put under requisition for some purpose by the farmer of horticulturist—even the little slips of patches of earth, sometimes found between the rails of the road and the embankment on each side of the road, are filled with succulent plants, & the fields are generally in small grain or grass all laid off into beds from 4 to 15 ft wide, perhaps even 20 ft. and the seeds so carefully put in that they appear to have been drilled. We arrived at Manchester in the afternoon early, in about 2 hours on the Railway and stopped at the Queen's Hotel. Sallying forth after a few mouthfuls of dinner, we [exited near?] public buildings having time only to inspect them on the outside, the Infirmary, St. Ann's Ch., St. Mary's Ch, and the Cathedral which we entered at the time the bell was ringing for

[1] Several of the Tennesseans went to Ireland instead of heading for London. Randal McGavock does not identify them. (**Pen**, p. 191).

evening services. We walked through the spacious building, every aisle of which on the floor was filled with slabs covering the bodies of the dead. The whole grave is filled in the same way—the inscriptions on many are scarcely now legible having been worn away by the constant passing over of persons walking. What perishable memorials these appear to be set off in various parts for officials. Thus some are marked for **magistrates**—guardians of the poor—1st Statesman, 2nd Statesman, 3rd Statesman, etc. This last designation I do not understand. Being very unwell with dyspepsia I returned as soon as I could to my Hotel and retired early to bed.

May 13, Tuesday, Rising early I walked a mile or more on the London road: on enquiring learned that the managers of the manufacturing establishments were very reluctant to admit visitors, so I made no applications. Passed Anderick green, a pond with swans, etc. Apsley Place— many houses and residences have notices stuck up—**"to let" "to be sold in chief &c** [etc.]." Met with a poor man in St. Thomas Ch: yard who informed me that for three weeks his family has not tasted a morsel of meat, that he is willing to work but could get no employment, that there were hundreds in his condition etc. Took the Coach at qtr. til 11 A.M. for Rowsley in Derbyshire. 4 inside and 18 outside—first came to Stockport a few miles from Manchester and a manufacturing town through which which the N.W. Railway passes over an immense number of arches of brick. The next place I remember is Buxton celebrated for the resort of Rheumatics to its baths & there is here an immense Hotel or Houses for the accommodation of visitors, and also grounds laid off into walks or promenades adjacent to a fine looking church founded 1811.[2] Leaving Buxton we pass various points of great interest which are minutely described in guide books & from which the accounts of travellers and letters are chiefly made up. There is Aswood dale Miller's dale etc. nothing more nor less than gorges through which a fine turnpike road wends along a stream called the Wye. The "cliffs" occasionally butting over the road are described in the English books in such terms as might lead the reader to suppose that there was no hill of mountain Scenery in the world, equal to or comparable with it. Addington is a small village of stone houses exceedingly antequated in appearance, with its striking little church. Ashford comes next, then Bakewell & lastly Rousley at which place we stopped at about 4 P.M. to visit Chatsworth as we intended. We determined nevertheless to employ the evening in a visit to Haddon Hall,

[2] Buxton is one of the oldest spas in Britain as the Romans used its waters. About 1780 the fifth duke of Devonshire began promoting its popularity. (**Shell Guide to England**, edited by John Hadfield [NY, 1970]. p. 648).

the property of the Duke of Rutland. After getting some dinner at the Peacock Inn[3] at Rousley where we had put up, over the interior door of which is the carving of a strutting Peacock and underneath the name "John Stevenson 1652". We set out for the Hall a mile and a half up the Wye. On our way and on our return we saw **hares** of an enormous size & also partridges feeding in the enclosures and which no hand is permitted in any way to molest without permission from the ducal proprietor. On arriving at the Hall situated on the bank or side of a hill a short distance from the little stream dignified with the name of **River** Wye. The first thing that attracted our notice was some Irish eayew [sic] trees in the yard of the keeper's house cut and trimmed so as to form the figures of a peacock, a fruit basket and bear on his hind legs. The Castle or Hall is built of stone, the floors and steps generally of stone, cement,or English oak. The larger or principal entrance has in it a small opening through which we entered under the guidance of a female cicerone who seemed to have learned her lecture very accurately or at least to repeat it very glibly, giving us the names of all the apartments and the history of every object. The stone step at the entrance has been worn ankle deep from the number of persons who have trodden upon it in the same precise spot. The porter's lodge is first on the right on entering. Here we saw the buck-skin doublet and military boots of the Duke of Rutland worn by him during the wars of Charles the 1st with the parliament.[4] I put on the doublet which fitted me very tight. Went into the Court formed by the quadrangle made when the various apartments were united. The first I shall mention is the Chapel at the entrance of which is placed a stoup or basin that held the holy water. It was erected before 1452. Pulpit and reading desk are on the left with the confessional immediately behind and reached by a flight of steps. The communion table or altar, is I judge, on the North end of the Chapel. Elevated above the Communion table is a window of stained glass now somewhat shattered and injured by pilferers, containing various figures Saints, Angels, etc. & also this inscription "Orate pro animabus Ricardi Vernon et Benedicta uxoris ejus, qui fecerunt Anno Dmi CCCCXXVII." [Pray for the souls of Richard Vernon and Benedicta his wife who erected this in the year of our Lord 1427.] A baptismal font stands in the South aisle. The floor is paved with rough stone slabs which must have been hard kneeling boards. The benches are equally rough and uncomfortable.

[3] McGavock, **Pen**, 192, identifies the inn as the Red Cock, very old but comfortable house.
[4] As the dukedom of Rutland was not created until 1707, the bishop errs; he should have used the title of earl. John Manners, the 8th earl, was the supporter of Charles I. .John Henry Manners (1788-1857) was the duke in 1851. (Burke's **Peerage and Baronetage**).

In the entrance part of the great hall to which we next proceeded after surveying the keep or prison, is a rude Roman altar found some centuries ago. It bears the following description according to Camden[5] who is perhaps the best authority DEO. MARJS. BRACIACAE. OSS[S?]IOUS. CAECILIAT. PREAFCI. IRO V.S. [a dedicatory inscription to the god Mars by a man who apparently held the office of prefect and who was a member of the senatorial order].

We entered the Banquetting Hall, a place which looked as though it was well suited for the rude entertainments of the Middle Ages when men went nightly to mingle strong drink. In the wall next to the door was fixed a kind of a hand-cuff in which was fastened the hand of the guest who refused after dinner to drink the prescribed quantity of liquor and the same was poured down his sleeve. The private dining room contains over the fire place the initials G. V. and the motto "Drede God and honor the king"—In the entry to this room is a picture of Abraham offering Isaac—also a very striking one of "Time destroying Youth," an athletic figure crushing a child in his hands—also the Transfiguration. The walls are generally hung with tapestry said to have been wrought by the hands of the ladies of the family. The ball room is very large, a card table or round table perhaps for refreshments in a recess on the side. A picture hung of Tomyris[6] [sic] queen of Scythia attended by her warriors, having the head of Cyrus thrown into a vessel of blood. At first sight I thought it was to represent the scene of the decapitation of John the Baptist, certainly a better subject in the ball room than in the former **State bed room**, an old bedstead 12½ feet high 6 feet long, once slept in by Queen Elizabeth—last by George IV.[7] The hangings are exceedingly rich, velvet lined with satin. Portraits in the ante chamber are of Queen Elizabeth, Charles I,[8] Prince Rupert[9]—Eugene.[10] Copies from Vandyke.[11] In the bed chamber is a looking glass called Queen Elizabeth. The frame is of brass and tortoise shell. I looked into it & thought of her who in her last moments exclaimed "my kingdom for an inch of time." We passed to a

[5] William Camden (1551-1623) was an antiquarian and historian. (**DNB**).

[6] According to a tradition Cyrus the Great of Persia (d. 529 B.C.) was lured into the Steppes of Russia by Tymiris, queen of the Sarmatians. When he was slain, she raised his head to allow the blood to drain. The Sarmatians were between Persia and Scythia (Harold Lamb, **Cyrus the Great** [Garden City, N.Y.: 1960], p. 271).

[7] George IV, king of Great Britain (1820-30).

[8] Charles I, king of England (1625-49).

[9] Prince Rupert (1619-82) was a nephew of Charles I and son of Frederick the Winter king of Bohemia. Rupert went to England and was a Royalist general in the Civil War and returned again after the Restoration. Later he was the first governor of the Hudson Bay Company. (**DNB**).

[10] Eugene of Savoy (1663-1736) was one of the great modern military commanders. His Holy Roman Empire army combined with Marlborough's to defeat the French at Blenheim (1704), Oudenarde (1708) and Malplaquet (1709). (**The New Columbia Encyclopedia** [NY, 1975] Hereinafter **NCE**).

[11] Anthony Vandyke (1599-1655) was a Flemish artist whom Charles invited to England in 1632 and knighted in 1634. (**DNB**).

room from which Dorothy Vernon[12] is said to have eloped with Sir John Manners, from which a flight of steps leads to a terrace in the rear of the hall where we found aged yew trees whose dark & funereal branches almost sweep the earth. History says that this domain in which H. [adden] Hall is situated was granted by William the Conqueror[13] to Wm Perceval his natural son. It remained in the family about two generations and was then given to a retainer named Avenell and finally about the time of Henry VI[14] became the property of the Vernon family. By the marriage of Dorothy Vernon to Sir John Manners the property passed in succession to the present Duke of Rutland.[15] The first duke of Rutland was created by Queen Anne.[16] The view from the terrace which is reached by a flight of stone steps, very narrow steep and winding, is very fine. The Wye meanders through meadows & lots of moist lovely grass is bordered by trees in places & meadow is stocked with the finest sheep. Saw at the Peacock Inn an original autograph letter of Lord Byron to the Editor of Galignani's magazine.[17]

Thursday May 14. Early this morning arose and took a stroll through the village of Rousley with Danna [sic][18] passing on our way the School house and chapel erected by the Duke of Rutland & of which I shall have more to say in another place. Also the Derwert & Wye the streams by which Issac Walton[19] meandered in his angling excursions. After breakfast which I did not relish having been very unwell since I left Liverpool, we took a carriage and horses from the Peacock Inn & proceeded three miles to Chatsworth the splendid mansion of the Duke of Devonshire. We entered the grounds, properly termed the park or deer-stalk I presume, through a gate, immediately after crossing the Derwert on a stone arched bridge, and drove slowly along a good macadamized road to the village of Edensor also the property of the Duke of Devonshire. We left Chatsworth to the right, passing it on purpose as the rules of the establishment permitted no entrance before 11o'clock A.M. The village of Edinsor is an exceedingly quiet place. The houses are constructed of red

---

[12] Dorothy Vernon died in 1584. (**DNB**).

[13] William the Conquerer was king of England from 1066 to 1087. According to the account on William the Conqueror in **DNB** there is no substance to the charge that he fathered Wm. Perceval or was ever unfaithful to his wife. **Shell Guide England**, repeats Otey's version.

[14] Henry VI was king of England from 1422 to 1461.

[15] In 1851 John Henry Manners (1778-1858) was duke of Rutland, being the fifth. (Burke's **Peerage and Baronetage** is a compendium listing the holders of the titles and descendants).

[16] Anne, queen of England from 1702 to 1714.

[17] Galignani's **Messenger**, a Parisian journal, was started in 1814 by John Anthony (1796-1873) and William Galignani (1798-1882). Having been born in London, they favored cordiality between England and France. (**DNB**).

[18] Benjamin Dana, Jr. (1830-98), from Watertown, Massachusetts, was a fellow passenger on the **Waterloo**. In 1870 he settled in England. (**Pen**, p. 185).

[19] Issac Walton (1593-1683) wrote **The Complete Angler or the Contemplative Man's Recreation**.

sandstone, all nearly new, built in the Gothic style of architecture and after the fashion of English cottages. The first object that attracted our attention was fine sire of the Durham stock, three years old of immense size, very fat—in so much that his lips seemed to be filled with flesh & his back rounded off in all directions. His legs and feet were small and neat as those of gentlemen dressed for the ballroom. Walking through the church yard & peering into the windows of the Ch: we saw some objects that excited our curiousity and led us to seek admission. This we did by calling on the Clerk of the village who led us to the door and showed us everything that was to be seen. This was not much. Behind the Chancel was a marble figure of the first duke of Devonshire, placed as in the tomb, hands folded and the body shrouded. The face was sculptured from a cast taken after death. Said to be very good. By the side of this figure reclines a skeleton, made of marble, representing human remains and intended as a memorial of the Brother of the Duke of D. whose remains were transferred to this place and reinterred. To the right and left ot these figures are the statues of Mars and Minerva in professional costume and very little becoming the sanctuary of Him who was the Prince of Peace. Besides these again are two figures with armorial bearings, & in a sense to the right Heft of the Chancel are representations of the Coats of Arms of the Dukes of D. In the vestry room or anti-room to the Church, for I could not exactly tell what it was, I saw a tablet containing a record of the names of individuals who had made bequests from time to time for the benefit of the poor of Edinsor. The present Duke is said to be very kind to his tenants. The comfortable dwellings in the village are rented at a mere song. Thus a building which cost £700 is held at a rent of £1.18 sh. Leaving Edinsor we soon arrived at the gates of Chatsworth. It is impossible for language to convey an adequate conception of the magnif-icence and taste of many things which combine to make up the concise [?] beauty & surpassing elegance of this imposing mansion. The gates are of wrought iron and partly overlaid with gold. Nothing it seems to me can surpass their gorgeous richness and splendor. After waiting for the introduction of a party who had preceded us a few moments, our turn came and we were ushered by the porter into the ample courtyard of the place. A gentleman and some ladies were left behind at the gates—He muttering & complaining but the porter paid no attention. Every party it seems is admitted seperately & in its turn. We were conducted to the Entrance Hall, called the painted Hall, so designated perhaps for the large pictures which form the sides and ceiling of the apartment. The subjects are a sacrifice to the Gods by Caesar, who appears in the foreground wearing something like a crown; His assassination in the Senate chamber, and his deification. The stair steps leading from this entrance Hall are supported by polished Derbyshire spar which receives the most beautiful gloss from the chizel [sic] of the artist besides being mostly of itself of admiration from the variety & richness of its colors. Over the Mantel Piece in this room is a Latin inscription giving a brief account of the foundation of the building & its completion in 1840. It was begun by the celebrated Countess of Shrewsbury[20] who was one of the most remarkable women of the day and certainly managed skilfully to advance her children in the World.

This remarkable woman had in her charge for sometime the celebrated Queen of Scots, Mary Stewart.[21] Entering a long Corridor from this apartment we were shown a variety of paintings, some coffers of artistic workmanship and a clock of the same description from Rome. Passing through various apartments, corridors, halls, chambers all adorned with tapestry or ornamented with paintings we came to a corridor that presented original sketched of nearly all the great masters by their own hands, a very curious collection. The Hall of Statuary presents some of the very best specimens of the greatest modern artists, Canova, Thorswalden [Thorswaldsen], Chantry and Powers.[22] The first that attracted my attention was Achilles, prostrate & drawing the arrow which had infixed his heel—shot by Paris, next a bust of Ed. Everett[23] by H. Powers and lastly a Napoleon & his Mother by Canova. The last figures I thought very fine. Their features were as perfect as ever delineated. It would take a volume to describe all the exquisite specimens of sculpture here exhibited. I must not however omit to mention one more, A Hebe by Canova & yet another, a Venus by Canova, I believe. The great state room is a magnificent apartment. Here are portraits of several members of the Royal family George 1,2,3,4th[24] Charlotte,[25] Mother of George 3rd; also the chairs used at the coronation of George 4th and Victoria which

[20] Elizabeth Talbot, Countess of Shrewsbury (1520-1608). She accused her husband, George, the sixth earl of having an affair with Mary Queen of Scots who was in his custody from 1566 to 1584. Mary briefly was confined in Chatsworth while she was in the custody of Sir Amais Paulet. For a recent short account of her activities see Israel Shenker, "Bess of Hardwick was a woman to be reckoned with," **Smithsonian** Vol. 22, No. 10 (January 1992), pp. 69-77.
[21] Mary Queen of Scots (1542-1587).
[22] Antonio Canova (1757-1822) Italian sculptor; Sir Francis Chantry (1781-1841) English sculptor; Hiram Powers (1805-73) American sculptor; Albert B. Thorwaldsen (1770-1844) Danish sculptor; Sir Richard Westmacott (1775-1856) British sculptor.
[23] Edward Everett (1794-1865) American statesman who is better known for having delivered the forgotten oration at the dedication of the Battlefield Cemetery at Gettysburg.
[24] George I (ruled 1714-27); George II (1727-60); George III (1760-1820); George IV (1820-30).
[25] Charlotte of Mecklinburg-Strelitz (1744-1818) was the wife of George III and mother of George IV. Augusta of Saxony (1719-72) was the mother of George III.

articles the Duke claims in virtue of his office as Lord Chamberlain.[26] A great many smaller objects than these but very interesting I can but refer to without attempting a description—Portraits of the Emperor and Empress of Russia,[27] a very fine engraving of Napoleon, of Wellington & others, especially Ch: J. Fox,[28] of the Duke of Devonshire, his Bro & other members of his family, especially Lady Burlington;[29] Also two of the exquisite carved vases of Malachite, presents from the Emperor of Russia; also a clock of the same material by the same.

A room called the Court room has in it a canopy, the tapestry of which was the work of Mary, Queen of Scots and has been recently transferred to a ground of black velvet. Also in the same apartment two chairs of the same kind of workmanship by the same hand. In one of the windows was a case containing an alabaster preparation intended to represent the al(legor)y (?) [blurred] of the dead on the morning of resur(rection?) [blurred]. It is one of the most affecting and effective representations I ever saw. The crust or covering of the tomb is presented as bursting & is very natural & beneath this the head of a child arising and a female head looking up expressive of the mingled emotions of fear, joy, confidence and hope. Leaving the mansion so replete with ornament in every part as even to weary ones unaccustomed to such profuse ornateness, we commenced our stroll through what may perhaps best be termed the pleasure grounds of Chatsworth. We were first shown into a greenhouse, containing an immense number of Japonicas of all varieties, most of them at this time out of bloom. Next we looked at a great number of flowers here and in the open air. Then crossing an extensive grass plot, plot, perfectly smooth, and soft as velvet, we advanced to a waterfall that descended by a succession of mimic cataracts from the high hill in the rear of Chatsworth & was finally conducted by subterranean passages to reservoirs nearly level with the floor of the mansion. While we were looking at this fixture, our guide gave a signal to a man near the foot of the hill above us and forthwith two fountains began to play & send volumes of snow white spray, 15 or 20 feet high. From the fountain to the place where we stood was about 350 or 400 yards and all the way in the

[26] The Lord Chamberlain theoretically manages the royal household. Today this hereditary office is primarily ceremonial and functions on occasions such as a coronation.

[27] The tsar and tsarina of Russia probably were Nicholas I who reigned from 1825/26 to 1855 and Charlotte of Prussia (1798-1870).

[28] Charles J. Fox (1749-1806) was a British statesman, sometime cabinet member, and proponent of liberal parliamentary reform. (**DNB**).

[29] In 1851 William Spencer Cavendish (1790-1858) was the 6th duke. His younger brother George Augustus became earl of Burlington and married Elizabeth, daughter of the earl of Northhampton. She probably was the lady Burlington mentioned by Otey. As the 6th duke died without direct heirs, the title passed to the 2nd earl of Burlington. (Burke's **Peerage**).

bed of the artificial stream was a succession of terraces rising one above another three or four steps at a time, each successive ascent of the terraces. After the fountains had nearly ceased playing we observed a minature flood of water descending towards us and at each descent from terrace to terrace or from step to step presenting a gradual lengthening belt of silver unfolding itself and approaching our feet until the whole was an uninterrupted stream of white glittering in the sunshine & seeming so beautiful was the whole scene. Pursuing our way along a gravelled walk that winded among rocks piled up as one would imagine by the hand of nature & along the foot of frowning precipices & under arched ways over which rocks hung pendent & some of which were so accurately balanced that you could by a slight effort set them to moving or oscillating, we at last came to a more than usually wild looking spot hemmed in on every side by rocks. Behind one of them our guide stepped & in a moment a tree apparently fresh & green began to send forth jets d'eau from every stem, branch, twig & leaf and so encrusted itself in a shower of silver. It was enchanting. Never had I witnessed such a display of art and cunning from the hand of the artificer. Here was something that excelled Xerxes tree of pearls[30] & requiring infinitely more skill to construct. The tree was made of copper & unless attention had been particularly called to it, the passer-by would hardly observe that it differed materially from a hundred other evergreens around it.

Passing under a natural archway of rocks—natural as it seemed—though it was all made by the hand of men & even the cliffs that were butting above us had been formed by cementing small fragments of rocks together, till they assumed the gigantic proportions of those vast masses that frown on the mountains brow. Passing by a narrow passage under the arch before us, we came to a large mass that appeared completely to block the way. I was just about to propose to push one of the party over the obstruction when our guide with his hand turned the whole mass upon a pivot and opened an anple passageway at both ends. After viewing many strange and novel sights, in which it appeared impossible to tell whether nature or art had the principle part in forming, we passed to an immense conservatory or green house made of glass and executed by the same gentleman, Mr. Patten [Paxton][31] who designed the Crystal Palace.

[30] Perhaps Otey meant Xerxes' plane tree instead of tree of pearls. According to Herodotus when Xerxes was enroute in 481/80 B.C. to invade Greece, he saw a beautifully formed plane tree near the River Maeander (Menderes) in western Asia Minor. The Persian ruler was so pleased that he ordered it decorated with golden ornaments and placed an "immortal" in charge of it. (The immortals were the elite corps of his army.) The plane tree has broad leaves which make it a favorite shade tree.

[31] Sir Joseph Paxton (1803-65) began as a gardiner and became estate manager at Chatsworth. His design of the conservatory there served as the model for the Crystal Palace in 1851 which he also designed and for which he was knighted. (**DNB**).

Here were hundreds & thousands of tropical plants & trees and shrubs flourishing in a tropical climate. The whole building is warmed by pipes filled with hot water which traverse the building often enough to extend in a straight line to a distance of four miles. Many rare & delicious fruits flourish in this conservatory which appear to waste their sweetness on the air with the fragrance of myriads of flowers blooming around, for the Ducal proprietor is seldom here to enjoy them. Like Solomon of old he has gathered around him all the delights of the sons of men. Two or three hundred servants obey his beck & nod in the lordly mansion. His streams abound with fish. His fattings [?] strong in every mead sheep by hundreds & deer by the thousands wander the hills and recline under the far spreading and deepening shades of his forests, a library rich with the productions of ancient & modern lore spreads its treasures before him and gold & precious stones are at his command to satisfy even a morbid taste for them & with them all, we may ask, is he contented? is he happy? No one can, I opine, answer that question except himself & Him who knows his heart. I returned to [from?] Chatsworth really oppressed with a feeling of satiety which the eyes had suffered in the number & variety of beautiful & rare things which I had seen. After dinner or rather lunch taking a carriage & horses, we rode to Affreton (Afferton) in the neighborhood of Newstead Abbey, and put up at the George I Inn, kept by Mrs. Rebecca Allen. Here I became acquainted with a Rev. Mr. Morse, a deacon of the established church who appeared to be a well meaning & good man. I walked with him to his church but through a mistake as to the key brought, we could not get admittance.

(Friday May 15,) Taking a carriage after breakfast we drove 8 miles or perhaps 12 to Newstead Abbey, situated in what appeared more like a native forest than anything else we have seen in England: some open grounds, in which we saw numbers of Rabbits [sic] or hares, lie to the right & left of the road in its winding course from the entrance or public highway. A pond appears on our left somewhat in the rear of the building & another a little to the right in front. Several pleasure boats were lying at anchor on its still bosom. Driving up to the principal entrance, we were quickly ushered into an ante-room & the housekeeper quickly made her appearance to conduct us through the various apartments. I pretend not to give a description of this ancient pile, so famous for being the residence of Lord Byron & from whom it derives its chief interest. It is in Sherwood forest once the haunt of Robin Hood & his band of outlaws that loved the greenwood & is said to have been founded [.......blurred insert] by Henry II shortly after the assassination of Thomas a [sic]

Becket.[32] The front of the building is accurately portrayed in most of the drawings which we find in the parlor books & galleries of magazines which are found on almost every center table in our Country.

Ivy the inexorable accompaniment of all ancient buildings is seen creeping over the walls & climbing up to the very battlements of the towers. In the entrance room we saw a Canadian Canoe, almost the only object of attention. The floor above this is in joined arches. Hence we entered the Monk's reception room & were politely requested by the Housekeeper to record our names in a book kept for that purpose. We were next ushered into Lord B's sleeping apartment which looks out on the sheet of water in front of the House. Everything in this chamber is kept in as nearly the same condition as possible as when occupied by the great poet. Very few ornaments are here, the portrait of Ch: J. Fox & some views of Cambridge & Oxford constitute the whole. Adjoining this chamber is a sleeping room & in it a portrait of a favorite tenant called "Old Joe Murray" pipe in hand. Next we entered a room called the Pope's room and sometimes the haunted chamber because it is said it is yet visited by the ghost of some restless monk. We from this place entered the Library; a fine collection of books, all most conveniently arranged. The portraits in the library are those of the Countess of Rutland, Nell Gwynne,[33] Mrs Hughes [?], Earl of Rutland, Sir Jno. Byron first lay owner of Newstead, and the portrait of Col Wilderman[34] & his brother.[35] Here also is seen a very curious bell from Pigpo[36][?] without a tongue or clapper & is sounded by being struck, as a gong. Passing through a corridor having several pieces of antique furniture we entered the Tapestry bedroom, fitted up expressly by the Byrons for Ch: II. Portraits of Ch 2d and his mother Hen[retta] Maria[37] are here seen. Also the state bed is here highly ornamented. This apartment was occupied if I remember right by Wash [sic] Irving on a visit to Newstead and he gives

[32] In December 1170 four knights thinking they were acting in accord with the wishes of King Henry II (ruled 1154-89) slew Thomas à Becket, archbishop of Canterbury in his cathedral. The spot where he fell promptly became a shrine and Thomas was declared a saint in 1173. ("Thomas à Becket, Saint" **NCE**).

[33] Nell Gwyn (1650-87), an English actress who was a mistress of Charles II, bore him two sons. (**DNB**).

[34] In 1817 Major (later colonel) Thomas Wildman (1787-1859) bought Newstead Abbey from Thomas Clawton for £95,000. He had been a schoolmate of Byron's at Harrow and served in the fighting on the Iberian Peninsula. At Waterloo he was an aide-de-camp to the earl of Uxbridge, later the marquis of Anglesey, and was slightly wounded. (Washington Irving, "Newstead Abbey" in **Crayon Sketches** [NY, 1889], p. 346; Frederick Boase, **Modern English Biographies** [London, 1897, Reprint 1965] VI, p. 875).

[35] John Wildman (1794?-1877), a younger brother of the colonel, was also a soldier having likewise served in the Light Dragoons from 1813. He was present at Waterloo and became a colonel in 1857. (**Mod. Eng. Bios.** VI, p. 875).

[36] Pigpo[?] — could the Bishop have meant Ningpo, one of the treaty ports opened by the Chinese to foreign trade after the Opium War. It was known for its temples and monasteries. From 1911 to 1949 the city appeared on the maps as Ninghsien. (**NCE**).

[37] Henrietta Marie (1609-69) was the wife of Charles I and daughter of Henry IV of France and Marie de Medici. Henrietta left England in 1644 and returned for a few years after the Restoration of Charles II. (**DNB**).

a detailed and minute description of everything in it. Irving also slept in Byron's Chamber and in his bed. From this room we have a view of the monument erected by Bryon over his dog called Boatswain and here I may as well say all I shall say about the dog. An inscription on the monument set forth the following

"Near this spot
are deposited the remains of one
who possessed beauty without vanity,
strength without insolence,
courage without ferocity,
and all the virtues of man without his vices.
This praise, which would be unmeaning flattery
if inscribed over human ashes
is but a just tribute to the memory of
BOATSWAIN a dog
who was born at Newfoundland May 1803
and died at Newstead Abbey, November 18, 1808"

Alas poor Yorick![38] alas for poor Byron! who would find nothing better in God's world upon which to lavish affection than a dog! He should have said his dog was **whelped** and not **born** and **in** Newfoundland—**at** refers to a particular locality. **Tapestry dressing room**—the chief thing worthy of note here is a most expensive figure of time, also a portrait of Sarah Jennings the Duchess of Marlborough.[39] **King Edward 3rd[40] bedroom** used by that king on a visit. Here are seen a cabinet inlaid with glass mirrors, a dressing table with a glass cover and a tripod stand once the property of Queen Elizabeth. Portraits, Queen Mary of England,[41] Mary of Scotland, Richard III, Henry IV, Henry 8th,[42] Duke D' Artois.[43] The bed stead [?] bears the date 1630. Henry 7th[44] lodging--the carvings of chairs as well as the coverlets of bed in this and several other rooms is the work of Mrs. Wildman who seems to have great taste in this crewel [?] of female industry. Portrait of the unfortunate duke of Monmouth,

[38] Yoirck is the jester of the king of Denmark in Shakespeare's **Hamlet**.

[39] Sarah Jennings (1660-1744) was the wife of John Churchhill, duke of Marlborough (1659-1722), and a confidante of Queen Anne until they quarreled over Whig cabinet appointments. (**DNB**).

[40] Edward III reigned as king of England from 1327 to 1377.

[41] Queen Mary who reigned from 1553 to 1558 was the daughter of Catherine of Aragon and half sister of Elizabeth.

[42] Richard III was king of England from 1483 to 1485; Henry IV from 1399 to 1413; and Henry VIII from 1509 to 1547.

[43] The Duke d´Artois probably is the Comte d´Artois, later Charles X of France from 1824 to 1830 when he lost his throne in a rebellion. He was the younger brother of Louis XVI and Louis XVIII.

[44] Henry VII who reigned in England from 1485 to 1509 was the first of the Tudors.

natural son of Charles 2d & beheaded by James II is here.[45]

Next to this apartment comes the duke of Sussex's[46] room chiefly noted for a fine portrait of **Boatswain**, the faithful and honored friend of Byron. After leaving this room we entered the large drawing room, a magnificent apartment and adorned with many and exquisite specimen of art. The portraits are the most attractive objects of attention viz: dogs and stag finely conceived and executed, portraits of Sir John Gardiner[47] and lady, of George I, Mother of Geo III,[48] Geo: II, Queen Mary wife of Wm 3rd[49]—of Lord Byron by Phillips[50] (We were informed that Phillips had to take three portraits before he succeeded in getting one to please the poet), of Wm 3rd, George III, Earl of Arundel,[51] etc. At the west end of the room is a full length portrait of the late duke of Sussex Col & Mrs Wildman & other members of his family.

At the east end stands a richly ornamented cabinet, the depository now of Lord Byron's drinking cup or bowl. It is the skull of a monk which was found in a stone coffin in or near the Abbey, and which Byron had bound with silver & polished: an act in keeping with many other parts of his short and sad history. The inscription is well known: beginning "Start not, nor deem my spirit fled." From this splendid apartment we entered the large dining room, once the refectory of the Abbey. It is hung around with the stag's antlers, various specimens of ancient &c [etc.] of modern armor. Among the latter are four helmets, breastplates & of cuirasseurs taken from the field of Waterloo. In the deeds of which "well foughten field" the present proprietor of Newstead bore an honorable if not conspicious share. He was aid de camp [sic] to the Earl of Anglesea.[52] Adjoining the banquetting Hall is a room called the breakfast room--remarkable only for a very exquisite portrait of Rembrant [sic][53]

[45] James Scott, duke of Monmouth (1649-85), a son of Charles II by Lucy Walter (1630-1658). His claim to the throne rested on whether Charles had married Lucy as some contended. After James II came to the throne in 1684, Monmouth led a rebellion which was suppressed by Sir John Churchill and was beheaded for treason. (**DNB**).

[46] Augustus, Duke of Sussex (1773-1843) was the ninth of George III's thirteen children. His secret marriage to Lady Augusta Murray was declared null even though two children were born to it. He then married Lady Ceclia Gore. (**DNB**). Wildman was an equerry to the duke. (Boase, **Mod. Eng. Bios.** V, p. 875).

[47] Major General John Gardiner was knighted in 1838 (Wm. A. Shaw, **The Knights of England** [Baltimore: 1971], I, p. 234).

[48] The mother of George III was Augusta (1719-72), dowager princess of Wales. (**DNB**).

[49] Mary II, a daughter of James II, shared the throne with her husband as William and Mary (1688-93). On her death he reigned as William III until 1702.

[50] Thomas Phillips (1770-1845) painted two portraits of Byron and also one of the duke of Sussex. (**DNB**).

[51] The Earl of Arundel probably is Thomas Howard (1585-1646) who excavated statuary in Rome and later gave it to Oxford University. A society to promote public interest in art has been named after him. (**DNB**).

[52] At the Battle of Waterloo William Henry Paget (1768-1854) was known as the earl of Uxbridge and was second in command of the British forces. He was wounded and lost an arm. For his role in the victory he was created Marquis of Anglesey. Along with Colonel Wildman and twenty-five other officer veterans of the battle he helped Wellington celebrate the thirty-sixth anniversary of the event on 18 June 1851. (**Times**, 19 June 1851).

[53] Rembrandt van Rijn (1606-69), a Dutch artist.

by himself and the Infant Saviour by Van Eyck.[54]

The Chapel, a small room fitted up with reading desk, communion table for divine worship, the seats for the proprietor & family are elevated above those intended for domestics which are nearly on a level with the chancel. In a glass-stained window over the pulpit are figures of the Twelve Apostles.

I quitted Newstead Abbey with a feeling of weariness and also sadness. I saw much and heard much that made me feel sorry for poor Byron while it depressed him in my estimation. The only true and solid reputation must be built upon virtue.

Leaving Newstead we drove by several pretty villages, among them Annesley famed in Bryon's verse till we came to Hacknall [Hacknell] in the church of which the poet is entombed with several other members of his family, his mother and other ancestors. An inscription on a plain marble slab makes mention of the fact of his burial in St. James Church, the date and place of his birth and burial, etc. Retiring from the Church which was undergoing repairs for the first time in fifty years we found ourselves the objects of the intense curiosity on the part of the men, women & children of Hacknal [sic]. They followed us in crowds wherever we turned. At last I stopped and said "My good people why do you gaze at us? Did you never see strangers before? Is it because we came from a foriegn land?" Yes, they said. We hope you will excuse us; but never seed people from so far as we know on ye. Well said we are glad to see you and hope you are glad to see us. Look as much as you chose. This little speech seemed to please them very much.[55] And when we drove off they almost shouted "**goodbye** goodbye!" Taking the cars at Hacknall station we were soon brought to Nottingham once famous for the wearing of stockings. Its noble old castle appears to be in ruins. It was at this place that the Unfortunate Ch:I first displayed the royal standard in the fatal contest on which he entered with his parliament & made an appeal to arms.[56] From Nottingham we soon reached Derby and shortly after arrived at Birmingham the great manufacturing town of England and stopped at the **Hen & Chickens**.

Friday May 16. Heard nothing from Mr. E. T. Morris to whom I wrote

[54] There were two Van Eyck brothers, Hubert (c. 1370-1426) and Jan (1390-1441). The work mentioned by Otey probably was by the younger man.

[55] According to McGavock the citizens were attracted by his red beard and 6 ft. 2 frame and the black skins of Frank Parrish and Mary, the servant of Felicia Eakins. Parrish was Edwin Ewing's servant. His status is not clear. If he was a slave why did he have a gun that he used that December in Egypt when the party McGavock, Ewing, and Parrish were travelling with up the Nile. Their boat was attack by some villagers who were driven off. One of the natives knocked the gun from Parrish's hand and then used it to wound him. (**Pen**, pp. 193, 288-90).

[56] In 1642 when Charles I raised his standard in Nottingham, it signaled the opening of the Civil War.

last night and was therefore obliged to rely on some other resource to get into the factories. This was more easily done than I expected: the proprietor of the Hen & Chickens gave us tickets and we first went to the Paper Mache works. The whole very curious & the products were marvellously beautiful. Next to the patent electro plate factory this was more wonderful and splendid still & lastly to a glass manufactory. It would occupy more days than hours taken to examine the manufacturing establishments of Birmingham. The operatives in the main appeared healthy. I was struck at the smallness & apparent frailty & age of the buildings in which the various works were carried on. Leaving Birmingham a little after 12. (Saw at the station Gen Sir Ch: Napier,)[57] We passed Coventry with its beautiful spires and here turned off the main railway to go to Kenilworth, Warwick, &c. We arrived at Kenilworth in half an hour & were conveyed by an omnibus through a considerable village to the views of the Castle. The ruins are striking & grand indeed. The old entrance to the Castle is in appearance a castle itself. It was here that the proud Earl of Leicester[58] received, entertained and even courted the prouder Queen of England, Elizabeth. It was here that poor Amy Robsart fell a victim to his arts. Here she was kept in a dungeon to prevent intercourse with Elizabeth with whom nevertheless she did have an interview & to whom she related her story. The walls are mantled wherever standing with ivy. The castle was rectangular with an open court. Each angle flanked with towers, one built by the Romans 1500 years ago & 16 feet in thickness—the whole surrounded by a moat. Originally it must have been a place of great strength. The walls and stones are now fast crumbling, the stones being held together by the interlacing of the ivy. I picked up a fragment of a stone in the dungeon of A. Robsart and a stick in the court yard which I brought away as memorials. Kenilworth now belongs to Lord Clarendon.[59] We proceded to Warwick & sought admission to the Castle.[60] We were too late and were refused. I resolved to try here for the first time whether the name and office of a Bishop had any influence with a British nobleman, most of whom are reported to feel great respect and

[57] Sir Charles Napier (1782-1853) was the British general whose forces conquered the Indian state of Sind in 1843 and was its governor until 1848. (**DNB**).

[58] Earl of Leicester, Robert Dudley (1532?-88) married Amy Robsart (1532-60). When she was found dead, rumors circulated that her husband had her murdered. An investigating jury returned a verdict of accidental death. (**DNB**).

[59] George W.F. Villers, fourth earl of Clarendon (1800-70), was the Lord lieutenant of Ireland (1847-52). As such he attempted to ease distress from the famine. (**NCE**).

[60] Today Warwick Castle is owned by Madame Tussaud's of London which acquired it for $3 million in 1978. The present earl, the 8th, then Lord Brooke, sold the castle as it was deteriorating. Yearly over half a million people tour it paying $10. (**New York Times**, 4 Oct. '78, p. 70. As a result of a strike the paper was not published. The articles that would have appeared are thus numbered).

reverence for the Church. Accordingly I sent my card to the Earl with a message by the porter to the effect that we desired admission to the grounds & not to the castle itself. The porter returned in a few minutes with my card in hand with a message from his Lordship that he deeply regretted that the hours for visiting the establishment passed. The porter said his Lordship was very angry with him for admitting a party just before us who were then in the grounds. All of which story we believed to be an apparent falsehood by the porter. Had he delivered by card, it would have scarcely have been returned and besides he took us up afterwards to the castle and let us look in upon the exterior of the buildings, conducted us throught the portcullis and entrance to the inner courts whence we had a view of all that we could have expected or could have hoped for with our limited time. This he would not have dared to do had his Lordship been angry at him as he represented. Returning to the Porter's lodge I asked him to give me a stick or cane from the trees and shrubbery. He gave us three or four and here indeed he showed some apprehension lest his lordship or an official might see him for he worked rapidly & looked anxious. We told him repeatedly not to do anything contrary to duty or orders; that we would by no means have him do that might endanger his place.

At the Porter's lodge we were shown the armor of the famous Guy of Warwick,[61] a giant 8ft. 6 inches high, his sword weighed 22 lbs and was at least 6 feet long. His casque or helmet sat on head as a mould, a dinner pot: his breast plate & shield & battle axe, as well as the stirrups & head piece for his horse were of the same proportions. His walking staff I should say was ten feet long and his tilting pole at least 16 or 18. But the most remarkable thing of all was his porridge-pot, a hugh kettle of copper or brass or both together holding 120 gallons and which we were told by the porter's wife, our chronicle for all the preceding concerning Guy, is filled three times on the day with punch when the eldest son & heir of the Earl of Warwick attains his majority. This was done it was said, when the present heir, Lord Brooke,[62] became of age.

Leaving Warwick Castle we drove rapidly through a beautiful farming & stock country to Stratford on Avon, [sic] the birth place & burial

[61] Guy of Warwick is a hero of romance whose origins hark back to Saxon times. Later he was made into a medieval Paul Bunyan. The dinner pot often called Guy's Porridge Pot is a garrison pot of the Sixteenth Century. The armor is horse armor of the same period. ("Guy Warwick" **DNB**).

[62] In 1851 the earl of Warwick was William Henry Greville (1779-1853), the third earl. The seventh earl, Charles Greville (1911-84) was interested in the stage and in the 1930's went to Hollywood where he was described as a descendant of the "Kingmaker earl of Warwick," Richard Neville (1428-71). MGM paid the later earl a weekly salary of $960 under the name of Brooke. (**Washington Post**, 27 Jan. 1984).

place of the great Shakespeare. So much has been written respecting all these that I have less need to be minute in my observations. The town is much larger & better built than I had expected. We stopped at the Red Horse Inn & at night my party except the servant & Mrs. E's [Eaken] child attended the Theater, for it seems that the **locale** of the immortal bard must be distinguished at least by a playhouse.

Saturday May 17, Rising very early as is my habit I took a stroll through the village or town and soon came to a church which I took to be the one containing the remains of Shakespeare. It was only the Chapel of Ease[63] to the Church which I found on the borders of the town & near the banks of the Avon. It is surrounded by aged forest trees and the whole yard, walks & all are filled slabs & tombstones marking the places of the dead. The sexton was engaged at that early hour in opening a grave into which a body had been previously placed—first the mother & now the daughter. Verily in this country kindred do mingle their ashes together. The family of Shakespeare are interred in the Eastern nave of the church just without the Chancel rails. A mural tablet representing a rudely carved bust of the poet recounts the date of his birth & death and an inscription of quaint a character I here give it verbatim et litteratim

> Iudicio Pylium, genio Socratem, arte Maronem
> Terra tegit, populos maeret, olympus habet
> (Wisdom of Pylos, genius of Socrates, art of Maro
> Earthholds, people mourn, Olympus possesses)[64]
> Stay passenger; why goest thou so fast?
> Read if thou canst whom envious death hath plact
> Within this monument: Shakespeare, with whom
> Quick nature dide; whose name doth deck ys tomb
> Far more than cost: sith all yt be hath
> Leaves living art but page to serve his wit.
> Obit Ino Dei 1616
> AEtatis 53 Die 23 Ap.

Immediately below this monument, on the 2nd step of the Chancel and receding from the Wall is a slab which marks the spot where Shakespeare's wife is buried: it bears the following inscription on a brass plate set into the stone.

"Here lyeth inteered the body of Anne [here Otey put a + and at the top of the page +Anne Hathaway—her maiden name] wife of William Shakespeare, who departed this life the 6 day of Aug 1623 being of age

---

[63] A Chapel of Ease originally was for the ease or accommodation of parishoners who lived too far away to attende the parish church.

[64] Pylium refers to Nestor who according to Greek mythology was the wise king of Pylos. Maro was the cognomen of Vergil, the poet.

— 41 —

67 years:

> Ubera tu mater, tu lac vitamq[ue] dedisti,
> Vae mihi pro tanto munere saxa debo,
> Quam mallem amoveat lapidem bonus Angelo ore,
> Exeat [ut] Christi corpus imago tua:
> Sed nil vota, valent, venias cito Christi, resurget,
> Clausa licet tumulo mater et astra petet."
> [Woe to you mother, you gave me milk and life,
> And for so great a favor, I gave you only a stone.
> Oh, might some good angel remove its weight,
> That your form might go forth as Christ's body:
> But my prayers avail not: I ask Christ that you rise up
> Mother, though closed in this narrow tomb, to the stars.
> Translation W. D. Burgess, Jr.]

Next to this comes the gravestone of the immortal bard and bearing an inscription which has effectively defended his grave from desecration & prevented the removal of his remains to Westminster Abbey. It is as follows:

> Good Friend for Jesus sake forbear:
> To dig the dust enclosed heare:
> Bleste be a man yt spares these stones
> Curst be he yt moves my bones."[65]

The next stone is over the remains of Susannah Hall, the daughter of Shakespeare & this seems to have comprised the whole family.[66] The Church in which S. rested was during the parliamentary wars desecrated and despoiled of everything that could be carried away. The clerk gave me as a memento of the place a piece of oak that formed part of the chancel railing next to which Shakespeare's grave is situated. Leaving the Church we visited the house in which S. was born. It has been purchased by a club of gentlemen in London, to prevent it, as is alledged, from falling into the hands of Barnum[67] the great show manager. It is a poor looking building in Henley Street, not worth the pen, ink and paper to describe it: walls & ceiling are entirely covered with the names of visitors who in this way have sought to render themselves immortal! myself

---

[65] Although Ann wanted to be buried with her husband, the sextons of the church refused to open the tomb fearing the curse (Joseph Quincy Adams. **A Life of William Shakespeare** [Boston: 1923], p. 482).

[66] In addition to Susannah, William and Ann had the twins Hamnet and Judith. Hamnet's dates are 1585-96 whereas Judith lived until 1662. Her three sons died at an early age and left no heirs. (**Ibid**).

[67] Phineas T. Barnum (1810-91), an American showman famous for his extravagant advertising spent the years 1844 to 1847 in England and Europe with his famous midget, General Tom Thumb. While abroad he continually sought attractions for his museum in New York City. In 1850 he sponsored Jenny Lind, the Swedish nightingale's tour of the United States.

among the number!!

Taking horse and carriage we set out for Oxford and passed a beautiful section of the country and many fine villages on the way. Among the places of interest, was Blenheim,[68] with its avenues of venerable and large oak trees, the seat of the great Duke of Marlborough. It was too late in the day to stop and see it, and we came to Oxford, the most celebrated seat of learning in the world and connected with so many associations of the past by means of the great men who have been educated here & the moving events of which it has been the theater. It never entered into my dreams three months ago that I should see Oxford! Yet here I am!

Sunday May 18. Rev. Mr. Cox of Hartford, Conn:[69] called on me last night with Mr. J. H. Parker, bookseller.[70] I was very pleased to see him. Mr. P. called this morning a little before 8 A. M. and took me to the Chapel of New College .[71] I was introduced to the warden, Rev. Dr. Williams, who very politely conducted me to the Chapel, where I heard the morning prayer & partook of the Holy Communion. It was the first time, I had enjoyed the opportunity, since I landed in England, of partaking of the holy ordinance, and I trust, I participated in it, with benefit. At 10½ A.M. I heard the University Sermon or Bamptom[72] lectures by Rev. [blank] in St. Mary's Hall, a poor affair altogether!! At 2 p. m. heard an eloquent discourse from Archdeacon Wilberforce,[73] author of the Incarnation. At 6 P.M. went to St. Paul's Church at the request of the clergyman. I pronounced the absolution & the Benediction. Returning stopped a little while at Mr. Rogers, who politely invited me to make his house my home too.

[68] Blenheim was built for John Churchhill, first duke of Marlborough, and named for his victory over the French in the War of Spanish Succession (1701-13) at Blenheim (1704), a village on the Danube in the Germanies. He was an ancestor of Sir Winston Churchill. ("Blenheim Park," NCE).

[69] A. Cleveland Coxe (1818-96), later bishop of the Protestant Episcopal diocese of Western New York, and celebrated hymn writer, reported Otey was despondent over an affliction which led him to feel no great disposition to live longer unless it should prove the will of God. (A.C. Coxe, "A Letter from Bishop Coxe," in William M. Green, **Memoir of Rt. Rev. James Hervey Otey, DD, LLD, First Bishop of Tennessee** [N.Y., 1885], p. 351. Hereinafter Coxe, "A Letter" in Green, **Memoir**.)

[70] John Parker was the English publisher of Coxe's popular **Christian Ballads** and probably of the English edition of Coxe's **Impressions of England or Sketches of English Scenery and Society**. (This information came from the library card).

[71] Oxford University consists of a series of resident colleges, each with its own corporation of scholars and masters, rules, property, customs and almost complete autonomy. University College (1249) is the oldest. Others mentioned in this account or in the footnotes with their dates of founding are: Baliol (1263), Oriel (1326), Exeter (1314), New (1379), Magdalen (1458), Christ Church (1546), and St. John (1555). ("Oxford University," NCE).

[72] Bampton Lectures were founded by John Bampton (1690-1751), an English cleric. The bequest stipulated eight lectures annually on the Christian religion. The series began in 1779. Coxe found the lecture by Mr. Wilson of St. John's not only dryly read but in conflict with the doctrines of the church. (**Impressions of England or Sketches of English Scenery and Society** [Philadelphia, 1863, 5th ed.] pp. 133-34.)

[73] Robert Issac Wilburforce (1802-57), brother of the bishop of Oxford, was an archdeacon. His administrative territory was the East Riding portion of the diocese of York. In 1854 he joined the Roman Catholic Church and later took priestly orders. His paper on "The Doctrine of the Incarnation of Our Lord Jesus Christ," written in 1848, was an appeal for the unity of teaching among churchmen. (**DNB**).

The most interesting spot I have seen in Oxford as yet, is a cross planted in the street opposite Baliol College, designating the precise spot it is said of the stake at which Latimer and Ridley[74] suffered. I went to it with Rev. Mr. Cox. I could scarcely repress my tears—involuntarily lifted my hat & thanked God for the testimony which his servants had borne to his truth! May England's Church never want a Latimer and a Ridley to lay down their lives when demanded as a sacrifice in her defense! How any man living at Oxford can turn papist with the Martyr's Monument before him is to me an inexplicable Mystery.

Monday, May the 19th. Today has been one of high gratification to me on many accounts. First I went to the Chapel of St. Magdalen's College—called by everybody St. Maud's--where the Choral service as it is called, was to be celebrated at 10 A.M. Shortly after our arrival the officials of the College & others with a number of little boys dressed in surplices entered & the service very soon began. I attempted at first to join in the service but very quickly had to desist finding myself continually before or behind in time. I was therefore a quiet spectator & listener. It appeared to me to be a sort of mournful recitation. Many parts of the service were pronounced with the same sort of tones which I have heard from illiterate Baptist and Methodist ministers. In the softness of voice and variety of inflexions and solemnity of sound: if these things are esteemed the chief excellencies or beauties of the choral or antiphonal service, our negroes can far surpass the Oxford Choristers, if they are but taught the same words. After leaving the Chapel we strolled through the grounds and along the walks attached to St. Mauds. The most noteworthy things are the beautiful tower with its pinnacles and the celebrated Mr. Addison's walk[75]—a sequestered spot, shaded with trees, a stream of water by its side and by its silent beauties seeming to invite to contemplation. I travelled the whole extent with Mr. Mariott,[76] fellow of Oriel, listening to his conversation, but with my thoughts wandering off after those dear ones who have passed to the land whither Mr. Addison's spirit has long since fled. Returning fron this long stroll, I called with Mr.

[74] Bishops Hugh Latmer (1485?-1555) and Nicholas Ridley (1500-55) were burned at the stake the same day for their refusal to renounce Protestantism when Mary tried to restore the Roman Catholic Church in England.

[75] Addison's Walk is named for Joseph Addison, the poet and creator of Sir Roger de Coverly.)A.R. Woolley, **The Clarendon Guide to Oxford**, 2nd. 4d. [Oxford, 1972], p. 46).

[76] Charles Mariott (1811-58) was an Anglican divine and friend of John Henry Newman. Unlike the latter Mariott did not go to Rome but remained loyal to the Church of England. Reputedly he was as effective as anyone in stemming the movement toward Rome. (**DNB**).

[77] Dr. Edward B. Pusey (1800-82), canon of Christ College, headed the Oxford Movement after Newman withdrew from it in 1841. Two years later his right to preach was suspended for two years as a result of his sermon on the Real Presence. This doctrine holds that Christ is really present in the communion. (**DNB**) Coxe later wrote that Otey displayed deference and humility "in the presence of that great scholar." (Coxe, "A Letter," in Green, **Memoir**, p. 351).

Mariott & Mr. Cox at Dr. Pusey's[77] rooms; and had a few minutes pleasant conversation. Pusey's head is certainly a remarkable one, the upper portion of the cranium spreading out & as it were overshadowing the base, somewhat like the top of a palm tree or even a burr-artichoke inverted. There is nothing striking in the expression of his countenance further than its seriousness approximating to anxiety, and a very fine blue eye that lightens up on any remark that rouses his attention. I remarked to him that the most precious fruits of Christian character were produced under trial and trouble and that I trusted the present days of rebuke, reproach & fear to the Church of England was but preparing her for the great & glorious things that God intended to accomplish through her instrumentality. His face brightened as I made the remark and with that & a shake of the hand I left him and preceded to the Bodleian Library,[78] one of the largest & most valuable in the world. A description of its wonders & treasures would require far more time & space to do them justice than I have opportunity to bestow. We passed around its quadrangle with its galleries one above another & the alcoves on each side with the thousands upon thousands of volumes of all languages & tongues neatly arranged on shelves with convenient steps to reach them and desks furnished with pens for the use of those who seek this vast repository of the learning of the world. Some of the manuscripts which the Bodleian official showed us were represented to be 12, 14, 15 hundred years old. The copies of the authorized editions of the Bible and the first ever printed was also exhibited besides many other things rare & curious. The collection of writings in Sanskrit is large enough alone to form a respectable library. And then there is a room appropriated to the reception of all the best periodicals from every country on earth, an assemblage of works which in ages to come must be exceedingly valuable. From looking at the thousands of volumes and manuscripts we went to the room containing the **Arundelian** Marbles, so called from Thomas Howard Earl of Arundel, by whom they were procured in Greece & brought to England. I did not examine the various objects with their inscriptions with any minuteness. It would have required too much time to decipher them & besides these have been published with full & accurate account of every article in the collection with a drawing of the same. After this I strolled through various apartments belonging to the different colleges. Examined the fine collection of portraits of great & good men that once were con-

[78] In 1602 the Bodleian Library replaced the Duke Humphrey Library which had been destroyed during the reign of Edward VI. Sir Thomas Bodley (1545-1613) who initiated the project, was a Greek scholar and teacher at the university and later a diplomat. He gave the library his collection of books and manuscripts. (**NCE**).

nected with their respective colleges as scholars, fellows, and masters. Among them was that of good Bp. Horne.[79] Viewed the towers & buildings, and finally entered Exeter College to dine with Mr. Sewel,[80] fellow of Exeter College. Here I met a good number of gentlemen. Their names I do not pretend to remember except Mr. Burgess, fellow of Oriel. We had a very pleasant meeting & after dinner entered Mr. Sewel's rooms for conversation, coffee, tea, fruit & wine. I took a glass of lemonade & no more.The conversation was very agreeable. I availed myself of the opportunity to ask many questions about our ritual, &c, in so much that I had to apologize to Mr. S. several times by assuring him that I was not trying him with hard questions as the Queen of Sheba did Solomon. My inquiries were received in a very kind spirit and all the information imparted that they possessed as to the matters of inquiry. The substance of the answers to the inquiry What is the judgement if the Priest constitutes the notorious evil living for which a man should be repelled from Communion, was this — That conviction of some offense charged & proven before some Competent Court to hear and determine the innocence or guilt of the party was requisite. I confess I do not like this interpretation: for surely a man might get drunk & thereby offend against the laws of Christ's Church & never be convicted by any judicial sentence for such an act or scandal and yet it is plain that he should not be allowed to come to Holy Communion, nor could he without offending the congregation.

From Exeter College we went to the banks of the Thames to witness the boat races among the different colleges. An immense crowd was out. Each college has its boat long, narrow, light & elegant equipped with eight oars & as many rowers & a helmsman. The stream being narrow they do not race abreast; but one after another according to a fixed inteval between each boat. Procedure in starting is regulated by success in former races. In the race if any boat touches the one in advance of it (which touching is called a bump), the boat so bumped has to stop & yield the victory & this is the great object for which they labour, each boat behind is striving to touch or bump the boat ahead. This race commenced before we reached the spot at which we were aiming to get a fair view, and in a few minutes the competition swept by almost with the fleetness of an arrow. The young men were bare headed & stripped of their clothing to the pantaloons & silk shirts fitting tightly to their bodies.

[79] George Horne (1730-92), dean of Canterbury, then bishop of Norwich (1790-92). (**DNB**).
[80] William Sewell (1804-74) left the Oxford Movement when he saw its drift toward Rome. He was famous for burning in a classroom a copy of J.A. Froude's novel **Nemesis of Faith** thereby making the novel a best seller. (**DNB**).

They worked most beautifully and with no less skill & energy. Each man seemed to lay himself to the work as if he thought the fate of England depended upon his personal prowess. Three boats of the whole number received bumps and Baliol College I heard was victorious. The pastime is itself innocent withal healthy if not pushed to excess & hence it is rather [illegible] than otherwise. The crowd which lined the banks of the river up & down for miles rent the air with their shouts as the boats shot by in the race and hastened to the goal.

Returning from this exciting scene I went with Mr. Rogers[81] to Mr. Mariot's rooms where I met a number of gentlemen with whom the evening was passed very agreeably in conversation — chiefly so far as I was concerned, about the Church in America. The persons present were very kind in the expressions and interest, etc. and I hope I left them at 11 p.m. favorably impressed.

Tuesday 20th. According to appointment I went this morning to breakfast with Mr. Burgess of Oriel College. He received me very courteously & very soon three other gentlemen came in evidently for the sole purpose of seeing me. We had a pleasant session. Mr. Barker, nephew of Dr. Pusey, entered into conversation with me respecting the Athanasian Creed[82]—why it was left out of the prayer book in our Church. I gave him the reasons as I knew them and said to him that our office of visitation instructed us to say to the sick that if he believed the Articles of the Apostles Creed, he believed as a Christian man should do & of course this was all that was necessary especially for the common people who were not fitted to enter into the deeper things of God as they were announced by the Athanasian Creed in the form of dogmas, reasoning or argument and proofs—that I thought that the morning service of the Church was a better exposition of Christian doctrine than could be made in a sermon by the ablest divine—that it contained everything necessary to be known in order to salvation, etc. It was replied to all this that the terms of the Creed required explanation and I was asked how I would reason with a man about the nature of Christ, his having a soul & not divinity to supply the place of a reasonable soul. I thought the point, an unlucky one for my opponent, so I said I would treat with him thus: I would bring him up to authority which he trusted, not to a creed which he might debate, because of human origin: but to the word of God with

[81] This could be Frederic Rogers (1811-99) later Baron Blachford, a friend of J.H. Newman and of Sewell. After 1844 he became involved in government work for which he was created a baron. (**DNB**)

[82] Athanasian Creed is an exact and elaborate statement on the Trinity and the Incarnation which is accepted by Roman Catholics, Anglicans, and Lutherans. One time Athanasius (297?-373) was considered the author, now scholars think it was written in Western Europe about the 6th Century. (**Oxford Dictionary of the Christian Religion**, 2nd edition [London, 1974].)

that word spoken by David & quoted by David as referring expectedly to Christ: "Thou will not leave my **soul** in Hell etc." This came very near overturning my opponents but while they were rallying for a reply the "**Bus**" called for me & I took leave of these Brethren with the expression of mutual and I doubt not sincere regrets. A few minutes brought me to the depot from which I was whirled along in an hour and a half or ¾ to London by the express train a distance of 63 miles.

The Great Exhibition

And here I am in London—that exceeding great city, the modern Babylon as it is sometimes called, less I hope on account of its abominations than the variety of its languages & richness of its merchandise—the Capital of the British Empire upon whose dependencies the sun never sets—the Commercial Emporium of the World. Here I am in this mart of Nations where I never expected to be and here I am first met by intelligence in a letter from my dear wife, of the death of Mrs. Dr. Hayes[83] & of Judge T.H. Cabal.[84] I have read my letters from Mr. Tomes and others & feel thankful to God that my family have been kept in health, peace & safety. May he enable me to show my gratitude by living a godly, righteous & solemn [?] life for J. Christ's sake. Amen!! I commenced writing a reply to my wife's letter this evening expecting to finish it in time for the steamer on next Saturday which I understand sails from Liverpool on that day.

Wednesday May 21. This morning while engaged in writing my wife I had the pleasure of receiving from her another letter dated the 29th April and conveying the pleasing intelligence that all were well. God be praised therefor! In a little time after breakfast accompanied by Mrs. Eakin and Miss Bass I went to the World's Fair in Hyde Park, and now having gazed at the wonders of nature and art there congregated I am seated to record an account, however meager, of what has fallen under my observation, but first let me say that the building itself is a world's wonder furnishing a most remarkable example of the triumph of human genius and skill to accomplish a work of great difficulty. It was to provide for the display of the specimens of human industry whether directed

---

[83] Ophelia C. Hayes according to the 1850 census was born in 1813 in Tennessee and her husband John B. Hayes was born in 1794 in Virginia. (**1850 Census, Maury County, Tennessee**, transcribed and printed by Ms. Deane Porch, Nashville, TN, 1966).
[84] Terry H. Cabal (1802-51) was a member of the 21st and 22nd General Assemblies of Tennessee. From 1843 to 1850 he was chancellor of the Middle Tennessee Division of Chancery Court. (**Biographical Directory of the Tennessee General Assembly** 1796-1861 [Nashville, 1975] I, pp. 107-8.)

to the creations of nature or the productions of art in the smallest allowable space and in a light to afford opportunities for a fair examination. In a word order and system now to be secured in an assemblage where from the multitude of objects & visitors, confusion and disorder were to be feared. An immense building raised on iron frame work, the interstices on the sides, ends & tops filled with glass effected the object of the free admission of light the divisions into compartments for the reception of the various offerings of industry and these divisions marked with the name of the various countries & states of the earth from which they came very effectually secured the object of system or order in the exhibitions. Also a great advantage was gained in this, that the arrangement enabled the examiner to compare the products of one country with another. Almost the first thing that arrested my attention on entering the place of exhibition was that I saw congregated before me men of many different nations. The lively Frenchman neatly dressed and restless as if a nettle were in his breeches, passing quickly from object to object, could not fail to be discerned from the heavy Dutchman, who with hands crossed behind his back a la [sic] Napoleon, surveyed each specimen in the great collection with the keen eye of a Jew intent upon & gaining the advantage in driving a bargain. The grave looking Turk was there with his flowing robes and turban of ample folds encircling his head: and the Persian with his pants drawn tight around the ankles and the seat of the pants descending below the calves of his legs and a loose jacket thrown over the shoulders and a species of turban betrayed his Eastern origin too plainly to be mistaken. The Spaniard was known by his proud look and the American from the U.S. by his free and independent bearing. The Tunisian by his olive complexion, moustaches and queer looking blue cap and abundance of beard, and the Chinese by his eyes with the outward corners turned upward, the head shorn except on the top and back, a long queue descending almost to his heels, and his dress like a woman with petticoats without an upper garment. The Italian was presently known by the brown complexion and dark hazel eyes, and lastly the Englishman with his half open mouth as he waddled along among the glorious products of industrial skill, heading for Cricket and thinking of ale & roast beef and ready to swear that the English excelled all people on Earth. So much then about the vanity of men at the World's Fair, though the subject so far from being exhausted has only been of concern. It would be an useless attempt on my part to attempt a description of that which beggers all description unless a man should undertake the task of writing a volume and even then it would be [no easy work?]

Through avenue after avenue, court after court and gallery after gallery and still I had not begin to see the middle section. Here are all sorts of new objects, infinite in variety and interesting in their beauty or usefulness upon which I had as yet bestowed no attention. It would occupy too much space in this diary to specify the different classes of objects to be found in this imposing collection from all the nations of the earth, to say nothing of the tediousness that would surely attend any effort at description in detail. The 'tout ensemble' [the whole] far surpasses any expectations which I had formed as to the number, beauty, and variety of objects and the taste manifest in this display. I must therefore content myself with reference to a few only of the many specimens of art, which attracted and unchained my attention. Near the center of the Crystal Palace, as it is called, stands a large French organ from which pealed the notes of Old Hundred filling the vaulted roof above & all the space around with inspiring and elevated associations carrying one's thoughts to the worship of the sanctuary and kindling emotions that find their counterpart only in the inspired harmonies of Heaven. It was a powerful instrument and withal exceedingly mellow. Hard by was gathered a group of people who seemed intently engaged in the examination of some object which I could not see without close inspection. Upon approaching nearer I observed that the celebrated "Koh-i-nor" or "mountain of light"—the most remarkable diamond, & as some say the largest in the world—was the great object of attraction. It was placed upon a framework of gilded bars, and this within another, and the jewel itself laid on a velvet cushion, in a way to display it, to the best advantage. The size of this precious stone, for the possession of which bloody wars have been waged, is that of a common hickory nut or walnut. It is neither so large, nor so brilliant as might be imagined from the descriptions which have been given it. The British authorities came into its possession during the war with Afghanistan.[85] Wandering off from this spot to the apartment into which the productions of the United States had been received, my attention was directed to a number of daguerreotypes, and among them whose should I recognize but the happy & smiling face of my own dear child Mary? To met with it at such a time and such a place was almost too much for my nerves and like Joseph when he knew his brethren, I would [faded] have sought a place where I might weep. Any further notice of the objects in this very complete collection from the dif-

[85] For generations prior to 1302 the Koh-i-nor diamond had been the possession of the rajahs of Malwa. From them until 1849 when the British acquired it, the stone passed through many hands. The diamond Otey saw weighed 191 carats. Later it was recut to 108 and made the center stone on the queen's state crown. ("Kohinor Diamond," **Encyclopedia Britannica**).

ferent tribes and states of men, I must reserve to another opportunity, after I shall again have visited it.

Returning to my lodgings fatigues in mind & body I employed the remainder of the day in writing to my wife & to Henrietta.

Thursday May 22. Today after dispatching various notes of introduction to different persons and letters to my wife & Retta, I went to the British Museum and devoted several hours to the examination of the immense and exceedingly valuable collection of works of nature and art that have been gathered together. It is doubtful whether any similar collection from the animal, vegetable, and mineral kingdoms, equal in extent & value, can be found in the whole world. The largest number of books—of specimens in the arts both in ancient & modern times—of fossils & minerals illustrative of geology—of animals both birds & beasts & reptiles with creeping things, are to be found here and furnish subjects of study both for the student and the artist. The building which is of huge dimensions is most conveniently arranged in the form of a quadrangle with long apartments above & below on the four sides and connected together in such a way that one may pass entirely around the square or quadrangle either on the 1st or 2nd floors.

In the rear of the ante-room or entrance hall the first objects which strike the attention are two colossal figures discovered by Layard[86] in his researches among the ruins of Ninevah. One is called the great Winged Bull with the face of a man, the other the great Winged Lion. Opposite to these are two gigantic human figures having a basket in one hand & some sort of fruit in the other. These statues are about 15 ft. high. To the right of the door in the same room is a marble statue of Sir Joseph Banks[87] with an inscription Aet. 76 yr 6 m. 6 d. Ob: XIII kal. Jul. A.S. 1820. The next room displayed many curious things. Among these a Latin Psalter printed at Mentz [Mainz] 1457 being the first book so far known that was printed with the date & the first example of printing in colors. Very similar in Execution [?] to this is the bull of indulgences issued by Nicholas V[88]—Pope—in favor of those who should assist the King of Cyprus against the Turks in 1455—in vellum print, large and

[86] Sir Henry Layard (1817-94) was an English archeologist and diplomat who excavated around Nineval between 1842 and 1851. (**DNB**).

[87] Sir Joseph Banks (1743-1820) traveled as a naturalist on the voyages of Captain James Cook (1728-79). Sir Joseph served as president of the Royal Society from 1778 until his death. The society was established in 1662 as a scientific organization. (**NCE**).

[88] Nicholas V (1397-1455) was pope from 1447 to 1455. He was the Renaissance pope who established the Vatican library. Following the fall of Constantinople to the Turks in 1453 he attempted to assemble a fleet to fight the Turks but received little support. (**New Cath Ency**).

[89] Charles V, Holy Roman Emperor from 1519 to 1555.

distinct.

Is where the Autographs of Chs:V, Emp.[89] in a codicil to his will; of Mary Q. of Scots. A carte-blanche signed and sealed by Ch:II and sent to Parliament to save his father's head & an original letter from the duke of Monmouth to the Queen dowager[90] begging for his life. Autos of Henry IV of France;[91] Gustavus Adolphus,[92] **beautiful** writing. Francis I of France;[93] Peter the Great of Russia,[94] a miserable fist; Catha. de Medici;[95] Napoleon; Frederick the Great.[96] Also the great seals & autographs of Wm. I, Henry I, Richard II, Henry IV, V, VI; Ed IV, V, Rich. III, Henry VII, VIII, Cath. of Aragon, Anne Boleyn, Ed. VI, Lady Jane Grey,[97] Queen Mary, Elizabeth, Mary of Scotland, James I, Ch: I, Ol. Cromwell,[98] Ch: II, James II, Wm. III, Q. Anne, Geo. I, II, III, of 24 [?] seals from Ed. I to Geo. III all are perfect except that of the Commonwealth which appears to have been broken with the spheres stuck together. Autos of Erasmus,[99] Knox, Cranmer, Luther, Ridley, Bonner (partly burnt),[100] Calvin, Melancthon,[101]Latimer, Wolsey[102] Sr. Th: Moore,[103] Sr Ph: Sidney,[104] Burghley,[105] Michel [Haynes?], Hampden,[106] Galileo, Drake & Hawkins,[107] Sr. W. Raleigh. Of all these Cranmer wrote the fairest hand.

[90] Catherine of Braganza (1638-1705) was the dowager Queen of Charles II. After his death she remained in England until the accession of William III in 1694 (**DNB**).

[91] Henry IV, king of France from 1589 to 1610.

[92] Gustavus Adolphus, king of Sweden from 1613 to 1632.

[93] Francis I, king of France from 1515 to 1547.

[94] Peter the Great, tsar of Russia from 1682 to 1725.

[95] Catherine dé Medici (1519-89) was the wife of Henry II of France who reigned from 1547 to 1559. She instigated the Massacre at St. Bartholomew's Eve. (1572).("Catherine dé Medici," **NCE**).

[96] Frederick the Great, king of Prussia from 1740 to 1786.

[97] Lady Jane Grey was queen for nine days in 1553 when her supporters put her on the throne in place of Mary who reigned from 1553 to 1558. (**DNB**).

[98] Oliver Cromwell was Lord Protector of the Commonwealth of England from 1649 to 1658.

[99] Desiderius Erasmus (1466?-1536) was an outstanding Renaissance personality who is known as the Prince of Humanists. He made three trips to England, knew both Henry VII and Henry III, and was a friend of Sir Thomas More. (**Encyclopedia Britannica** [1970]).

[100] Edmund Bonner (1500-69) had been bishop of London, lost the see under Edward VI, had it restored by Mary and went into exile when Elizabeth became queen. (**DNB**).

[101] Philip Melancthon (1497-1560), friend of Luther and drafter of the Augsburg Confession (1539), the statement of the Lutheran doctrinal position. (**NCE**).

[102] Thomas Wolsey (1473?-1530), archbishop, cardinal and chancellor. He lost the latter office because he was unable to get Rome's permission for Henry VIII's divorce from Catherine of Aragon. (**DNB**).

[103] 'Sir (Saint) Thomas More (1473?-1535), author of **Utopia**, chancellor of England was canonized by the Roman Catholic Church because he refused to take the oath recognizing Henry as head of the church in England, a decision that cost his life.

[104] Sir Philip Sydney (1554-86) an Elizabethian courtier who is better known for his influence on English poetry.

[105] William Cecil, Baron Burghley (1520-98) chief advisor to Elizabeth. ("Burghley, William Cecil," **NCE**).

[106] John Hampden (1594-1643) a member of Parliament who refused to pay "ship money," was brought to court and nearly won his case against the crown. (**NCE**).

[107] Sir John Hawkins (1532-95), an Elizabethan "seadog" and kinsman of Sir Francis Drake.

[108] Edward the Confessor, king of England from 1042-1066. William the Conquerer claimed Edward gave him the English throne.

[109] Stephen, king of England from 1135-1154.

Magna Carta, original & copy beautifully written on Vellum. Charter original of Ed Confessor,[108] Henry I, Jno: Articles of Magna Carta, Henry II, III, Stephen,[109] Rich: I with seals metal, clay or wax.

Autos of Bacon,[110] Locke,[111] Pope,[112] Newton, Dryden,[113] Voltaire,[114] Addison, Leibnitz,[115] **Franklin**, Sully,[116] Pr: Rupert, Wellington, Conde.[117] Marlborough, Napoleon, Turenne,[118] **Washington**, Nelson.

I saw also a large collection of manuscripts written on the leaves and bark of the talipot tree, on reeds, on sheets of ivory in the Burmese, Cingalese, Tamil languages, etc. Persian romances with pitures illustrating the story and in deed from the number of these pictures one might well conclude that the address was made to the eye rather than to the understanding in relating the story. The odes of Hafiz[119] the Persian poet were illustrated in the same manner. there were a great many works in Sanskrit and many drawings made in India to portray manners and customs which are seen in the same collection. Close by, my eye fell upon a Roll of the Pentatuch in Hebrew very large and belonging to the XIV Century. It was written on goat skins.

Next I saw a manuscript copy of the Bible beautifully illuminated of the time of Charles the Bald of France, AD 840, said to have been revised by Alcuin.[120] Here also was an autograph copy of a work by

[110] Sir Francis Bacon, Baron Verulam, Viscount St Albans (1562-1626), English statesman, essayist, and philosopher. He is highly regarded for his arguments in behalf of the experimental method to prove theories. (**DNB**).

[111] John Locke (1634-1704), English philosopher and founder of British empiricism.

[112] Alexander Pope (1688-1744), a well known English poet.

[113] John Dryden (1631-1700), an outstanding English poet and dramatist.

[114] Francois de Voltaire (1694-1778), probably the best known French writer of the eighteenth century, was born Francois Marie Arouet and added the de Voltaire about 1718. (**NCE**).

[115] Gottfried, Baron von Leibnitz (1646-1716) a German philosopher and mathmetician who developed calculus three years before Newton did (**NCE**).

[116] Maximilien de Béthune, Duc de Sully (1556-1649) advisor and friend of Henri IV. (Sully, Maximilien de Béthune. (**NCE**).

[117] Louis II de Bourbon, Prince de Condé 1621-86) called the Great Condé, a French marshal. (**NCE**).

[118] Henri de la Tour d'Auvergne, Vicomte de Turenne (1611-75), one of France's greatest marshals. He is buried in the Invalides. (**NCE**).

[119] Hafiz (d. 1389?) Persian lyric poet. (**NCE**).

[120] Alcuin or Albinus (735?-804) English churchman and educator invited to Aachen or Aix-le-Chapelle) by Charlemagne (742?-814). Here was the moving spirit in the Carolingen Renaissance. Alcuin's Bible consists primarily of the Gospels in which the Latin is correct and the text without grammatical or orthographic errors. (**DNB**)

[121] Torquarto Tasso (1544-95), an Italian, wrote "Jerusalem Delivered" which is lauded as the greatest poem of the Catholic Reformation. (**NCE**).

[122] Felix Lope de Vega Carpio (1562-1635), a Spaniard, was the author of nearly 1800 plays. (Lope de Vega Carpiô, **NCE**).

[123] Codex Alexandrinus is an early 5th Century manuscript of the Greek Bible. Within a short time after its arrival in England scholars were using it. (**Oxford Dictionary of the Christian Church**).

[124] Cyril Lucar (1572-1638), an Orthodox patriarch, who studied in Geneva and was influenced by Calvinist doctrine. He became patriarch of Alexandria in 1602 and then of Constantinople in 1612. Between 1620 and his death he was deposed seven times. He gave the Codex to Sir Thomas Roe, English Ambassador to Constantinople. The patriarch was strangled by troops of Sultan Murad and his body was thrown into the sea. Through Cyril Calvinistic teachings had a short-lived influence on the Orthodox Church. (**New Cath Ency**).

Tasso[121] & by Lope de Vega.[122] A very interesting vol called the Codex Alexandrinus[123] of the Vth Cent. and said to have been presented to Ch: I by Cyril,[124] Pat[riarch] of Constantinople, came next under observation, together with a copy of what is called St. Cuthbert's[125] gospel, the illumination of which employed 22 years from 698 to 720. After this I saw the title of a very curious work which I should like much to have examined. It was the **prophecies** of the **Ten Sybils** written in English verse and by Jane Seager presented to Q. Elizabeth in 1578.[126]

Among curiosities of the book kind [?] must not be omitted a manuscript copy in Latin of the Gospels, belonging to VII & IX Cents. in ancient binding covered with plates of silver and set with gems. Within the covers are preserved the relics of some of the saints. The bull of Pope Leo X[127] conferring the title of "Fidei Defensor" [Defender of the Faith] on Henry VIII is scarcely legible. In the same condition is the original Mag. Car. both having been injured by fire. The bull of Innocent III[128] receiving in fee the kingdom of England from John 1214 and taking it under his Apostolic protection is here preserved. If John had any right to give the kingdom away, I suppose Henry VIII had a right to take it back; if he could, and he did.

It was interesting to see here the first book printed in America. It is entitled Doctrina Christiana, Mexico A.D. 1544.

Leaving the apartment containing books of which the editions are as far as I observed very beautiful and the best—many of them first editions, as for example Horace[129] in folio, besides others. I entered a room appropriated to Egyptian antiquities. Here again I must forego descriptions and content myself with a slight reference to striking objects. Among these may be named many colossal figures with faces of lions and other animals having human bodies: also immense and ponderous sarcophagi. The statue of Rameses 2 or 3 18th dynasty from Thebes,[130] Amenophis III 18th Dy[nasty] Thebes.[131] Some I think make this the Pharoah of Joseph's time. Two vast stone baths as I take them to be, covered with hieroglyphics, captured by the British Army in 1801 and pre-

[125] St. Cuthbert's Gospel, an illustrated Latin text, is better known as the Lindisfarne Gospel because the work was done prior to 700 on Holy Island, the location of Lindisfarne where Cuthbert was bishop from 684-686. (**DNB**).

[126] Jane Seagar's work "Prophecies of the Ten Sybils" has disappeared from the proper folder in the British Museum according to Dr. Colin Baxter, a colleague who looked for the pamphlet in 1990. He found it listed by topic and not by author. Perhaps it was not returned to the proper folder following its display in 1851.

[127] Leo X, pope from 1513 to 1521. During his pontificate the Reformation started.

[128] Innocent III. His occupancy of the Papacy from 1198 to 1216 marked the zenith of Papal power.

[129] Horace (65-8 BC), one of the greatest lyric poets, is famous for his **Satires** and **Odes**.

[130] Rameses II (reigned from 1292-1225 B.C.) an Egyptian pharoah who erected many statues proclaiming his greatness.

[131] Amenophis III reigned in Egypt from 1411 to 1372 B.C.

[132] Ptolemy V ruled Egypt from 205-180 B.C. The Rosetta stone was found at Rosetta, Egypt.

sented by George III. Here was a curious writing in Enchorial [ancient Egyptian] & Greek characters taken from the Rosetta Stone, a decree in honor of Ptolemy V[132]—by whom made is not said—Elegant & elaborate Sercophagus of Amasis queen of Thebes. Colossal heads of kings and a representation or figure in stone of a human fist [foot?] weighing several tons. From the Egyptian collection of sculptures etc I proceeded to that made by Layard among the ruins of Ninevah. It is exceedingly interesting, but as accurate drawings have been given in Layard's work accompanied by descriptions, it would be useless for me to attempt anything of the sort here. I may mention that I was struck with the degree of preservation even to minutia which makes these wonderful relics of far gone ages. The nails as developed by sculpture on the hands and toes appear to be perfect.

Leaving all these things behind I entered the apartments in which are found preserved specimens of animals, birds, beasts, etc. I suppose that a specimen of every known animal in the world is to be found in this collection. I could not but admire the great variety in the deer species from the gigantic & stately moose, deer & elk to the diminutive but elegant little creatures found in Africa, perfect in its form but not larger than a rat or squirrel. Other striking objects new camelopards {giraffe] 18 to 29 ft. high — the huge Rhinoceros—the unwieldy Hippopotamus—Walrus—White, Black and Grizzly bear—all the feline race from the lion of Zaharn [sic] or Tiger or Bengal to the cat besides others to name which would be tedious. Curiosities from Australia & Isles of the Pacific & East generally were seen in infinite profusion. Mexico, the Northern parts of America, So. America & Africa furnished their contributions & India with gods or divinities innumerable. Here was seen a model of the temple of Juggernaught—then a curious ruin of what I could not tell—the shield of Achilles full of emblematic devices as described by Homer, modeled by Flaxman.[133] Also a curious representation, by an artist of the East, of Thugs accompanying a traveller, finally murdering & hanging him and then dividing the spoil.[134] If any part of the British Museum can be said to be preeminently rich over other parts in collections, it perhaps may be claimed for that department devoted to birds. The number, variety & beauty of the species almost surpass belief. The case of humming birds is especially rich & abundant. Some of them are indescribably beautiful and incredibly small while their colors in the back & crests are

[133] John Flaxman (1755-1826) English sculptor and draftsman, also made medallions of Benjamin Franklin's son, William, the governor of New Jersey, and of the latter's son William Temple Franklin. (**DNB**).

[134] Thugs were members of a Hindu sect who murdered as a sacrifice to the goddess Kali. The act was usually done through strangulation. Over a period of years the British were able to suppress the group by mass arrest and execution. (**NCE**).

brilliant to a degree scarcely to be conceived of by imagination—burnished gold, emerald green, deep blue, shining and dazzling violet, all these are but faint terms to convey the impression which sight gives. The Scarlett Tanager is a brilliant speciment of the bird kind. The variety of Parrots is nearly as striking: blue, green, white, red, black, brown, grey, & varigated. Pheasants with capes and tail-feathers 2 or 3 yds. long—pencilled pheasants also very remarkable [Otey drew something like this.] the crown pigeon[135] from China is worthy to be remembered for its singularity & beauty.

Mineralogical & Geological Cabinet is perhaps the most interesting of all. I regretted exceedingly that I had not more time to spend in its examination. I staid long enough however to see the original specimens of formation from which drawings have been made in the works of Mantel,[136] Murchison[137] & Miller: and to mark their great accuracy. They are indeed most curious & wonderful. I must close by saying I saw a curious Tortoise wrought out of Nephrite or Jade found on the banks of the "Jumma" [or Yamuna][138] (India). Also a rock crystal from Ireland at least 16 or 18 inches by 12 or 14, clear as water—& lastly the **ornithorynchus**[139] [sic] from New Holland—that most curious of all animals having webbed feet and legs like a frog behind, like a mole before with the bill of a duck, the head of a bat & hair for feathers and which hatches its eggs in its own body. The British Museum is the most wonderful and interesting of all things I have seen and examined as yet.[140]

May 23. This morning I had determined to go into the country but the rain and other things led me to change my purpose and to spend the day in visiting places of interest about the Metropolis. The first to which we turned our attention was Westminster Abbey, one of the most venerable and interesting structures in the whole kingdom.

> "Through the aisles of Westminster to roam
> Where bubbles burst of Jolly's dancing form
> Melts if it cross the threshold." Wordsworth[141]

This venerable pile was founded by Henry III[142] about six centuries

---

[135] The crown pigeon is the goura of New Guinea. ("Goura," **Webster's New Twentieth Century Dictionary Unabridged**).

[136] Gideon Mantell (1790-1852) an English geologist who discovered the Iguanodon, an extinct thirty foot reptile.("Mantell," **DNB**; "Iquanadon," **NCE**).

[137] Sir Roderick Impey Murchison (1792-1871), a British geologist who became director general of a geological survey of England in 1855. (**DNB**).

[138] The Jumna or Yamuna, its present name, is a major tributary of the Ganges and joins that stream just below Allahabad.

[139] **Ornithorhynchus anatinus** is the platypus of duckbill, a mammal which lays eggs.

[140] Randal McGavock who accompanied Otey on both the 22nd and 23rd wrote they spent four hours in the British museum. (**Pen** p. 195).

[141] William Wordsworth (1770-1850), an English poet laurate.

[142] Henry III was king of England from 1216 to 1272.

ago: and has received many additions since that time as the piety or pride of successive monarchs led them to make them. After taking a survey of the most striking objects in those parts of the building which are at all times open to public inspection, we then placed ourselves under the conduct of a servitor or guide, who led the way to the various chapels bearing the names of the kings by whom they were chiefly used or erected or else those of some of the saints. It is a place peculiarly adapted to serious thought and comtemplations. I never before felt the effect, upon my mind, of "the dim religious light" that fell into the aisles and other parts of the vast structure, through the wonders of stained glass. These windows are the most beautiful I have ever seen. The monuments to consecrate the memory of the dead—the mighty dead—are all around us. Here sleep the illustrious men who have adorned life by their virtues, or enlightened the world by their labors in the various departments of human knowledge, who have reigned as Fathers of their people, ruling in the fear of God or have governed with an iron rod and in the indulgence of their passions have violated every law human and divine. Their ashes repose here in peace, their souls are with Him who gave them being and will hereafter call them to stand at the bar of eternal judgement. I was forcibly reminded while looking at the various memorials of the sleepers below of the expressive words of the late Mr. Jno: Q. Adams:[143] "This is the end of earth!" The monuments are by no means rich and imposing which mark the resting places of the truly great. Thus Milton's[144] is a plain mural tablet and so is rare "Ben Johnson's:[145] But the sepulchres of the Kings are somewhat different. Here we find great effort made at the grand, the ornate, & the beautiful. Mary styled the bloody Mary and her sister Elizabeth both repose in the same tomb and one monument covers them both. I looked with melancholy interest on the monument erected by James I in honor of his mother "Mary queen of Scots." Among many interesting objects shown to us was the chair used at the coronation of the Kings & Queens of England. It was made in the reign of Edward the first,[146] and presents nothing remarkable for beauty of form or costliness of material. Immediately under the seat if fixed the stone of Scone from Scotland which was formerly used at the crowning of Scottish Kings. The chair itself is as plain as Daniel Boone's and appears to have been hacked and carved with pen knives, not a little, by persons desireous of cutting their names upon the coronation chair of English monarchs. The

[143] John Quincy Adams, sixth president of the United States (1825-29), died 1848.
[144] John Milton (1608-74) English poet.
[145] Ben Jonson (1572-1637) English dramatist and poet.
[146] Edward I king of England (1272-1307).
[147] Major John Andre (1751-80) was captured and hanged for his role in Benedict Arnold's betrayal.

unfortunate Maj. Andre,[147] adjutant Genl. to the British army in America during the war of revolution, has a monument erected to his memory in the south aisle: it sets forth his melancholy end, the estee, in which held both by his friends and his foes and concludes by stating that his remains had been deposited in An[no] 1821 in a grave near to the monument. I left the Abbey with a feeling of reluctance and determining in my own mind to avail myself of the first favorable opportunity to revisit it—to sit down solitary and alone and devote a few hours to the contemplation which the place and the associations connected with it can not fail to inspire.

A few minutes walk brought us to Westminster Hall noted as the place where the high Court of Parliament voted the sentence of death against the unhappy Charles Stuart I. Hard by were the Inns of court and committees of the House of Commons: we entered into one of these merely to see some of the lawyers dressed, as they were, in gowns, whigs & bands. Crossing Westminster bridge we took a carriage and drove to the Thames Tunnel[148] through which we passed on foot from the Surry to the Middlesex side of London. In passing through the tunnel we saw stalls nearly all the way for the sale of refreshments and bijouteries &c From the tunnel we went to the Tower of London a place rendered illustrious in the annals of history by reason of the many great and good men who have pined under the hand of tyranny within its massive walls and who passed from its gates to exchange a miserable life for one immortal, happy and glorious! On our first entrance we passed through a long room arranged in such a manner as to show the costumes in armor of knights on horseback from the times of Henry I,[149] till its use (that is of armor) was superseded by the inventions of modern times. Swords, pistols, guns, ramrods, etc. were arranged in a very forciful [sic] manner, so as to represent stars, plants, etc. We were shown the apartment in which Sir W. Raleigh[150] was confined, in which he wrote his own life and from which he was led to the block. Opposite to the door of his bedroom are a block

[148] The Thames tunnel was begun in 1825 by the famed engineer Marc Isambard Brunel. Construction resumed in 1836 and completed in 1842. Because the promoters did not have enough money to build approaches, the tunnel remained a walking one until 1865 when it became part of East London Railway. ("Thames Tunnel," **London Ency**).

[149] Henry I, king of England (1100-35).

[150] Sir Walter Raleigh (1554?-1618), English soldier, explorer, courtier and man of letters was beheaded for treason.

[151] Arthur Elphinstone, Baron Balmerino (1688-1746) who was captured at Culloden Moor in 1745, was executed for his role in the Jacobite uprisings of 1715. Following their suppression he fled to France and returned with the Bonnie Prince. (**DNB**).

[152] William Boyd, Earl of Kilmarnock (1704-46) supported the Bonnie Prince although earlier the Hanoverians. He was executed primarily because the Duke of Cumberland (1721-65), the victor at Culloden Moor, thought the earl had given the order: no quarter! (**DNB**).

[153] Simon Fraser, Baron Lovat (1675?-1746) was another executed for attempting to put Bonnie Prince Charlie on the British Throne. (**DNB**).

& axe for execution, which appears to have been used, and the last time at the decapitation of Lords Balmerino,[151] Kilmarnock[152] and Lovat[153] in 1746. The Jewel room for holding the crown Jewels is worthy of a passing notice. Before entering it, we are passed by one or two guard rooms with soldiers in attendance, and required to leave canes, umbrellas and everything which by possibility could be converted into an offensive weapon. The Jewels are tastefully arranged within a strong iron railing and canopy, and a glass jar, an immense bell glass covering the treasures. The queen's crown is beautiful and rich—in the front of the band is the largest and most beautiful ruby I ever saw—above it an emerald, and below a sapphire, the whole surrounded with brilliants. The value of this crown is estimated at one million of pounds sterling. There are 4 or 5 crowns in the collection all richly ornamented with diamonds & other precious stones, together with sceptres [sic] globes or orbs, swords, etc. The communion service appears to be massive gold and is very beautiful and large. There are also salt cellars, a large silver wine fountain and a baptismal font. In a small room near the entrance of the way leading to the Jewel room, were found the bones of the young prince and princess [sic] murdered by order of Richard Duke of Glouchester.[154]

Leaving the tower, our next object of examination was the celebrated Cathedral of St Pauls, it is in the form of a Cross, the whole surmounted by a magnificent dome, elevated to a height that is actually painful to behold. The interior is grand and impressive. A great part of the space inside seemed to be unappropriated to any useful purpose or particular object. Many niches and spaces are filled with figures of Warriors & Admirals & other officers slain in the service of their country. Of 48 monuments erected in St Paul's Cathedral 41 commemorate the services of warriors on land or by sea, whereas only 7 perpetuate the memory of those distinguished in the arts of peace. I omit any further account of this immense structure & its contents as I am not qualified to do justice to either. I returned to my lodgings weary; was very sick at night.

Saturday May 24. After breakfast this morning I walked first to the British museum to see the Rev. Mr. Norm who in a note written yesterday expressed a desire that I should call. I did call but he was not in his rooms: The British Museum is not open to visitors on Saturday. From the

[154] The children Richard of Glouchester is accused of having murdered were his nephews, young Edward V and younger brother. On their disappearance the duke took the throne as Richard III. (**DNB**).

[155] Ernest Hawkins (1802-65), prior to becoming secretary of the SPCK had been an under librarian at the Bodleian in Oxford and was once considered for the post of Keeper of the Printed Books at the British Museum. (Edward Miller, **That Noble Cabinet, A History of the British Museum** [Athens, OH: 1974], p. 148).

[156] The Society for the Propagation of Christian Knowledge was founded in 1698 by Dr. Thomas Bray and some of the laity for the purpose of "promoting Religion and learning in any part of His Majesty's Plantations abroad, and to provide catechetical Libraries and free Schools in the Parishes at home." Today it is headquartered at Holy Trinity Marylebone Church. ("SPCK", **London Ency**).

museum I threaded my way through a labyrinth of streets to Pall Mall to the Rev. Ernest Hawkins,[155] Sec'y to the venerable Society for the Propagation of Christian Knowledge,[156] whose rooms are No. 79. He received me with much cordiality and kindness and afterwards accompanied me to the house of the Bp. of London[157] who was out when we called. Hence I walked to the American Minister at 138 Picadilly, where I met my travelling companions and many other Americans & among them Mr. Haddock Charge to Portugal.[158] Mr. Lawrence[159] was very kind in proferring his services to aid us in any way that I might desire them. From this we proceeded to the Queen's Mews, or the place where the horses, carriages and equipments of the royal household are kept. We saw a very large number perhaps a hundred or more very fine horses, in fine keeping, in snug & comfortable stalls attended by grooms, etc. Some of the horses were remarkable for their beauty. I saw one of a rich cream color, his hair glossy as silk his tale [sic] swept the ground and his mane hanging down to his breast would descend to his knees but that animal as we were told was in the habit of biting it off. We were also shown the harness & various other caparisons of the horses. The carriages which were also shown to us were very beautiful, substantial and well made. The State Carriages, used only on great occasions—such as the opening of Parliament, the prorogation of it, or at a coronation—is a magnificent vehicle, very massive and rich with gold plating and weighs eight tons. It is drawn when in use by eight horses.

After leaving the mews we drove by Buckingham Palace, the present residence of the Queen and which is a very imposing structure fronting St. James park, [sic] to the Zoological gardens in Regents park. [sic] This is a most interesting locality to visit and is reached by one of the most delightful drives which the Metropolis furnishes. Of almost every thing of the animal kind, of which we saw stuffed specimens in the Museum, we here find exemplifications in the living animals. The first things that attracted my attention were very large white bears. They must be very formidable in a state of nature. The collection of Parrots is very complete—some of them very diminuitive not larger than sparrows, but very beautiful in form and plumage. The ducks, black swans, flamingoes, &

[157] Charles James Bromfield (1786-1859) was bishop of London from 1828 to 1856 when he resigned for reasons of health. During his tenure 200 new churches were built and other steps taken to strengthen the church in his diocese and elsewhere in England. (**DNB**).

[158] Charles Brickett Haddock (1796-1861), a nephew of Daniel Webster, was appointed minister to Portugal by President Fillmore, a post he held from 1851 to 1856. (**DAB**).

[159] Abbott Lawrence (1792-1855) made his money as a manufacturer of cotton textiles. He also served in the US Congress in 1835-37 and 1839-40. In 1848 he was appointed minister to Great Britain and held the office until 1852. (**Ibid**).

[160] According to legend "The Wandering Jew" was an individual who mocked Christ on His way to crucifixion. For this, the man was condemned to wander until the Second Coming. The origins of the legend go back to the 13th Century and perhaps earlier. ("Wandering Jew," **NCE**).

pheasants were also curious and very interesting. The hyena from Africa is a hideous looking animal. The lions, tigers, cougars, and leopards reminded me of Le Mort in the "Wandering Jew."[160] After strolling about the grounds and listening to the Horse-guards[161] band til near the hour of 5 p.m. I returned with Mrs. E[akins] to our lodgings.[162]

Sunday May 25. Attended Church this morning at St. George the Martyr's—heard the morning prayer by Rev. Mr. Mason and a sermon by Rev. Mr. Short and partook of the Holy Communion. The congregation was respectable in numbers & behaved well during the service & sermon which was a plain & practical discourse & better delivered than any I have yet heard in England except Dr. McNeil's[163] at Liverpool. After the sermon, the congregation retired and then the Communion was celebrated. In the afternoon I attended worship in the same Church. Mr. Short read prayers & Mr. Mason preached on the character of St. Paul. It was an instructive sermon. I did not feel inclined to seek the opportunity of hearing some distinguished preacher. I find that when I listen to a great man my mind is too apt to be dwelling upon the man to the forgetting of his subject. I felt to day [sic] that I must act in conformity with my own saddened thoughts. They have dwelt much upon the memory of my beloved Sarah, the anniversary of whose death is near at hand. And yet the recollections of it and all its attending circumstances from years ago is just as fresh in my mind now as the occurances of yesterday. Merciful Lord! grant me the graces of meek resignation of thy will, of humble submission to thy Providence. I have striven to worship God to day with an humble mind and sincere heart! yet am I sensible of my imperfections and feel that my best efforts need to be regarded compassionately By Him, I strive to serve!

Monday May 26. Mrs. Eakin and friends went this day to visit Windsor Castle. I remained at my lodgings employed in writing. I addressed a letter to the Archbishop of Canterbury,[164] in reference to his circular addressed to the American Bps: concerning the Jubilee of the Venerable Society for the Propagation of the Gospel in Foreign Parts. A note to the Bp. of London accepting an invitation to Breakfast on the 31st. And to Rev. Mr. Hawkins engaging to preach at the Jubilee of the Society, the 22nd June. I then took a cab and rode to the Thames, embarked on a

[161] Horse Guards is the cavalry component of the guard regiments. The two mounted troopers who sit almost like statues in front of the Horse Guard office at Whitehall are part of this organization.

[162] The Tennesseans lodged at Miss Lawson's, No. 46, Great Orman Street, Queens Square, Bloomsbury. (McGavock, **Pen**, p. 195.)

[163] Hugh McNeile (1795-1879) was a lawyer before he became a clergyman. From 1848 to 1867 he served at St. Paul, Prince's Park, Liverpool and from 1868 to 1875 was dean of Ripon. Some of his sermons were published. (**DNB**). According to McGavock who did not accept Otey's invitation to go to church on 11 May, Dr. McNeile "has the character of being one of the best preachers in Great Britain." (**Pen**, p. 191).

[164] John Bird Sumner (1780-1862) was Archbishop of Canterbury from 1848 to 1862.

steamer and landing at London bridge proceeded to the Custom House to enquire after a box of charts which I had sent from Liverpool. It was there. The officers were very polite and suggested to me the method by which I should have it passed through the Custom House without charge, &c. Returning I met with a stout athletic man who opened & shut the Cab-door for me and then asked for a copper—a penny. Why, I said, must I give you a copper my good fellow? Because it is my business to wait upon gentlemen in this way, and it is the only way I have to get my living. "I am licensed," said he, pointing to a brass-plate suspended from his neck. I gave him the penny and said to him, "if you will go to my country I will given you work and wages to set you up, and make you a decent living." "Would to God I could go," said he "But I have no means to get there!" "Can you dress a garden and do you understand farming?" "Indeed, Sir, I do not!" I was struck with the man's open countenance and the apparent honesty in his answers & felt sorry for him. But how many thousands of others are there in this immense city who are in the same and even worse condition than this man! The vast majority of those whom I see on the streets appear to be poor, their dress for the most part indifferent, often dirty and sometimes squalid. I observe also that many things here are offered for sale as food which I never saw put to that use in America—as chicken's heads and feet, the heads and feet and legs of sheep, etc. Returning to my lodgings I addressed a letter to Mr. Lawrence our Minister respecting my box and hope speedily to obtain an order from the Lords of Treasury for its release from the keep of the Custom House. Rev. Mr. Short called today and also Dr. Shelton[165] of Buffalo, N.Y.

Tuesday May 27. This day is so near the anniversary of that day in the year which brought with it the most distressing event which I had then ever known, the death of my dearly beloved Sarah[166]—that I feel no disposition whatever to go out this day and to mingle with men engaged in the ordinary pursuit of life. Yet I shall be compelled to go forth for a little time on necessary business: let me then dispatch it as speedily as I can and return to thoughts & meditations more suitable to one who feels that

[165] William Shelton, D.D. was born at Fairfield Connecticut in 1798 and died there on a visit in 1883. Meanwhile for fifty years he was rector of St. Paul's Protestant Episcopal Church, Buffalo, New York and rector emeritus. He was a pastor rather than an theologian. (**Appelton's Cyclopedia of American Biography**, [N.Y.: 1888] vol. 5).

[166] Although Sarah was the third of Otey's children to die, her death seems to have effected him the most.

[167] Lucien Campbell Duncan, a lawyer from New Orleans, was appointed United States Commissioner to the Great Exhibition. The flag he took for display in the Great Crystal Palace was woven by some women in Philadelphia and carried on a staff from a sapling grown at Mount Vernon. At the close of the exhibition Duncan took the flag to various parts of Europe and Jerusalem where the patriarch blessed it. On Duncan's death a young nephew inherited it. In 1857 Bishop Polk prevailed on young Herman Duncan to take it to the meeting at Lookout Mountain where Sewanee was chosen as the site for the future University of the South. Twenty-eight years later the lad, now archdeacon of the Episcopal cathedral in Alexandria, Louisiana, presented the flag to the university where it hangs, glass enclosed, on a wall of the chapel. (**Purple Sewanee**, a reprint of "Sewanee" by permission of the copyright owner, Charles E. Thomas...Copyright 1961. pp. 93-94).

in the death of his child he had suffered at least one of the greatest earthly calamities that could befall him. After having been engaged a great part of the forenoon in writing I went to see Mr. Lucius Duncan[167] in Hunter Street.[168] I had forgotten the number of his lodgings & could not find him. Returning to my lodgings I met with Mr. McGavock and reached Westminster Abbey at the time of the celebration of the evening service. There was a considerable congregation present and the service was more than half concluded before we entered. The choir was engaged in singing an anthem and I thought I had never in my life heard any music that was so soul-thrilling and touching. The notes of the organ which were deep and mellow mingling with the fine silvery voices of the boys in the choir, rose into the lofty and fretted roofs of this antiquated building or rolled along its extended aisles and dying away in the deep recesses above, seemed like the music of the Heavenly World. There was something mournful and plaintive in the character of the plain song that was deeply affecting to my spirit. It seemed to call me away from earth and earthly things and draw my thoughts up to high & heavenly contemplations. If the music of Earth have such an effect upon the mind in this state, what must it be to hear that unnumerable company that surrounds the throne "harping with their harps," of the thousands of thousands who sing the song of Moses and the Lamb; the sound of whose voices is as the sound of many waters & of mighty thundering? O Lord! let me [undecipherable] live under the influence and powers of the world to come! let me have not only my thoughts, but the affections of my heart also fixed upon the prize of life eternal; & let all that I think, or design, or say, or do, be so directed by thy grace as to bring me on the way that leads to thy favor—and to a blissful reunion with those whom I have loved & lost in thy heavenly and everlasting kingdom at last!

After the conclusion of the service in the Abbey and taking a turn through the aisles and viewing the monuments which crowd the niches, walls, recesses, I went into the gallery of the House of Commons and listened to the debates for the space of an hour or longer. It did not strike me as a dignified body. The members were very generally engaged in conversation or moving about even when a member was speaking and all sat covered except him who for the time occupied the floor in speaking. The chairman very frequently had to call out Order! Order!! Very tart and occasionally acrimonious language was used in debate. Most generally however it was hypothetical and in the end qualified, so as to be harmless or was retracted. The men in support of the government or administration and those opposed occupy opposite seats in the chamber.

[168] Hunter Street is in the Bloomsbury section at Brunswick Square. (**London Ency.**).

[169] George D. Campbell, Duke of Argyle (1823-1900) succeded in 1843 as the 8th duke. (Burke's **Peerage**).

I went next into the House of Lords, who meet in a spacious and elegant room. It had the appearance of an orderly & dignified body. The duke of Argyle[169] was addressing the House. I was struck with this fact in all the speaking I heard in the House of Lords & in the Commons: a degree of hesitation or halting which gives to an address any thing but the appearance of ease & grace. The oratory of Americans in the legislature or on the stump, is far superior to anything I have heard in this country.[170] The duke of Argyle is a small, red-haired man, very youthful in his appearance and is said to be one of the best speakers in the House of Lords. If his speech was not distinguished for its finished rhetoric, it was at least creditable to his good sense. I saw but three Bishops[171] in the House which very soon adjourned.

Wednesday May 28th. Day ever to be remembered as bringing the saddest recollection of may past life! A day which I fear must be devoted to the indulgence of sorrow! How this poor heart yearns after that beloved child which death tore away from my embraces just four years ago this day! I remember how I sat by her dying couch, and held her hand, and watched her failing breath, till she breathed her last breath, and departed without a struggle or groan! O My God! Can I ever forget the overwhelming agony of that moment? Even now the remembrance, tears my soul, and makes life bitterness [sic] and covers the world with gloom. Yet my most merciful Father who seest into my heart, then knewest that it is the very desire of my soul to be humble and resigned—to let no murmuring thought find a place in my heart, and no word of complaint escape the door of my lips! I pray that I may be as a weaned child before thee & lay my hand upon my mouth because thou hast done it! Be still! my heart! be still!—still!—still!! Remember the rod and who has appointed it!

I walked with Mr. L. Duncan today & called at the Bp. of St Asaph's[172] who received us kindly and courteously. Then we went to see

<hr />

[170] This remark is in sharp contrast to comments made in his diary on 15 September 1852 about a speech by General Sam Houston in Columbia, Tennessee. "Upon the respective merits of Gen: Scott and Pierce for the Presidency, I do think that I have never in all my life listened to a speech that was filled with more low vulgar slang and nonsense. Not a single thing did I hear worthy of the subject and worthy of the exalted station which Houston holds as Senator of the U. States. There was a constant effort to be witty accompanied with an attempted criticism of Scott's generalship! I left the ground disgusted utterly with all that I heard & saw! Alas! for my country!" (This diary is volume 8, James Otey Papers, Southern Historical Collection, Wilson Library, University of North Carolina at Chapel Hill).

[171] In 1851 all twenty-seven bishops of the Church of England had a seat in the House of Lords. Today as there are forty bishoprics, membership in Lords is on a seniority basis with the exception of the archbishops of Canterbury and York who along with the occupants of the sees of London, Winchester, and Durham always have a seat. The bishop of Soder and Mann is not seated because the Isle of Mann has its own legislative assembly. Thus the bishop of this diocese was usually transferred to another on a vacancy. (**Whitaker's Almanac** (1993), pp. 167 and 223).

[172] Thomas V. Short (1790-1872), bishop of St. Asaph (1846-70) had been bishop of Soder and Mann (1841-46). St. Asaph is in the northeast corner of Wales near the Dee River. (**DNB**).

the archeological collection of a Mr. Hertz, to the inspection of which I had been specially invited by Mr. David Hoffman who is very desireous that the collection should be secured for some institution in our country. There are here some of the most interesting specimens of antiquity, as well as most curious that have ever fallen under my observation— Among them a kind of mirror or speculum which looked at with the light falling on it appears to be a green glass with an embryo head in the centre elevated[?] & of metal & the rim of the speculum is surrounded with metal globules or hemispheres. The metal portion is apparently as opaque as any metal preparation can be: until you turn and hold the speculum between the eye and the sun or a strong light and then the whole becomes transparent presenting a beautiful emerald green appearance. By what art the ancients were enabled to do this in the preparation of this speculum it altogether incomprehensible. I returned from this examination & of a bazaar between Gt. Marlborough St. & Oxford Street weary and exhausted. Met the Rev. Dr. Moore of New York at M. Hertz's rooms.

May 29, Thursday. Still a day of sad reminiscences. This day four years ago the grave closed its jaws upon an object than which few in the world were so dear to my heart: and since that hour I have found no rest to my spirit, and what has this world been to me or what can it ever, but a theater hung around with darkness and the shadow of death!. Yet O God! who art compassionate and merciful even to the ungrateful & sinner, grant me grace to submit to thy dispensations without murmuring and to receive them as wholesome medicines to the soul.

To day I have walked a great way through London with Mr. L. Duncan of New Orleans an exceedingly amiable and pleasant gentleman and kind in his disposition. He is about as remarkable for his low stature and broad build—filling up exactly my idea of Zaccheus'[173] personal appearance— as I may be for my height and thinness or leaness. We presented so striking a contrast in size &c, as we walked, that it was very manifest that we attracted the notice of all who were not too busily engaged to permit their attention to be diverted from their occupations. To make the disparity between us more noticeable my friend, my "fidus Achates,"[174] would in

[173] Zaccheus was the small man who climbed a tree in order to see Jesus when the Lord was in Jericho. (**Luke** 19: 1-6).

[174] Achates was the faithful companion of Aeneas in the **Aeneid**.

[175] A prison was built in 1615 at Clerkenwell. It was demolished in 1804. The one Otey saw was erected in 1845-46 (**London Ency.**).

[176] Newgate had been the site of a prison since the 12th century. The one mentioned above was built in 1780-83 replacing a structure burnt in the Gordan Riots in 1780. (**Ibid**).

[177] At one time the Smithfield Market's occupied a ten acre area. Not only were cattle slaughtered here but also humans were executed by hanging or burning at the stake. Over 200 martyrs were burned during the reign of "Bloody Mary" for stubbornly holding to their Protestant beliefs. Today the place is the London Central Meat Market where over 350,000 tons of meat are sold annually. (**Ibid**).

[178] John Rogers (d. 1556) was burned as a heretic because he uttered anti-Roman statements. (**Ibid**).

the shade of the houses take off his hat and walk with it in his hands. We passed many noted places—Clerkenwell prison,[175] Newgate,[176] Smithfield market[177] where Jno: Rogers[178] was burnt and finally drew up at the Banking House of the Barings.[179] I deposited with them £200 in a check on the Bk of England, drew £50 for present use and left £150 upon which to predicate a letter of credit for my use hereafter. Went from the Barings to Allen and Anderson's Bankers &c. and left with them my letter of credit for £300 from New York, not expecting to use it. Mr. Anderson junior was very polite & invited me to dine at his Father's on Saturday. After this I went to the American Ministers and left our passports to be visad.[180] Finding that the day was nearly exhausted and having engaged to dine at **Verilan** House No. 3—Verilan Terrace Maida Vale,[181] with Mr. Jos: Miller & his sister Mrs. Harper the friends of Mrs. Trotter I set off to fulfill the engagement and to my surprise I arrived nearly an hour before the hour appointed. Making my apologies to Mrs. Harper who presently appeared and received me very cordially I sat down to dinner about 8 p.m. and passed my time as pleasantly as I could in a country the manners of whose people are cold, stiff and all the time constrained. These folk here when they would even treat you with marked civility, seem nevertheless to act and speak with an air of constraint—as if they feared they might lose something of that dignity or consequence which they claim or affect to claim to belong to their rank or station. Wealth here is establishing a species of affected aristocratical superiority and the manifestation of this superiority is as apparent as between our planters and their menials and at the same time far more unpleasant.

Mr. Jos: Miller & Mrs. Harper are brother and sister: the latter was taken to Albemarle Va at the age of 12 was there educated and married. She had lost all trace and nearly all remembrance of her Bro: and they both thought each other dead. At the end of 24 years, enquiry through a friend going to America was made by Mr. Miller as to the place where his sister had lived and been buried. The enquiry led to the development of the mutually interesting fact that the sister & brother were both alive. In due time Mrs. H. crossed the Atalantic to see her Bro: who is an invalid from his gout or rheumatism, and she now lives in the house with him in the enjoyment of every luxury wealth can furnish.

[179] The banking house was established in 1763 as John and Francis Baring and Company. In 1803 the name was changed to Baring Brothers, an establishment that is still family controlled. (**NCE**).

[180] Otey's visit to the office of the American minister requesting a visa is the only time his name appears in its official records (Sally Marks, National Archives, Washington DC, to Edwin T. Greninger, 19 July 1988).

[181] Maida Vail was a recent development with most of the terraces and mansions being built in the 1840's and 50's. (**London Ency**).

[182] John Miller, according to McGavock, was the American agent. Before leaving on his tour of the British Isles McGavock left his trunk with Miller and on his return collected it and mail (**Pen**, pp. 201 and 212).

[183] Token House Yard is on the north side of the Bank of England and is the location of stock brokers and solicitors. (**London Ency.**).

May 30 Friday. This morning after arranging some matters for myself and Mrs. Eakin with Mr. Jno: Miller[182] I walked to Token House[183] place near the Bk of England to see Mr. A.G. Ralston Dr. Balch's brother in law & to whom the Dr. had specially commended me. I delivered the letter & entered into conversation but the gentleman whom I took to be Mr. Ralston seemed to be very little disposed to interest himself about me or my concerns or the wishes of Dr. Balch to bring me into intercourse with his friends in England—So I very soon left and walked to Dr. Russell's[184] Devonshire Square. If my reception at Token House was cold, it was icy here. The servant that met me at the door informed me that Dr. Russell, who had sent me his card without any advances from me, was engaged. I told him to present my card to the Dr.—that I was tired and had walked too far to come there again &c. He disappeared and in a minute or two returned with the answer that the Dr. was particularly engaged. I took my hat and as we say in America **"Mosied."** There was a meeting of some kind at Dr. Russell's with the clergy I presume. I heard something like a voice in earnest discussion. But no matter what was the occasion or business at hand, the Dr. should have had at least politeness enough to offer an excuse in person. Such I am sure is the treatment he would have received in America. From this place I went to call upon the Bp. of Nova Scotia[185] and the Rev. Drs. Binney & Townsend—all of whom were out. At 7 went to the Bp. of St Asaph's to dine. Here I met with the Bps of Ripon and Soder & Mann and several gentlemen and ladies. The same stiffness and formality as heretofore observed at other places. There is no positive want of politeness here but a manifest deficiency in efforts to make a guest feel easy & as we say in America "at home." I ate but very little of the good things set before me and still less did I drink of the many I suppose generous wines that were passed round the table. A Dr. Wilson,[186] physician to St. George's hospital, rather annoyed me by the quantity of his talk concerning some young American and the interest taken in him by his Countrymen. The English are mar-

[184] John Russell (1787-1863) could be the Dr. Russell mentioned. He graduated from Oxford in 1806 and received a D.D. in 1820. In addition to being a canon of Canterbury (1832-63) he was rector of St Botolph's Outside Bishopsgate and treasurer of the Society for the Propagation of the Gospel. Among his publications were a Latin grammar that had three editions and an English grammar that was issued nine times. (**DNB**).

[185] Hibbert Binney (1819-78) was the new bishop of Nova Scotia having been consecrated on the 25th of that March. The previous bishop, John Inglis, who had died in London on 27 October 1850, was the son of the first bishop, Charles Inglis who, prior to the American Revolution, had been a rector in New York City. Binney was the first Canadian-born bishop of Nova Scotia although he had been educated in England because his father who had had a parish in Halifax returned to England while Hibbert was a child. (Philip Carrington, **The Anglican Church in Canada, A History**, [Toronto, 1963]; **Two Hundred and Fifty Years Young, Our Diocesan Story 1710-1960** [Nova Scotia] p. 24).

[186] Wilson, James Arthur (1795-1882) was physician at St. George's Hospital from 1828 to 1857. In 1850 he delivered the Harveian lecture at the Royal College of Physicans, the school founded by William Harvey. (**Mod. Eng. Biog.**, III).

vellously [sic] given to talk all themselves and to keep right on without stopping when you would interpose an observation—that is when once they begin to talk.

At 10½ p.m. went to the American Minister's, a large and elegant party were present—and among them the Duke of Wellington—an old looking gentleman with face rather broader that I expected to see. There is nothing very different in his appearance from that of any other old man! Several of my countrymen were introduced to him I suppose I might have been: but feeling that I had nothing to say to him nor he to me I did not seek the opportunity to be introduced: but feeling very unwell *[Material appears to be missing. The account resumes the following morning at the breakfast to which Otey was invited by the bishop of London.]* as it is called, I was ushered into the presence of his Lordship who presented me to his lady and to the Venerable Archdeacon ++++++ [sic] and presented afterwards to the Bishop of Oxford.[187] There were several other gentlemen and ladies present but I was not introduced to them. It appears to be the custom here not to introduce persons unless it is desired by the parties and in mixed assemblies it often leads to meetings that are anything but pleasant. When an evening party is assembling, the practice is for doorkeeper to announce the name of the invited guest as soon as he arrives and the name is repeated from servant to servant until it reaches the master or mistress of the house at the drawing room door. The breakfast this morning was plain and simple enough and passed off quite agreeably. I was also presented to the Bishop of Glasgow[188] who seemed glad to see me and invited me to visit him at home. There was too much appearance of formality—an air of constraint in the bearing and speech of all around to make the party as pleasant as a similar assemblage in our own land.

After breakfast I returned to my lodgings and have remained within doors all the balance of the day. I had accepted an invitation to dine this evening with Mr. Anderson in Hyde Park at 7 p.m. Upon the approach of the hour I felt too unwell to fulfill the engagement.

Sunday June 1. The first day of Summer—a clear day, if there be any such thing in London. The Bp. of London having yesterday furnished me with a ticket of admission to the Royal Chapel of St. James I drove thither a little before 8 a.m. with Mrs. Eakin and found no body in the

[187] Samuel Wilburforce (1805-73) was bishop of Oxford (1845-69) and of Winchester (1869-73). Not being a member of the Oxford Movement he attempted to take the middle ground between the High and Low Churchmen. (**NCE**).

[188] Walter John Trower (1805-77) was born and educated in England and held a parish there before becoming bishop of Glasgow and Galloway (1848-59). Later he was chosen bishop of Gibralter where he served from 1863 to 1868. From then until his death in 1871 he was rector of Ashington. (**Mod. Eng. Bios.** IV, pp. 1024-25).

chapel but the verger and the Duke of Wellington. Several persons afterwards entered among them the Duke of Rutland and a person whom I
took to be Col. Wildman of Newstead. The clergyman read the antecommunion service, preached a short and practical sermon, and then proceeded with the communion office. After he had consecrated the bread
and wine and was in the act of receiving himself, I went forward according to the invariable usage and kneeled at the chancel railing to receive
the Communion according to the requirements of the Rubric as a Bp. The
practice of administering to the clergy first did not seem to be understood
here, as I find many other things equally neglected, overlooked or disre-
garded. I had hardly composed my thoughts for the solemn act I was
about to perform when I found the Duke of Wellington kneeling at my
side, a lady on my left and the railing of the chancel nearly filled or occupied by communicants. So the communion was administered to us without distinction and upon reflection I was rather gratified that it was so.
Here was a curious or interesting circumstance at least to myself. That
the Conqueror of Napoleon shd. kneel by my side at the same altar pro-
fessing his faith in the Saviour whose blood of atonement was poured out
for the sins of the world and to give life to the world—and should there
join with me in the performance of the most solemn act of our holy religion was an incident which I surely never anticipated among the bare
probabilities of life.

At 10½ a.m. I went to St. James Church in Piccadilly, I believe The
Church was nearly filled—entering I saw an official and asked for a seat.
He said I should have one presently. After waiting sometime and looking
[unclear] in vain for the courtesy of an offered seat, I went to the same
official and told him that the Bp. of London had told me that I could get a
seat there. He replied that I could get a seat in the gallery and would
show me to a pew-opener. I followed him to the gallery stairs, went up—
no pew-opener was there and no seat was offered. I came down & meeting the official told him the difficulty and said it was the first time I was
ever in an Episcopal Church where I was denied the civility of a seat. He
said he would take me to a seat if he knew where one would be vacant,
but that he was compelled to wait until the pew owners came—that is I
suppose until service began when vacant pews might be thrown open for
the accommodation of visitors. I told him I should make no further effort,
but would return home. Proceeding to the gate the cab-man was gone and
I was obliged to return to the church, stand in the street or walk home. I
went back to the Church and ascended to another gallery where a lady
very politely tendered to Miss Bass & myself a seat in her pew. We

entered, heard the service, and an excellent sermon. At 3 P.M. went to Temple-bar Church, heard the Choral service as it it called and a very able discourse from the Bishop of Oxford. The only objection to it I think was, that it was far above the comprehension of hundreds of men and women present. This being the church at which the lawyers ordinarily attend many of them might have been present & heard & understood the learned prelate. His text was "Sin is the Transgression of the Law." The object of the sermon was to show that sin was something more than the violation of a law arbitrarily enacted by Him who had power to punish the violations, this was the common apprehension and was a great mistake. Sin, he argued, was something that followed naturally, or more properly **necessarily** from violation of the constitution which the all wise God had established. When God saw all his works which he created, he pronounced them very good. They were exactly fitted to answer the ends for which he had formed them. Man as he existed before the Fall, was the expression of the idea which had previously existed in the mind of the Deity. Now any change in his will or affections in opposition to the law under which he was placed was of necessity a deterioration—was in short sin essentially and must necessarily end in misery. The subject was managed with great ability. But the difficulty which might be raised: namely; how could the moral attributes of the Deity be manifested without the introduction of moral evil into the world, was a point not considered and discussed. It seems to me proper upon the whole to take for granted that sin is the violation of the law of a perfectly holy & just Being, and we need go no further than the positive declaration of scripture on such subjects—all reasonings upon such matters having a tendency to perplex rather than to enlighten the understanding.

The Water Cure

Monday June 2. This morning settled accounts with Miss Lawson and proceeded with Mrs. Eakin & Miss Bass to Euston Station[189] to take the road to Birmingham & thence to Great Malvern, the celebrated Hydropathic establishment of Dr. Wilson. Travelled through an exceedingly beautiful & well cultivated country until we reached the neighborhood of the village of Gt. Malvern where the country rising in bold hills and mountains assumed quite a picturesque appearance. Indeed I may well say that I have rarely if ever seen so beautiful a picture as that presented to the eye as one approached the village or town of Great Malvern. It is situated rather on the side of a mountain and commands the full view of a most lovely valley. Arriving between 8 & 9 p.m. we stopped at the house of Dr. Wilson where we had the pleasure of meeting Dr. Breckenridge,[190] Col. Grigsby and lady.[191] Let this entry suffice for the present as I have travelled from London since 12 p.m. a distance of some 160 or 170 miles.

Tuesday June 3. My first night and the best part of one day has been passed at Malvern. This morning about 7 a.m., the Dr. (Summes) [sic] came to my room, examined my condition and prescribed fomentations of warm water & flannel applied to my stomach and abdomen and afterwards tepid bath: all of which were speedily administered by the servant in attendance. I then dressed myself and went down to the sitting room till breakfast. After breakfast I walked through the principal park of the village with Dr. Breckenridge till we came to the Chapel of Ease now in the progress of erection for the parish congregation. The style of building is the early English as it is called. There is the appearance of a great deal of patch work about all such structures and what recommendation such a style of construction to modern tastes other than their antique fashion I cannot imagine. The buildings inside appear to be arranged consistently enough with open wood work roof—warmed by pipes running from a furnace in one corner depressed below the floor. Chancel as usual in a

[189] Euston is the oldest mainline station in London having been built in 1837 for the London and Birmingham Railway. It was rebuilt and opened in 1968 by Queen Elizabeth II. (**London Ency.**).

[190] William Lewis Breckenridge, DD (1803-76), pastor of the First Presbyterian Church of Louisville, left for Cincinnati on the same boat as McGavock and company. In 1874 he became president of Centre College. His tenure was short as ill health forced his resignation. (Wm. E. Connelley and E.M. Coulter, **History of Kentucky**, [Chicago, 1922], III, p. 17).

[191] John Warren Grigsby (1820?-77) was born in Virginia. In 1840 he was appointed American consul at Bordeaux, France. Following this he studied law and in 1850 married Susan Shelby, a granddaughter of Issac Shelby (1750-1826) the first governor of Kentucky. During the Civil War he commanded a Kentucky cavalry regiment and later a brigade under General John H. Morgan. In the fighting around Atlanta he commanded another brigade with distinction. Like Breckenridge the colonel was in Wilson's establishment for the treatment. He and his wife were not Breckenridge's travelling companions. (R.M. McGavock, **Pen** p. 201 and **Biographical Encyclopaedia of Kentucky of the Dead and Living Men of the Nineteenth Century** [Cincinnati, 1878], p. 723).

recess in the East &c.

Returning to my lodgings I have spent nearly all day within doors. I walked in the garden perhaps half an hour and have felt drowsy and have slept a good deal in my chair. Upon weighing to day I find that my exact weight is 145 pounds 2 ozs. Still falling off. I am much grieved and disappointed in getting no evening post. Retire at 9 p.m.

Wednesday June 4. Last night had a repetition of warm fomentation and slept comfortably. Between four and five the attendant came and applied as before warm fomentation and gave me a tepid bath and rubbed me dry. I feel less disposition this morning to Nausea or pyrosis. Dressed and strolled through the village and ascended the lofty hills that overhang or overlook the town and surrounding country for a great distance. The scene is one of the most enchanting that the eye of man ever rested on. It wants nothing to its perfection but water in the form of a sea, of Lakes [sic] or rivers. Below and just at your feet lies the village of great [sic] Malvern[192] with its beautiful houses built after the fashion of the Italian villas or English Cottages; garden, hedges & copses interspersed among them. Some of the dwellings seem as if they might slide down the hills— so entirely do they appear to hang in the air. To the Eastward lies the ancient city of Worcester about 8 miles distant, plainly distinguishable in the clear, bright morning, with its Cathedral town and Church spires & other lofty points of observation. The valley of the **Severn** highly cultivated & studded with farm houses lies to the South while to the North & West you look over Hertfordshire into Wales with its ranges of high & blue looking mountains. Nothing can be more lovely in prospect than the clumps of trees crossing here & there lofty hills & eminences, with the spire of a Church, or a town, or something of the sort attached to a private dwelling peering out of the trees & marking it may be the abode of contentment and peace. But over this whole scene of natural & artificial beauty there seems to rest a spirit of reserve or restraint—imparting to the mind the idea of stern repose that must not be disturbed. This felt by the spectator, the want of cheerfulness. The very sheep look as if they were afraid to bleat—the lambs lie on the hill-sides and do not race about in sport—but seem to anticipate the knife of the butcher. It is not so in America. When you stand upon the summits of her lofty mountains— there is a solemn stillness around occasionally broken and rendered more impressive by the sighing of the breeze as in passing it whispers to the

---

[192] Great Malvern was a village of about sixty houses until 1842 when it became a hydropathic center. The purity of the water made it an ideal location for these treatments. In 1862 a public school for boys, Malvern College, was established. Its priory church dates from 1085. (**Shell Guide England**, and **NCE**).

aged pines but you there feel inspired to raise your voice & shout and exult in that freedom of thought &d action which you realize to be your birthright. I advanced to the verge, to the topmost point of the hill before me and gazed with mingled emotions of pleasure and sadness upon a scene which brought back the recollections of childhood and the sweet memories of many loved ones who have closed their eyes forever upon the changes and chances of this mortal life. While standing here a sense of the divine power and goodness came strongly over me with the grateful remembrance of multiplied mercies and blessings which had crowned my past life. I bared my head to the cool breeze which fanned my cheeks, and which seemed by its very touch to invigorate every nerve in my body, and opening my lips I repeated aloud various passages of the Psalms expressive of the power and greatness of God. As for example "The Earth is the Lord's and all that therein is, the round [sic] world and they that dwell therein for He hath founded it upon the floods" &c. After indulging in this strain of memoriter recitation, until my fund of quotations was exhausted. I glided very naturally into prayer: and surely I felt that I prayed in sincerity on this occasion: My heart's desire was to be filled with the love of God—to be resigned to his will—to feel that I and all near & dear to me were in his hands & that we might be kept in the fear & love of God, so that we might be sanctified in soul, body & spirit & kept to his Heavenly Kingdom and that there we might at last be reunited to the Spirits of those dear ones whose bodies now sleep quietly in the graves, their souls we trust are happy in the Paradise of God.

Whenever this day comes it brings with it the recollection of what is called Hughes prophecy.[193] A wretched debtor in Richmond jail Va. was unable to pay his jail fees and his lawyer wrote a paper setting in the form of a prophecy the destruction of one third of mankind by means of a storm to occur on the 4th of June 1812. The pamphlet sold readily when printed and yielded a handsome sum of money. It spread especially all through Western Virginia and had the effect of greatly alarming the fears of many weak and credulous people. I well remember the 4th June 1812 and the very spot where I stood at Sunrise that morning with several members of my father's family. Someone remarked how brightly & clearly the sun rose. "So it did." said I, "on the morning that Noah entered the ark." Why I made such observation I knew not then nor have

---

[193] Unlike Hughes, Edgar Whisenant in his books **88 Reasons Why the Rapture Will Be in 1988**, and **The Final Shout: Rapture Report 1989** did not predict the date for the end of the world but the beginning of the end when Christ will begin his Thousand Year Reign before the final judgement. For both men their books were profitable if not prophetic. Whisenant's first book sold 4.5 million copies and brought the publisher $5.5 million according the author who claims he took no royalty, preferring to get his reward in heaven. (**Johnson City** [TN] **Press**, Saturday 26 August 1989, p. 11).

I ever been able to give a reason for it since. It was wholly unpremeditated and prompted at the moment, perhaps by my own childish fears. Nevertheless it was the brightest & most beautiful day that I have ever seen shine in this world from sunrise to sunset.

June 5, Wednesday. This morning after the usual applications of water, &c I dressed and ascended the summit of the highest hill that overlooks Gt. Malvern.[194] The ascent was long and fatiguing and must have employed fully an hour's constant toil. Upon reaching the beacon as it is called—a pile of stones with a pole stuck in them—I observed a thick mist or cloud from the west driving rapidly towards me which in a few moments enveloped the whole range of hills to the S.W. & N.E. I stood for a few minutes inhaling the fresh breeze as it rushed by, offered a short prayer, as I always feel inclined to do when I reach the top of a lofty hill or mountain, for myself and those near & dear to me and descended hastily to my lodgings in the village. It had rained most of the day. I am forbidden to write only a few lines and must not study. Have exercised under the sheds at some gymnastic fixtures & walked and thus this day closes without anything of interest.

Friday June 6. Up early—packed in wet towels—put in a cold bath—walk to St. Ann's well & return. It is now raining & the prospect is for a wet day. I had the happiness this morning of receiving letters by the post from my dear children Virginia & Ben and of leaning that they were all tolerably well. It is an inexpressible pleasure to hear from dear friends in a foreign land far from home and when you find yourself in the midst of strangers. This day has been unpleasant affording little opportunity for exercise abroad and I am forbidden to exert myself at all in the way of mental labor. I must however write a little every day, if only to record the events that are passing around however trifling they may be. There are in this house three clergymen of the Ch: of England, one of them a D.D. of Magdalen College Oxford by name Rev. Mr. Fisher &c.[195]—another the Rev. Mr. Law[196] brother of the Lord Ellenborough[197] and the incumbent it

[194] The **Shell Guide England** says on p. 583 and again on p. 584 that the Malvern Hills provide good walking country.

[195] When John Fisher (1805-1896) died in his rooms at Oxford, he was the oldest member of any college in the university. In 1851 he received a DD, the following year he became dean of the divinity school and bursar the next year. He remained a fellow of Magdalen. (**Mod. Eng. Biog.** vol. 5).

[196] William Towry Law (1809-86) was the youngest brother of Lord Ellenborough. He had been an officer in the army, later was ordained and became chancellor of the diocese of Bath and Wells. In 1851 he wrote an attack on "papal aggression." Slowly he began rethinking his position after Manning went over to Rome. As a result of his turmoil, Law took a six month leave which he was on when Otey met him. In October Law gave up his benefices and joined the Roman Catholic Church. Meanwhile his eldest son, Augustus, was also struggling with the same issue independent of his father. After leaving the navy he entered the Society of Jesus. He was serving in 1880 as a missionary when he died in Africa at the age of forty-seven. (**DNB; Bibliographical Dictionary of English Catholics**).

[197] Ellenborough, Edward Law, 1st earl of (1790-1871) was governor general of India (1841-44). He divorced his second wife, Jane Digby (1807-81) for her adulterous relationship with Prince Windischgratz, the Austrian ambassador. She was married four times and died in Syria. (**DNB**).

is said of a rich living—a third a Mr. Wood, who appears to be an hum-ble-minded man and who fills the office of curate to some Rector for 85£ a year.

The first named seems to fill up one's idea of a bon vivant—a good fellow—always ready to hear or tell a joke. He keeps the company laughing whenever he is present by the drollery of his remarks and seems to have practically as little sense of religion as nine men out of ten with whom you meet. His conversation never turns upon religious matters and if you should ask him a question about the affairs of religion or of the Church, it is altogether possible his answer will be "I am sure, I don't know!" The second Mr. Law appears to eat with the heartiness of a labor-ing man. He sets himself to the task of dispatching a meal with an air which you would at once pronounce to be "con amore." He has five rings on one hand and two on the other. I have been shocked at the bearing of these two clergymen: while the remarks which I heard from others who I know are not members of the church give me no great pain; inasmuch as I know that the Church is made to bear the obloguy which follow from the light & frivolous manners and worldly spririt of her ministers. What incalculable mischief may not a clergyman do by a heedless speech of by levity of a few minutes?

Saturday June 7. To day has been passed pretty much as yesterday. In the morning before rising warm fomentations for three quarters of an hour—then a tepid bath gradually cooled—at noon a lamp bath[198] and that followed by the water ablutions as before—at 5 rubbing with a wet sheet & dry frictions and at night fomentations at bed time. After each of these applications, except the last, I took long walks and worked at gym-nastics till I obtained a warm glow on the surface. I have had water brash slightly to day as on yesterday but the symptoms are diminishing in vio-lence and I hope to be rid of it entirely in a short time. Mr. R. McGavock arrived this morning and brought me letters from London. Among them an invitation from the Lord Mayor[199] and Lady to meet the Bishops at dinner on June 18th which I must fain accept & accordingly write a note to that effect to his Lordship. But I am reminded that I must write but lit-tle.[?]

Whitsunday June 8th. Early as I could get my fomentations and sub-sequent bath this morning I was out on a tramp with Rev. Dr. Brecken-ridge to St. Ann's Well or fountain. After quaffing the pure beverage

[198] The lamp bath is explained in Otey's letter to his wife, see p. 79.
[199] Sir John Musgrove was the Lord Mayor.

which God has provided so bountifully to quench the thirst of man we returned to our lodgings: and in my room we engaged together in reading the Scriptures and in prayer. At 11 a.m. I went to church which was filled with a large and orderly congregation of respectable looking people. The service was proceeded with as usual and afterwards a sermon preached by a clergyman who I afterwards learned was the vicar of the parish. It was a sound practical discourse upon the words of Ezekiel XXXVI 25, 26, & 27. After the sermon the clerk asked me to the vestry room where the Pastor requested me to assist him in the administration of Holy Communion. Accordingly at his insistance I pronounced the absolution, consecrated the bread and wine, administered first to the clergy present, them assisted in the distribution of the bread to the people and afterwards performed the post com: services. In the afternoon took a long walk and then returned to church by six o'clock where after the customary service I heard a plain sermon from same clergyman who had read prayers in the morning. Thus the day closed and it was pleasant to think that some of my family & children had been so employed during its passing hours; and that though far apart in Godly presence, a wide ocean rolling between us, yet we had this day been united in heart & spirit in the offering of prayer & praise to God of our lives & the Father of our spirits. May He for Jesus' sake graciously accept us and our imperfect services and bring us at last to meet as a family in Heaven, "No wanderer lost!"

Monday June 9th. After the usual treatment this morning I walked over the hills of Malvern lying to the North and took a long circuit before I returned. I think I must have gone five miles: and yet the air is so pure and invigorating that I did not find myself fatigued by the exercise. After breakfast Mrs. Eakin with her party left in the Post coach for Worcester, there to take the rail cars for Birmingham, Chester, etc. on the way to Ireland. They all expressed much regret in leaving me behind.[200] It is better for them to go and certainly expedient for me to stay: though I feel sad, in being left wholly in the hands of strangers. I can hear the organ in the church from my chambers where I am penning these lines, and its sounds take me back to distant scenes, and to the memories of other years, and fill my soul with inexpressible sadness. There are certain harmonies which invariably revive recollections of my dearly beloved & deceased children. their images rise before my mind in the vividness of a living reality, and the thought that I can see them no more, almost distracts me.

[200]McGavock wrote in his diary that Bishop Otey's health being delicate, he remained behind to try more effectively the hydropathic system. (**Pen**, p. 202).

I ask myself the question, can any state or enjoyment of future happiness compensate for the anguish of heart and soul which I have felt under my bereavements? Thou O God! alone knowest and canst alone, make up of thy fullness for our losses in this miserable world!

I have to day witnessed a singular and to me curious spectacle. It seems that Whitsunday is kept by the working classes and lower orders of the English people as a holiday. They assemble in the villages & towns to hold a sort of a fair and merry-making. The sides of the streets are filled with temporary stalls and tables for the exhibition of bon-bons, goodies, nut, cakes & jim cracks of all varieties and descriptions. Beer & malt liquors etc are abundant. Donkey carts & dog carts are seen standing here & there & serving as counters on which to expose wares for sale. **Cheap Jack**[201] occupies the most conspicuous position and his voice crying his goods like an auctioneer is generally heard above all others. There are gaming tables displayed all about the streets & all sorts of enticements to induce betting. There is usually spread down a cloth like oil cloth marked off in divisions—each division having the picture of some animal as a lion, cock &c or of an object as an anchor or a diamond or a heart such as we see on playing cards. There are two dice marked with corresponding figures engraved on the six sides. The player or better lays his money on one of the figures on the table, the dice are thrown by the owner of the table from a box or cap and if the dice show a face corresponding with that covered by the money the better wins & the owner of the table has to add to it a similar amount. If the dice show differently, the owner of the table takes the money. Others have a table with an iron pointer turning or a pointer which in its rotation will point to the figure on the rim of the table. The money bet is laid on one of the figures & the pointer is made to revolve, and if on stopping it points to the money laid down the better wins, otherwise the owner of the table wins. In addition to all this there has been parading all day a band of music with a banner accompanied by what is called a morris dancer,[202] a personage trigged off and bedizened with mock finery & tinsel in the most fantastic manner. He dances in the open streets and keeps time with the music all it seems for the amusement of the populace. There are hundreds of men, women, boys & girls who attend on this spectacle and

[201] According to the **Webster's New Twentieth Century Dictionary Unabridged** Second Edition, cheap jack is a hawker of cheap goods who will often reduce the price to make a sale.

[202] The morris dance appears to be a corruption of Morisco as supposedly the dance is Moorish in origin. Originally it was a fandango later combined with an older pageant dance honoring Robin Hood and his outlaws including Friar Tuck. (**The Book of Days, a Miscellany of Popular Antiquities in connection with the Calendar Including Anecdote, Biography, and History, Curiosities of Literature and Oddities of Human Life and Character**, R. Chambers, ed. [London and Edinburgh, 1878] I, pp. 630-31).

seem to be wonderfully delighted. There is also a species of gaming carried on for nuts. A boy puts down a penny on the table where the nuts are offered. The table owner hands him a small gun which when discharged makes a report like a cracker—sending off a small spike. If the spike strikes the center of the target the boy gets such a quantity of nuts for his penny; if in some other part of the target he obtains some other quantity and so on to nothing according to their rules. I was shocked today to see a woman presiding at one of the gaming tables and actually enticing children to bet!

A sprigg of yew taken from the spot where Mary Queen of Scots was imprisoned at Chatsworth[203]

Dr. Wilson's Water Cure Establishment
GREAT MALVERN

June 9, 1851

My dear Wife,

Having written to Mary a few days since that I was at this place, I suppose you will feel anxious to learn how I am getting along with the **water-cure &c**. It will be my purpose to keep you accurately informed as to everything respecting me and my movements, whether I hear from you or not. A great many steamers have arrived in regular time at Liverpool from New York since the date of your last letter April 29; but by all of them I have received only one letter from Tennessee and that was Mary's dated May 7. This week past I have heard from Ben & Virginia.

Everbody tells me that my health has greatly improved or rather that I have mended very much in my looks during the past week. I have been here just one week today, and certainly I have been kept as busy, as one could be, in the use of the prescribed remedies since my coming. I will endeavor to describe to you the daily & hourly routine of applications to a patient in this establishment. It is **water, water** all the time and nothing but water, which is most abundant & of the purest kind. First then in the morning generally about six o'clock **Sanders** the man that waits upon me comes into my room with a tin vessel of hot water—four pieces of flannel about a yard square, a towel and a blanket on his arm. The blanket is folded to the width of

---

[203] This note was written at the top of the page above the picture of the establishment. The picture is on p. 105.

two feet or twenty inches and laid across my bed between the sheets—one lone piece of flannel is dipped into the hot water and wrung in the towel and having been previously folded to the proper size, is laid over my stomach & bowels and the blanket on which I was lying wrapped tightly around my body so as to prevent the escape of heat & moisture. After remaining 8 or 10 minutes this flannel is taken off and replaced by another prepared in the same way until the whole four have been used. Then I rise, strip off everything and get into a tepid bath into which a cold stream is presently turned and kept running till it is chilling cold; after a few minutes I am taken out of this wrapped up in a dry sheet and rubbed until I am perfectly dry and my skin all in a glow. This is pleasant enough. Immediately after this I dress and hurry off for a walk to the top of some hill which you see in the rear of the house pictured on this sheet. These hills are 1,400 feet above the level of the sea and 900 feet above Dr. Wilson's house. It makes one blow to ascend to the summit of any of them. Returning from my walk a little above 8 o'clock I get ready for breakfast which is always announced punctually at that hour. Our breakfast consists of cold light bread either of bolted or unbolted flour—black tea—butter and milk and **nothing more— nothing more** for love or money, unless it be a boiled egg which is allowed to a visitor & not to a patient. After breakfast I am permitted to walk about as I please until 12 p.m. when I must sit down in a bath of water at 60 degrees for 4 minutes or take what is called here the lamp bath. This is given as follows. You sit in a chair prepared for the purpose and a lighted spirits of wine lamp is placed under the chair and you are then covered all over to the neck (having previously stripped off all your clothes) with sheets and blankets and there you sit till you become as hot almost as Tophet,[204] and continue to sit until the perspiration breaks out upon you and runs down in streams. Then you are put into a tepid bath gradually cooled till it is chilled and lastly rubbed in a dry sheet till your skin is red & glowing. You are then dismissed to walk around and drink pure cold water till dinner. This consists of the same sort of bread as before described—of mutton boiled or roast, sometimes a piece of beef or boiled chicken, Irish potatoes—macaroni and boiled cabbages & salt and nothing more. Neither pepper, mustard, vinegar nor a pickel is ever permitted to make its appearance on the table. For desert a nice pudding. I call this good living though some people profess to think it very poor.

[204] In the Old Testament a place where humans were the burnt offerings to Moloch.

About 5 p.m. I have a wet sheet thrown over shoulders and a stout man rubs me from head to foot and then dried off as before. Teatime comes and we have bread tea and butter as before. At breakfast there is one thing more allowed us—what we call **molasses** the English **Treacle**. We may have treacle with our milk & both are of first chop or quality. At nine o'clock I go to bed which is sometime before dark in this country and **Sanders** comes, puts the hot flannels to my stomach; I drop to sleep, **dream of you**, and awake between three and four o'clock in the morning. And then the only trouble I have begins. The water brash begins shortly after I awake and generally continues more or less till I have undergone treatment as they say here, am out on the hill for a tramp. I find however that my waterbrash is gradually lessening every day. I have not vomited since I came here and the accumulation of water from the salivary glands is much less. My appetite has improved and I have some relish for my food. My skin is looking a good deal better and some of my American friends tell me that I appear ten years younger than when I came. I don't believe this. But I am sure that I feel better & I think my looks are changed for the better decidedly. So far these things seem to promise fair; but I have been so often sorely disappointed by promising appearances in this world, that I indulge in no very sanguine hopes about this or anything else, but strive to live in habitual trust in & dependence upon God. Of one thing I am perfectly well persuaded that the water cure is no **humbug**. It is nothing more nor less as practiced here than the application of good science to the cure of disease by very simple & obvious remedies & regimen. If I were a Doctor, I would set up a water cure establishment near the Cumberland mountains or at the Beaver Dam Springs[205] as certain as I lived. It will be done by somebody before very long if I am not greatly mistaken. Dr. Breckenridge of Louisville is here and is improving very rapidly. Mrs. Eakins and her party consisting of Nephew [Randal McGavock], niece, child & servant left this morning intending to go to Ireland and Scotland and then to France. Health being so much more to me than seeing new & strange scenes and sights, and having sacrificed so much already in pursuit of it, I think it more than probably that I shall not visit Scotland or Ireland, but spend most of my time here, if I continue to improve. Should I get well and have time left I may visit the north

[205] Beaverdam Springs is in the southern part of Hickam County, Tennessee. It lies to the north of state route 100 and once was known as Nocome. Today a camp operated by the Presbyterians is located here and is called Na Co Me after the first two letters of the three presbyteries, Nashville, Columbia and Memphis. (Katherine Honour).

but hardly otherwise. However as I said before I will make no calculations so far ahead. I shall go to London next Saturday. This day week I am invited to dine with the Archbishop of Canterbury at the Bishop of Winchester's and this Wednesday following I have an invitation from the Lord Mayor of London & his lady to meet the Bishops at dinner at the Mansion House. I am in very poor plight to be fèted in this way as I can eat but very little and cannot drink wine at all. But these invitations I could not decline with any degree of propriety, for these are intended as marks of respect to the church of which I am a minister rather than as indications of personal consideration. So at least I have choosen to consider them. In other cases where I felt at liberty to decline civilities, I have done so upon the ground of feeble health.

A few nights before I left London I went by invitation to the American ministers where were assembled Lords, dukes & commoners. Among them the Duke of Wellington and all the foreign Ambassadors. I had been there but a few minutes before I was taken so sick that I was obliged to make my apology to the minster's wife, Mrs. Lawrence, and come to my lodgings and what pickel I should have made, had I staid longer! for I vomited from the hack window nearly all the way home! So you may be sure I don't intend to run any risk more than I can help in meeting the magistrates of the land. I desire that you will not mention that I have been invited by the Lord Mayor to dine, for though such a distinction may perhaps gratify you & the children (for that reason I mention it). Still my friends might very naturally think that my mentioning it was proof of my being vain and puffed up. But the Lord knows that I would rather dine with you & any friend that I have at Columbia than with all the Lord Mayors & dignitaries of England. I am sorry on Mrs. Eakin's and Miss Bass' account that I have been so disqualified by bad health to seek an introduction into the higher circles of society, and so give them the advantage of it, if any was to be gained. But the truth is I was too unwell and felt no disposition in the world to mingle in the ranks of fashion, dignity & all that. And the English people are not at all forward to give foreigners such an opportunity. **It must be sought after.** — There is a curious spectacle going on here today which I would like to describe to you. But I am transgressing all rules by writing as much as I have done already in this letter. It is **Whitmonday** and a universal holiday among the working classes and the streets are lined on each side with little stalls & tables, & donkeys &

dog carts all laden & stuffed with bon-bons—cakes—nuts—gim-
cracks and ten thousand little eatables & toys—among them tables
for betting and at one of them a **woman was presiding**—crying **"put
down your pennies gents! Only the anchor & the heart taken!"**
&c &c—and then she threw something like dice out of a horn cup on
the six sides of which are engraved the various figures as anchor,
heart, club or diamond which are on the table & the corresponding
shows the winner. It was all very amusing and I wish Mercer could
see it. — Dear wife! has the ice kept? Can you not make Jack and
George[206] put the spring lot in perfect order for grass—have every
stone picked and piled up. That lot if fixed as is done here would
almost support our family by the grass it would make. Don't waste or
give away the stone you have had taken up at the yard. My love,
dearest, to all at our own dear home & to all enquiring friends

Yours most affectionately **Ja: H. Otey**

Tuesday June 10. Nothing of interest to record this day which has
been wet and lowering. I spent the evening at the Rev. Mr. Rashdall's the
incumbent of the parish where I also met his colleague the Rev. Mr.
Davies, Sir John Kennaway,[207] Lady & daughter and a Miss Allen—all
very pleasant people. Mr. R. and his friends I can very plainly see are
what are called "Low Church." They asked me a multitude of questions
concerning the church in Americas—its constitution, canons, etc., etc. A
very strong desire was expressed that the Convocation[208] might be
restored to the Ch: of England having added to it a lay representation.

Wednesday June 11. Today has passed as yesterday without anything
worthy of note. I could record my thoughts but am forbid.

Thursday 12 June. As gloomy & unpleasant a day as any we have
seen. This month so far has been surely very unpropitious. Have
remained within doors nearly the whole day. Wrote B.B. Minor of Richmond, Va: Dr. Wilson returns from London to day about 4 p.m. I had an
interview to day with Dr. Stummes which gave me very little satisfaction. He directs that I shall to night apply a compress saturated with cold
water to my stomach & bowels, explaining the object to be to produce
heat or warmth in the region of the stomach; this application to be made

---

[206] These men were slaves or servants as Otey claimed. George Otey, a black, died in the Memphis Yellow
Fever epidemic of 1878.

[207] Sir John Kennaway (1797-1873) became the second baronet in 1836. His father was awarded the title for
persuading the Nizam of Hyderbad to enter an alliance against Tipu Sahib, sultan of Mysore in India. Sir John's
younger brother, Charles, a clergyman, published sermons and poetry. This third baronet was also active in church
affairs. (Burke's **Peerage**).

[208] For the background on Convocation see p. 8.

about 2 in the morning & to be followed at daylight with warm fomentations, bath cooled, etc. Now this seems to be a very contradictory sort of
practice and reason, if any, deducible from the Logicians rule of **lucus a
non lucendo**.[209] I will however give it a fair try.

Friday June 13. Have felt very much depressed by my condition today
which as far as I can judge is not improving one. The water brash is as
ever if not aggravated by the applications of cold water in the form of a
sitz-bath and compress. I have felt very much inclined to go to Liverpool
& take the steamer for America in the conviction that Summer spent in
the mountains of Virginia or Tennessee will do more for the restoration
of my health than any remedial agents in this country. I will however see
Dr. Wilson before determining upon any decisive step for as the recovery
of my health is the great and paramount object for which I am here and
have been sent away from home. I ought to leave nothing undone which
may give a reasonable hope for its restoration.

Saturday June 14. I had a long consultation with Dr. Wilson last night.
I hope I may trust him. He gave so accurate & minute an account of all
my symptoms, described my feelings so exactly as being precisely such
as he had himself experienced or witnessed in others, that he surely must
understand my complaint. He says my brain has been overtaxed, that my
physical powers have been overworked, that a whole years rest from anything like strong mental effort must be taken or that my whole system
will give way & that I will come down all at once & in a heap. He is of
the opinion that a stay at Malvern of a few weeks may wholly restore me
& will certainly set me up and put me in a way to get well if I am prudent
etc. I think I will follow his advice.

This morning after bathing &c I took a walk about the Malvern hills
and returned to breakfast with considerable appetite and feeling altogether better & in better spirits. After settling my bills I took my seat in
the coach for Worcester accompanied by some friends and arrived there
in time for the railroad train to London. The journey to London to day
had been wearisome & unpleasant. The cars were not easy & were too
much crowded to be comfortable. Upon reaching London at 6½ p.m. I
took a cab and drove to Mr. Geo: Gabain's No. 2 Nelson House Stoke
Newington.[210] This gentleman who had married a cousin of Mrs. Ann

---

[209] **Lucus a non lucendo** is an absurd derivation because lucus means grove instead of light.

[210] Stoke Newington was a village in Saxon times and perhaps earlier. It was long outside the area of London. However in the 1830s and 40s a building program began as the city reached out to it. (**London Ency.**).

[211] According to the 1850 census there were two Ann Reeds in Nashville. The one that Bishop Otey knew probably was the 37 year old wife of D. Reed. Since coming from Ireland they had prospered and acquired prop-erty worth an estimated $4,000. (**1850 Census, Davidson County, Nashville, Tennessee**).

Reads[211] of Nashville, had invited me to make his house my home while in London and on arrival received me as did his family in a very cordial manner; so that I felt quite at home. It is a quiet residence at least three miles from the heart of the city and although the streets are built up all around, it seems to enjoy all the peace, fresh air &c of a rural residence. The houses here generally have trees & shrubbery about them: and when I am sitting in my chamber I hear the birds singing as cheerily as in my own yard.

The Jubilee

Sunday June 15. Arose at 5 a.m. Sponged my body in cold water, dressed, put on a wet compress and walked about 2 miles for exercise. I thought surely I shall come presently to the open fields but none such came in view. This is certainly the most desireable part of the metropolis I have seen yet for residences. I see written on the walls in large letters but evidently with unskilled hands. **"No Popery!"** "No Wafer Gods!!"[212] These words paraded on the walls throughout London & indeed England in all public places are truly significant of the spirit that has been stirred up among the people. There is a deep feeling of indignation excited throughout the land and woe to popery and to the Establishment too, if it once finds vent in the aroused action of a people who feel that they have rights to defend and liberties to guard.

After breakfast went with Mr. Neitre[?], Lutheran minister from Bremen, to St. Paul's Cathedral. The service had already begun, though it was but a few minutes past 10 a.m. The part of the Cathedral, one of the chapels, was apparently filled and many persons were walking about in the larger unoccupied spaces of this immense building. I applied to an official for a seat. He directed me to call upon a verger. He was about to turn us away when my companion told him I was a Bp. in America. O, that being the case, he shall find a place—follow me! I was very much disposed to refuse & I believe now if I had reflected a moment I should have declined being a party to this unbecoming act of discrimination between persons in the house of God! However we entered by a side door and were seated just in front of the chancel where was room for 40 or 50 persons, double the number of whom were looking through the open iron work of the gates or entrances seeking admission. The service was **intoned**, prayers, psalms, creed & all except a small portion, one or two collects & the commandments which were read very appropriately by the Bp. of London. I soon discovered that there was to be an ordina-

[212] The statements painted on the walls were part of the reaction to the so-called "Papal Aggression."

tion. The sermon was too marked in its allusions to be mistaken in this aspect. It was on the text in 2 Cor: 2 ch. "Who is sufficient for these things?" and was made up of very commonplace observations. In the bidding prayer the minister most distinctly said among other things "let us pray for the dead who have departed in the faith & fear of God's holy name that we &c." After the sermon about 24 persons were ordained Deacons and the same number admitted to the Priesthood. The oath of Supremacy[213] and allegiance to the Queen was first taken by both classes of candidates: whereupon the ordination proceeded in all respects as with us.

The intoning of the service, as it is called, strikes me as exceedingly malapropos. Indeed it reminds me more of children's play than anything else. Besides depriving the people of their share in the service, it is objectionable from its wearisome monotony & indistinctness—so that it reaches neither the heart nor the head—neither the feeling nor the understanding. I can not but say to myself surely the authorities of the Ch: here have reached the period of second childishness & it is no wonder that the whole establishment is looked upon as effete and as visibly posting to decay & ruin. The masses have no respect for it, and are rapidly losing their love & veneration for the religion of their fathers; or rather that which has usurped its place. "And more's the pity."

I have already mentioned the spirit of discrimination as to persons, among officials etc. Sometimes it takes a turn which to Americans really seems ludicrous. Thus I saw in the congregation today seated among the most respectable people present, a black woolly headed negro—apparently as much at ease as any one there. In one respect this was right the negro ought to feel himself as much privileged in the house of God as the white man—but why an official in the indulgence of caprice should admit him & exclude the white-man [sic], I do not know or perceive any reason.[214]

Monday June 16. This being the day appointed to begin the celebration of the 4th Jubilee of the Venerable Society for the Propagation of the Gospel in Foreign Parts by appropriate services in Westminster Abbey, I got off from my lodgings at an early hour in order to be in readiness & to appear in my official dress should it be expected. I went first to Mr. Jno: Miller's where my robes had been left. They were still at the milliner's,

[213] The Oath of Supremacy is based on the acts of Supremacy passed in 1534 and then in 1558 following the accession of Elizabeth. This requires the recognition of the sovereign as "supreme governor" of both church and state.

[214] For confirmation of his attitude that negro had the right to feel "as much privileged in the house of God as the white," see p. 18.

probably unfinished. Next I proceeded to the rooms of the Socy. in Pall Mall[215] where Mr. Hawkins the Secy: informed me that I was desired & expected to appear & assist as a Bishop. Away I had to hasten to the Robemakers—the lawn sleeves had to be stitched on and the sleeves had not been washed—vexations—but to be endured & made the most of. After so long a time during which I read Mr. Tomes' letter which had just reached me, I got off with Mr. Hawkins to Westminster Abbey where I arrived in time to robe and join the procession of Bishops to Henry the 7th's chapel in which the services were to be held. And here was furnished another very striking evidence of the importance which is attached to station &c in this country even in trifling matters. The archbishop of Canterbury led the way followed by a trainbearer who held up, his gown or robes behind—the Bp. of London next—all this seemed proper—the rest of the Bps were to follow in the order of their consecration.[216] Then the English Bps took their places without the slightest reference to myself & the Bp. of Argyle from Scotland—not even in inquiring the date of our consecrations. Just as we were entering the body of the Ch: in the nave the Bp. of Argyle[217] asked me when I was consecrated and upon my replying "in 1834," he immediately fell behind saying "you are my senior." I thanked him for his courtesy and went forward. We all entered the chancel & took seats which had been arranged for us. The services began—**intoned** "again"—losing it seems to me very much of their impressiveness & effect. But people must be humored I suppose in this & in other things as well. The sermon which I thought was a good one, was preached by the Bp. of London. The Communion was first by the Archbishop of C. & the Bp. of London to the Bps. present & then the Bps. administered to the clergy of whom there was a large number present and then to the people. This service has been regarded as very grand and imposing and was of course intended to be so. But to me it had been divested of all that impressive effect which attends the performance of Christian rites & worship in their simplicity and connected with the plain announcement of the awful and concerning truths of the gospel. Habit it seems will accustom a man to any thing or rather I ought to write that

[215] Today the Society is quartered at 157 Waterloo Rd. (**London Ency.**).

[216] Had Otey been given precedence on the basis of seniority, he would have outranked at least six bishops such as Ripon (1836), Durham (1836), Worcester (1841), Oxford (1842), and Litchfield (1843).

[217] Alexander Ewing (1814-73), bishop of Argyle and the Isles (1847), was not an ordinary Scottish bishop. Shortly after becoming a deacon he spent three years in Italy recovering his health and again twenty years later but he never leaned toward the Roman Church. As a bishop he was on friendly terms with officials of the Church of Scotland and also of England. By participating in the communion at the Jubilee he became the first Scottish bishop in nearly a century to celebrate the Eucharist in Westminster with the archbishop of Canterbury, the bishop of London, and others. His courteous act to Otey was seemingly part of his nature. (Lochhead, **Episcopal Scotland**, p. 163).

custom will establish habits & make that easy & familiar which at first strikes one as unpleasant & withal novel. I cannot otherwise understand how it is that sensible men as many of the Bps & clergy appear to be can acquiesce seemingly with complacency and pleasure in practices that appear to be not only indefensible but positively puerile.

Tuesday June 17. Went early this morning with Mr. Gabain to the city & called on Messers. Wadeson & Malleson So. 11 Austin Friars—out— met Hamilton & Litton[218] on the Street—took L to Gabain, left and went to look for Ewing & Price whom I met on the street. Had a long walk with Ewing, saw parade in front of Buckingham Palace—called at Am: minister's spoke with him respecting Henry Fogg.[219] Went to Crystal palace. Frank Parrish in difficulty about his [move?], relieve him—walk about the various apartments of the exhibition. Examine particularly the lately received Russian articles. They are very magnificent and costly. I was led to make this reflection while considering them that none but crowned heads or very rich men could possess so very costly articles. How upon looking at the productions from the U. States it will be perceived that they are all with hardly an exception such things as are designed for useful purposes & generally speaking such as are within the ability of men in moderate circumstances to purchase. On the contrary the Russian articles must be estimated by ten, hundreds & thousands of pounds. Thus some doors of Malachite intended to serve I presume for a wardrobe are said to have been sold recently for £10,000 each! But I cannot undertake to describe that which it will fill volumes of description adequately to pourtray. [sic]

Returning from the Crystal palace I took a cab and drove to St. Martin's Hall to attend a meeting of the friends of the Venerable Socy: to be favored with the presidency of Prince Albert. The meeting had been already organized and the Bishop of London was speaking when I entered. He was followed by Lord Jno: Russell[220] in a style offensively magesterial & pompous as I thought. The amount of all he said was that the Bible was the great instrument of enlightening the world, rather insinuating that a ministry interpret it, well enough in its place, might yet be dispensed with. He was followed by several other speakers who had printed resolutions put into their hands to move and second. I might have

[218] Hamilton, Litton, Ewing and Price were part of the group which traveled to Europe on the **Waterloo**. Parrish was Ewing's servant.

[219] Henry Middleton Rutledge Fogg (1830-1862) was a Nashville attorney who travelled to Europe with Henry Maney. Fogg carried the names of his two grandfathers who signed the Declaration of Independence. He was killed in the Civil War. Alfred Leland Crabb, ed, "Letters Over the Waters," **Tennessee Historical Quarterly**, XVI (Sept. 1957), p. 265.

[220] Lord John Russell (1792-1878) was prime minister from 1846 to 1852 and 1865 to 1866. He was a younger son of the 6th duke of Bedford and was created Earl Russell in 1861. His grandson, Bertrand (1872-1970) was the 3rd earl. (**DNB**).

expected, I think I may say this without any arrogance or presumption, that I, as coming from a sister church in a foreign land, should be called on to address the meeting. I was not among the selected to do so. Some of the speakers made very friendly references to the American church & peoples and especially the duke of New Castle[221] [sic] who quoted in complimentary terms the language of an American Bp. When he had concluded and taken his seat I asked him whether he could not, would not make an opportunity for me to address the meeting. He said, he had nothing to do with it. I then said Sir! I am an Am: Bp. and I think it due to the occasion that I should be allowed to respond to the sentiments which have been kindly expressed towards my country and the Church of which I am a minister." This seemed to strike him with much force and he beckoned to the Bp. of London who spoke to Prince Albert. In a minute or so I was informed that his Royal Highness had granted leave to me to make a short address, confining my remarks to the particular topic on which I wished to be heard &c, that it was getting late & he wished to go. This I thought was John Bullism again. Nevertheless I determined to use the opportunity. So, as soon, as the Earl of Harrowby[222] had concluded, the Bp. of London announced my name to the meeting & I rose in my place and made the following addres as nearly as I can recall the words.[223] "May it please your Royal Highness! I beg leave to express my deep sense of the kindness which allows me the opportunity of addressing a few words through you to the large & respected assembly. It is in keeping with the manifestations of friendly interests toward the U.S. & the Protestant Episcopal Church: in America, which it has been my happiness to witness in every part of England I have visited. Believe me Sir, that the feelings of kindly regard is warmly reciprocated and carefully cherished towards the Church of England by the members of that communion of which I am in some sort the representative here today. I should not have sought the opportunity to say a word on this occasion but for the kind & even complimentary terms, in which reference has been made to the people and church in the United States by the speakers who have addressed your Royal Highness & especially by the Noble Duke who moved the resolution now under consideration. The merits of that resolution it is not my intention to discuss. I know that I must not detain the meeting at this late hour by making a speech. But his Grace

---

[221] Henry Pelham Hope (1811-64) was the fifth duke of Newcastle. (Burke's **Peerage**).

[222] Dudley Ryder (1798-1882) was 2nd earl of Harrowby.

[223] According to A. Cleveland Coxe who was present, Otey's request to speak created some consternation among the officialdom "as such volunteering was quite unusual" and that the Prince consort was bored. Later Bishop Wilburforce expressed to Coxe his pleasure over Otey's remarks. (Coxe, "A Letter," in Green, **Memoir**, pp. 352-53).

was pleased to quote the language of an American Bishop & adopt it as expressive of his sentiments. I am authorized to speak for that Right Reverend prelate as I am for some others in the Episcopate of the American Church[224] and I beg leave to say that he will & that we all shall feel happy at this and every other manifestation of love & kindness which our brethren on this side of the Atlantic shall give us; in the earnest conviction and hope that each and every such mark of friendly regard will strengthen the ties of amity between the two powerful nations & knit the members of our Communion together in the closer bonds of that fellowship called "The Communion of Saints." Before I take my seat I beg leave to say one word confirmatory of all that has been advanced here this afternoon, as to the importance of enlarging the number of Bishops in order to extend the Church. I mean not to argue this point but simply to bear my testimony founded upon personal observations and experience. When twenty-six years ago I moved to the state of which I am now Bp. there was not an organized congregation of Episcopalians within its limits nor was there á clergyman of the Church within 200 miles of my residence. Within eight years the ecclesiastical organization of the diocese was completed by the election of a Bishop & within five more, the number of clergymen had increased from 6 to 21. Such has been the result I believe without exception in the history of all our recently organized dioceses. And it is my firm persuasion that the Church of England cannot take a more direct and effective method to advance the cause of our Blessed Redeemer & his Church in this world than by having Bishops established in all the Colonial dependencies of the British Empire. [The following sentence was marked for insertion at this point.] (Here observations were made which escaped my recollections while writing but which I have jotted down at the close of this journal.) (I may be allowed to say that there is a strong obligation resting upon the people of this land to provide as far as they can for the religious instruction of those who emigrate to the British Colonies. I know what must be the condition of those emigrants from having seen the condition of emigrants in my own country. And I think I can here make an appeal to the hearts of every Englishman present that scarcely could be resisted. I remember with the distinctiveness of a yesterday's impression, so strongly were the circumstances all stamped on my memory etc, that years ago I was called on while awaiting the arrival of a steamboat at a small town on the banks of the Mississippi River, to visit a stranger then lying in the extremity of

---

[224] Otey had been authorized to speak for: William R. Whittingham (1805-1879), bishop of Maryland, consecrated 1844; Carlton Chase (1794-1870), bishop of New Hampshire, consecrated 1844; William M. Green (1798-1887), bishop of Mississippi, consecrated 1844; and George Upfold (1796-1872), bishop of Indiana, consecrated 1849. (Armentrout, **Otey**, p. 121).

sickness in that little man whom I helped. He was from a distant land. I spoke to him of Jesus & endeavored to direct his faith & hope to the blood of "lamb of God that takes away the Sins of the world." And then came struggle between weak faith & feeble hope on the one side and the [faded] conscience & the awful dread of the future on the other and the big tears gathered in his restless eye when memory called back, [faded] of his childhood & he spoke of the days when his Father & Mother went to church & taught him to clasp his infants hands and pray "Our Father which art in Heaven." It is not my purpose to detail what passed during the hours of that long & sorrowful night. He died so far as I know without the support of faith of the Comfort of hope in Victory.)[225]

It has been said by an American orator that the roll of the British drums does not cease at one of the military posts of this mighty kingdom, before it is taken up at another & attests then the warning sound of her power is prolonged and heard girdling the globe. We can scarecely forget that it will be 36 years ago tomorrow, since the [meteor?] flag of Britain floated high in air amidst the triumphant shouts of victory [Waterloo], but sir, it will be more to Britain's substantial honor & glory if the beacon lights of the Missionary enterprise planted by her sons shall be multiplied until their radiance spreading & intermingling shall at last so blend as to form a sea of glory & cover all the earth."

When I first rose there was great cheering as usual. After it had ceased and I had made this address, it was renewed in a manner which I have no doubt was intended to gratify my feelings and so far as I had a desire to please men it was grateful. But it strikes me that the indiscriminate applause bestowed on all speakers deprives it of its value. Of one thing I am pretty sure: I dont [sic] care one fig whether these people like what I say or not, if I can but keep strictly to truth & propriety in all I say or do. For they are the most proud, haughty, self important & churlish people altogether that I have ever seen in any land under any sun!

Wednesday June 18. Anniversary of the battle of Waterloo! I am invited to dine to day with the Lord Mayor & Lady Mayoress! Have remained in my room nearly all day engaged in writing. About 5¾ p.m. set off in a carriage for the Lord Mayors![226] An immense crowd in the

---

[225]The paragraph in the parentheses was the insertion and was on the last page of the journal.

[226]The banquet was held at Mansion House the official residence of the Lord Mayor and his wife who is known as Lady Mayoress. Sir John Musgrove began as an auctioneer and house agent. In 1842 he was elected an alderman, a position he held until 1872. He served as Sheriff of London and Middlesex in 1843-44, a requisite. In addition the Lord Mayor needs to be a person of wealth as his salary does not cover all the entertaining expected of him during the one year that extends from November to early November. Today the Lord Mayor receives a salary of £80,000, nevertheless some holders of the office have dipped into their private purse for as much as £68,000. (Whitaker's **Almanac**, p. 223). Musgrove was knighted in 1843 and raised to a baronetecy in 1851. (**Mod. Eng. Bio..** III).

streets, hard to reach the entrance, a larger force of the police present and enforcing order etc. Upon entering I was conducted by a gentleman Usher, gorgeously apparelled as all officials were on this occasion, to a Servant who took my hat and gave me a ticket with a number written on it, a maneuver which I did not at first understand but which, upon my going away, I discovered to be, for the purpose of identifying the rightful ownership of my hat. Next I was conducted to a master of ceremonies at a table upon which the said "Magister ceremoniarum" glanced his eye repeatedly, but could find no card marked "Bishop of Tennessee." Here was a predicament, presenting me thus: the fault or neglect of some body, in the attitude of appearing at the Memorial festival of the Lord Mayor of London as of an uninvited guest. I stood at the table waiting to learn what disposition was to be made of me. The search for the name of the "Bp. of Tenn." meanwhile proceeded by an under official while the head man in this part of the business continued to conduct the guests as they successively arrived to the reception room of his Lordship, where their names were formally & pompously announced. While standing at the table in the entry I thought within myself, it is true I have no court dress—no official vestments, as I perceive every one has, but I certainly have and can produce the invitation of the Lord Mayor & Lady Mayoress addressed to the "Bp. of Otels" & directed to me & if any body else claims under that address to be invited to the Lord Mayor's to dinner this evening and has accepted the invitation, as I have done, then I shall give way and as we say "back out!" Still I was waiting—others coming in the foyer with cards, &c—The Bps. of London, St. Asaph, Winchester and others were just before me in the entry; but not one had the courtesy to come forward and relieve me from the embarrassing position, which my long standing where I was must have indicated to them, if indeed they regarded me with any proper degree of interest. I began to feel my blood warm considerably as the Master of Ceremonies approached the table the second or third time saying he "did not know how it was. There was some mistake of omissions &c" I said to him rather sternly "Sir! tell me where to go and don't keep me standing here in this state of unpleasant suspension." "I'll furnish you with a card Sir! You will go next to the Bp. of Bombay.[227] What is the name Sir?" "Bp. of Tenn: or Bp. Otey as you

[227] Early in 1851 Thomas Carr, the first bishop of Bombay, was forced by his health to resign this seat which he had held since 1837. Eight years after his return to England he died. On learning of the resignation the arch-bishop of Canterbury appointed John Harding (1805-74) who was consecrated in Lambeth Palace on 10 August 1851. The region around Bombay must have been unhealthy because he took sick leave in 1867 and went back to England where two years later he resigned the bishopric. Although Otey gave no hint, Harding most likely was the unidentified bishop of Bombay. (M.E. Gibbs, **The Anglican Church in India 1600-1970** [Delhi, 1972], pp. 168 and 412; "John Harding," **DNB**).

please" I said. I advanced to the reception room where another usher called aloud "The Bishop of Ten-**es**sy!"[sic] the **"es"** was ludicrously emphatic. I could scarcely repress laughing outright! The Lord Mayor advanced. I made a very fine bow I know: for I felt large and perfectly at ease. His Lordship extended his hand which I observed he did not give to all—and taking mine which was put forward to meet his said, "I am very happy to see you Sir and to welcome you to the hospitality of the good city of London"! [sic] I thanked his lordship and passed on. But the pro-nounciation of Ten-**ess**-se still rung in my ears and made me for a moment or two forget every thing but to remember how ridiculous it would be, should I laugh. Thus thinking I totally forgot to pay my respects to the Lady Mayoress until I saw others so occupied on their entrance. So believing it not too late to retrieve my oversight I asked the Bp. of Winchester[228] whether he could be kind enough to present me to her ladyship, that I had in my ignorance of the customs, omitted on my entrance to pay my respects to her. He very readily consented, so I made my salaam—scraped my foot backward, bent forward with my hand on my heart, and my eyes cast modestly down & then timidly raised to see if I was regarded with any attention at all and perceived her Ladyship incline her head with a smile intended to be gracious. My error said I to myself is now corrected and my reception is finished. I took my stand in the company, resolved that I would make advances to no one, but that if any were made, they should come from others. This I very soon found made me an object much sought unto. Very many persons sought an introduction to me and expressed the high gratification they felt the day before in hearing my speech at St. Martin's Hall at the meeting of the friends of the Vene: Society under Prince Albert. Among others I had the pleasure of seeing the Rev. Th: H. Horne, D.D.[229] author of the "Introduc-tion &c" and Archdeacon Robinson the friend of the lamented Heber,[230] both of whom asked to be introduced to me. While engaged in conversa-tion with a lady who also solicited an introduction & who was the Bp. of London's daughter and as I judge a very charming woman, dinner was announced & the Magnates paired off with the ladies present. I had no body to escort and finding that the crowd were proceeding to the ban-

---

[228] Charles R. Sumner (1790-1874), brother of the archbishop of Canterbury, was bishop of Winchester 1825-69. He resigned for reasons of health. (**DNB**).

[229] Thomas H. Horne, D.D. (1780-1862) was a biblical scholar and senior assistant in the books department, British Museum. His **Introductions to Critical Study and Knowledge of the Holy Scriptures** went through sev-eral editions. He was a canon of St. Paul's Cathedral. (**DNB**).

[230] Reginald Heber (1783-1826) was the first bishop of Calcutta (1823-26). He is better known for his hymns such "From Greenland's Icy Mountains." Perhaps Otey who obviously admired Heber named his eldest son after the man. (**DNB**).

quetting Hall with a speed, almost amounting to a rush, which seemed to say in rude phrase "Devil take the hindmost," I also quickened my pace and getting sight of the Bp. of Bombay and remembering that I had no card as I supposed the others had to indicate their places, & recollecting what the gentleman usher had told me that I was next to the Bp. of Bombay—seeing I say the Bp. of Bombay—for Bombay I pushed & upon drawing up in order at the table I found before me a card inscribed **"Bp. of Tennessee"**. After all were seated and soup served, the toastmaster who stood just behind the Lord Mayor, cried with a loud voice, "My Lords & Gentlemen! hear grace!" We all rose to our feet and the grace was sung in most excellent taste & with sweet voices by a choir provided specially for the occasion. After this wines & meat & fish & in short every thing good in this & almost every land was served up and offered to us. I ate very moderately and drank not a spoonful of wine. I did barely touch the liquid to my lips in return to the civility of the Lord Mayor & the Bp. of St. Asaph, who asked me to pledge them in a glass: also The Rev. Mr. Cox of Hartford Conn. When the dinner, desert, fruits & all being ended—interlarded as it was by several excellent pieces of music exquisitely executed by the choir—the regular toasts of the evening began. Before every toast the Toastmaster made proclamation, "My Lords & **Gentlemen**! Charge your **glasses**"—Gentlemen emphatic and glasses more emphatic! Then followed "Hear the Lord Mayor"! The Lord Mayor would rise and preface the reading of the toast with a few observations in reference to each toast; and in this I thought his Lordship was peculiarly felicitous. I here record the thought that struck me most forcibly the first time His Lordship addressed us, & I had a fair view of his face. He is more like my nieghbor **Genl. G.J. Pillow**[231] in features— the whiteness of his hair excepted, & in his voice than any man whom I have ever seen!

A great many toasts were proposed and drunk to all of which responses were made in the form of speeches or addresses from those whose names were specially connected with the sentiment delivered. The proceedings having been reported and printed there is less occasion for my entering into any long detail in this place. I may however and perhaps ought to record my own particular share in the actings and sayings of the evening. A toast was proposed by the Lord Mayor expressive of good wishes for the prosperity of the Church in the U. States and my name

[231] General Gideon J. Pillow (1806-78) had been a law partner of President Polk. In the Mexican War he was a brigadier general and in the Civil War a major general in the Tennessee Provisional Army and a brigadier in the Confederate army. He was second in command at Fort Donelson and escaped before the surrender. (**DAB**).

connected with it. Whereupon as it was expected, I rose and said as nearly as I remember as follows: "My Lord Mayor, ladies and gentlemen, I beg leave to express my acknowledgements for the honor done to me by connecting my name with the sentiment which has just been proposed to this company, and to return my thanks for the kind terms in which you have expressed your good wishes towards the Church of which I am a minister. I am perfectly sensible that it is not in consideration of any personal merit that my name has been associated with the Church which I here represent; but rather from that feeling which binds us together as members of one body. I assure your Lordship that the kindly feeling of which I have had an expression this evening and of which I have seen manifestations in every part of England is mainly reciprocated by members of the Prot. Ep. Church in the U. States. It is a feeling which I am sure they will continue to cherish.

It is not my purpose to make a speech to your Lordship & this worshipful assembly and that for two very substantial reasons. First, I am forbidden by my Doctor and 2nd I do not feel myself capable of entertaining this company in such a way as to justify my occupying their time & attention. I take occasion, however, to say that I feel a peculiar satisfaction in bearing testimony on this occasion to the deep interest which is felt in America towards the people & Church of England. I believe it is reciprocal: why should it not be so? We are of the same blood. We are descended from you. We have the same laws and nearly the same institutions. It is to our mutual interest to cultivate friendly relations and we are in a great measure necessary to each other. We want your surplus labor to fell our mighty forests, to construct roads — open the navigation of our rivers, and develop the rich resources of our great & growing country. You want our raw materials — the products of our soil — to give employment to your manufactories. You have evidences of our friendly disposition in the readiness with which some years ago we supplied some portions of your suffering population with food, when famine was apprehended, in Ireland especially, from the failure of the crops. You have had more recent evidence of the same sentiments of friendly regard, in the responses made by the Bps. of America to his Grace, the Archbishop of Canterbury. There is indeed a bond of Union more sacred than all others—a bond more indissoluble than that which unites man and wife! What is that, you will ask? It is the bond which unites us, in the fellowship or "communion of saints." All other unions, even the nuptial tie, lasts only "till death;" but this is for eternity. We shall still be one in Christ Jesus when the changes & chances of this mortal life are over, and

eternity shall have closed in, with all its mysteries and changeless solem-
nities. I will detain you but a moment longer Sir: for as I said before, I
am forbidden to make a speech. America and Gt. Britain now present a
most interesting aspect for comtemplation to the philanthropist, the
statesman & the Christian. The world is at peace: and furnishes the most
inviting prospect or opportunity it has ever done to introduce everywhere
the blessings of civilization and religion among all the tribes and families
of man. Between our respective governments all causes of difference
have happily passed away. Our boundary lines to the north west as well
as the N. East have been satisfactorily adjusted, and the only object of
contest now before us seems to be, which shall be most active in diffus-
ing the light of the glorious gospel of God and our blessed Saviour. Does
any man shrink back from the magnitude of the work?

Let us but look at the beginning of Christianity and see the most striking instance of the moral sublime the world has ever witnessed: Eleven
Apostles and five hundred brethren at most undertaking to overthrow all
other systems of faith & hope and to establish in their stead the simple
system of the Gospel! Does any one ask for authority to undertake this
work? God has said "Go ye into all the world & preach the gospel to
every creature"! [sic] Who asks for higher sanctions than the commands
of the Heavenly King and this world's judge? There we have a righteous
cause and undoubted authority and these make right. Now, Sir, we have a
saying often quoted as originating with Bro: Jonathan, and which as it
embodies a sound principle of philosphy, and withal is frequently mis-
quoted, I beg leave to state correctly & to adduce as encouragement to us
all in the performance of our duty. The sentiment is not "Go ahead!" as
generally said, but "Be sure you are right, then go ahead."[232] We sure are
right in this cause: We have nothing to do but go ahead—(Gt. Laughter).

Sir, his grace the Archbishop a little while since concluded with a
quotation of Holy Scriptures. In humble imitation of his example I would
only say, as representing American Churchmen, to our Brethren in the
Church of England: "We wish you good luck in the name of the Lord"!
[sic]

The meeting at the Lord Mayor's passed off very pleasantly as much
so as any I have ever attended. There was a curious custom observed on
this occasion, kept up as I was told "time out of mind." The Lord Mayor
& Lady Mayoress, take each a large flagon of wine covered & pledge
their guests in a loving cup. The flagons are then passed to all the company & as they come around two persons rise — one takes off the top of

[232] Authorship of the "be sure you're right..." statement is usually attributed to Davy Crockett.

the flagon, the other drinks, replaces the top & the 2nd person presents the flagon to the next who takes off the top & the 2nd drinks—the first yet standing & so the cups are passed around. The custom is said to have originated in a prudent caution to guard against assassination which sometimes occurred in their cups among men of olden time.

The company separated about 12 o'clock at night. I was very agreeably entertained by the conversation of a very intelligent and beautiful woman who sat just to my left and whom it became my duty to pledge in the loving cup of the Lord Mayor & Lady. She had many questions to ask about America. I suspect she was the wife of the Rev. Dr. Jno. Thynne,[233] Dean of Westminster. After leaving the Lord Mayor's Mansion I accompanied the Rev. A.C. Cox to Miss Burdett Coutt's[234] party. It was a most maginificent assemblage of the nobles, gentry & ladies of England. The guests were, some of them richly, dressed. Miss Coutts must have had on diamonds & pearls to the amt. of half a million of dollars I should think. She received me very politely & conversed very affably with me as long as I staid. I think she wished to have my good opinion, by her whole manner & bearing toward me. I saw the Duke of Newcastle here who in a friendly way held out his hand and made a sort of apologetic explanation of his conduct the day before in not responding more readily to my request to him to give me an opportunity to address the meeting &c I thanked him & having paid my respects to Miss Coutts I left for my lodgings & went to bed between three and four o'clock in the morning!

June 19. At Messrs Wadeson and Malleson's No. 11 Austin Friars this morning Mr. Minor's business. A conversation with Mr. Wadeson elicits nothing definite. Report from [proctors?] daily expected, upon which a decree of Chancery Court is to be predicated. Information of the same to be communicated to Mr. Minor. Next to Mr. Jno. Miller's. Upon examining my robes discovered that the scarf was missing—sent to Cox's for

[264]Lord John Thynne, D.D. (1797-1881) was Canon of Westminster (1831-81) and sub dean (1835-81). He was a younger son of the Marquis of Bath and married to Anna C. Beresford. William Buckland was dean of the Abbey from 1845 to 1856. (A.P. Stanley, **Memorials of Westminster Abbey** [London, 1924], p. 491).

[265]Angelina Burdett-Coutts (1814-1906) was the granddaughter of the man who made Coutts the private bank of the Royal family and of some of the nobility. She inherited her money and the bank through her step grandmother. Angelina headed the bank until her death. She gave this Waterloo party in honor of the Duke of Wellington to whom she once suggested marriage. He deftly turned the hint aside with the observation that the age difference of 25 and 70 was against them. In 1871 Victoria created her a baroness for her charities. Ten years later she married W.L.A. Bartlett who was born in 1851 and who idolized her. Miss Coutts was famous for her jewelry. A few days prior to the party the **Times** reported that at a Royal reception she wore a string of emeralds and diamonds in baldric fashion stretching from her right shoulder to her left hip. (For her relationship with Wellington see: **Wellington and his Friends, Letters of the First Duke of Wellington**, edited by the 7th Duke, [London, 1965]. For William Lehman Ashmead Bartlett Burdett-Coutts [He took his wife's name] see **Who Was Who 1916-1928**).

it—could not be found. This man Cox for making a pair of lawn sleeves for my Episcopal dress had charged me three guineas; a piece of extortion & nothing less & now having taken my robes, rochet &c to wash & now he loses the scarf. It is too bad to endure patiently.

Friday June 20. Received letters this morning from my wife & Rev. Mr. Cressey. Also a note from Mr. Pierce Connelly[235]—formerly an Episcopal clergyman, whom I displaced from the ministry on account of his defection to Rome. He has again returned to the Communion of the Church of England, having renounced Romanism.

Saturday June 21. After calling at Mr. W.H. Manners, a miniature painter No. 41 Poultry & leaving with him my beloved Sarah's daguerreotype to be painted I went to Mr. Miller's where I saw Gov. N.S. Brown & Mr. Litton. Accompanied by the latter I visited Greenwich and had the opportunity of seeing the room of the paintings belonging to this hospital & also the Chapel. In the hall of paintings are to be seen the portraits of the most distinguished of England's naval heroes—Drake, Hawkins,[236] Duncan,[237] Vincent,[238] Hyde, Parker,[239] Hood,[240] Howe,[241] Collingwood,[242] Codrington,[243] Nelson, Hardy[244] & many others and several paintings of naval battles. Two glass cases or show boxes contain the uniform coat which Nelson wore at the battle of Aboukir[245] and the coat & waistcoat which he had on when mortally wounded at the battle of Trafalgar, The stains of blood are plain enough on the white marseilles waist coat. There is a painting of Nelson dying which I thought particularly fine.

[235] Otey deposed Pierce Connelly, rector of Trinity Church, Natchez, Mississippi because the latter while in Europe joined the Roman Catholic Church and was ordained in 1845. Before entering that priesthood Connelly and his wife took vows of perpetual chastity. She founded the Society of the Holy Child Jesus and died a member of that church. Meanwhile Pierce and his three children returned to the Episcopal Church. He was readmitted to Episcopalian priesthood later serving in Florence, Italy.

[236] Sir John Hawkins (1532-95), an Elizabethan Seadog who sold slaves in the Spanish West Indies, later became treasurer of the navy and commanded the **Victory** in the fleet that defended England from the Armada. (**DNB**).

[237] Adam Duncan, Viscount Camperdown (1731-1804), was given this title for defeating a Dutch fleet near this place in 1797. (**DNB**).

[238] John Jervis, Earl of St. Vincent (1735-1823), led a British fleet successfully against a larger Spanish fleet in 1797. (**DNB**).

[239] Probably Sir Parker Hyde (1739-1807) who commanded at the battle of Copenhagen (1801) where he was charged with irresolution and was recalled. (**DNB**).

[240] Samuel, Viscount Hood (1724-1816) lost to Comte de Grasse in 1782 during the War of the American Revolution. He captured Toulon in 1793 and Corsica in 1794. (**DNB**).

[241] Richard, Earl Howe (1726-99) was the British naval commander in charge of American waters from 1776 to 1778. (**DNB**).

[242] Cuthbert, Baron Collingwood (1750-1810) was second in command at Trafalgar (1806) and took over on Nelson's death. (**DNB**).

[243] Sir Edward Codrington (1770-1851) commanded the combined British, French and Russian fleet in the victory over the Turkish and Egyptian fleets at Navarino Bay (1827) in the war of Greek Independence. (**DNB**).

[244] Sir Thomas Hardy, Baronet (1769-1839), captained Nelson's flagship, HMS **Victory** at Trafalgar. (**DNB**).

[245] The Battle of Aboukir was fought off a promontory of the Nile delta in 1798. Sometimes this British victory over the French is called the Battle of the Nile.

Sunday June 22. Preached today in St. Marks Church, St. John's Wood,[246] London in behalf of the Society of the Propagation of the Gospel in Foreign Parts after the usual service by the Rector. I did not preach with much ease & satisfaction to myself feeling hurried in consequence of the length of the service prolong by the manner in which it was conducted—partly **intoned**.

June 24. Was very sick last night and this morning—returned by Rail Road to Malvern arriving by way of Cheltenham about 4 p.m.

From this time to Saturday, June 28 I have nothing to record no matters of interest personally to myself or others beyond the brief notices made in my pocket diary which keeps the memory of passing events. I may however mention that I have been somewhat annoyed by the application of a person who signs herself S.E.M. Warner, wife of the late Rev. Mr. Warner[247] of West Point, N.Y., for pecuniary assistance. I know nothing in the world about the woman or her claims to consideration. Certainly I am not in a situation to aid her and less so to be harassed by attention to such application. So I have written to her.

Saturday 28th. I took the Post Coach this morning for Worcester to visit the cathedral. The distance 8 miles was traversed and I soon found myself in this ancient city celebrated as the residence or burial place of many men of renown and famous for the battle [1651] in its vicinity, in which Cromwell defeated Charles II.[248] The first objects of interest which I went to see were the relics of this battle preserved in the Townhall & consisting of Helmets, breastplates, coats of mail made of small links of iron or steel—spears, swords &c. Here also were two pieces of brass ordinance taken from the French. In the upper room I was shown the portraits of Sr. John Pakington,[249] Queen Anne, Sr. Th: Winnington,[250] Ld.

[246] **Times**, 6 June 1851 carried the announcement that the Bishop of Tennessee would preach at St. Marks St. John's Wood as part of the Society for the Propagation of the Gospel Jubilee. St. Marks Church is on Hamilton Terrace, Maida Vail and was built in 1846-47 for nearly £10,000. One critic described it "as a large Gothic riding school" (**London Ency**, p. 732).

[247] Probably Thomas Warner who was ordained a deacon in 1821 and died in 1849 (American Episcopal Clergy, **Register of Ordinances in Episcopal Church United States from 1785 through 1904**. [Hartford, CT: 1970]).

[148] In 1651 Charles II came down from Scotland with a force that met Cromwell at Worcester. After his defeat Charles fled to France.

[249] Sir John Parkington, Bt. (1620-80) was four years old when he succeded to the title. He supported Charles II at the Battle of Worcester. For this he temporarily lost his estates. After the Restoration he sat in Parliament for Worcestershire. His wife, Lady Dorothy Parkington (d. 1679) is generally regarded as the author of the anonymously written **The Whole Duty of Man** (1658). (**DNB**).

[150] Sir Thomas Winnington (1697-1746) ws a Lord of the Admirality. (**DNB**).

[251] Lord Sands of the Vine was a barony created by Henry VIII. When the fourth lord died in 1629 the title ended but was revived through the Sandys who had married a sister of last baron. The nephew became Lord Sands. Two generations later the line died out. (Collins **Peerage of England**).

[252] Earl of Plymouth was probably Thomas Windsoe (1627?-87) who fought in the Civil War at the age of 15. He was created earl in 1685 when governor of Hull. (**DNB**).

[253] The first Earl of Coventry died in 1699, the 2nd 1710 and the 3rd 1712 aged 10. (**DNB**).

[254] Thomas, Lord Coventry, 1st Baron Coventry (1578-1640). The second died in 1661.(**DNB**).

Sands[251] Earl of Plymouth,[252] Earl of Coventry,[253] Thos: Lord Coventry,[254] Geo: III and Alderman Webb who still lives. Some of the portraits are fine paintings and some are very old.

Next I visited the Porcelain works of Chamberlain and Co.[255] the fine porcelain ware is manufactured from a sut [?] of granite & clay found in Cornwall & of bones ground to powder and prepared by filtering, drying &c for the hands of the potter & other operatives until the beautiful table furniture appears which serves us at our meals. I can not undertake to describe the various processes of the manufacture which were all curious enough. I was much interested in the appearance of a large number of females—some quite advanced in life, others in childhood—employed in burnishing the gilded porcelain. These females sit here 12 hours in the day and received for their labor 9/- [9 shillings] per week or 1/6 per day [1 shilling 6 pence]: and find themselves & this is thought in this country to be good wages!

Next I visited the Cathedral through a gateway, arched and hung in the center of the arch which is very large, a figure carved in stone, now much decayed by time and written underneath **"Edgar 975."** The Worcester Cathedral is among the most ancient in the kingdom, its foundation dating about 600 A.D.—It is 400 feet long 70 high & 70 wide and like many edifices of the same kind and age has cloisters for monks, crypts or concealed or secret chambers under ground for purposes which can now only be conjectured. There are many monuments in the different parts of the Cathedral, some of which I shall mention—St Oswald 992[256] & Woolstan[257] 1084 both Saxon Bishops interred in front of the chancel in one of the chapels—Bp Constantian 1298, Bp. Decantelope[258] 1262. A very fine figure of a Crusader Sir Wm. Harcourt 1220, Bp. [Deakinson?] of St. David 1840, Bp. Hurd[259] 1808, Ann Walton wife of Issac Walton 1662, Sr Jno Beauchamp of Warwick, Mr. & Mrs. Wilde of Worcester.[260] An exquisite monument of Bp Hough[261] by Rubouilliac.[262] Here is also seen the tomb in which rest the bones of Jno I sirnamed Lackland—of

[255] Chamberlain and Son was formed by Robert and Humphrey Chamberlain in 1786 and remained in competition with Worcester Porcelain Co. until 1840 when the two organizations amalgamated and formed a joint stock company. (**DNB**).

[256] St. Oswald (961-91) dedicated the cathedral to the Virgin. ("Worchester," **New Cath Ency**).

[257] St. Wulfstan (1062-95) began the present structure. (**Ibid**).

[258] De Cantelupe (d. 1266) became bishop in 1237. (**Ibid**).

[259] Richard Hurd (1720-1808) was bishop of Worcester from 1781 til his death. He declined Canterbury in 1783. (**DNB**).

[260] Mr. and Mrs. Wilde probably was John Wylde or Wild (1590-1660) who was a chief baron of the exchequer—i.e., chief justice of the court of exchequer. (**DNB**).

[261] John Hough (1651-1743) refused Canterbury in 1715 but accepted Worcester in 1717. (**DNB**).

[262] Louis Francis Rubouillac (1702?-62) a French sculptor who influenced English sculpture. (**DNB**).

[263] John Gauden (1605-62) authored **Eikon Basiliki: The Pourtraiture of His Sacred Majestie** [Charles I] **in his Solitudes and Suffering**. In 1662 he was rewarded with the bishopric of Worcester. (**DNB**).

Bp Gauden[263] of the time of Chs 2nd—Tomb of Prince Arthur son of Henry VII and of Godfrey[264]—Bp besides many others. The windows of stained glass are very fine and the sealing off of the stone in many places give the Cathedral a very venerable as well as striking appearance.

Monday June 30th. The birthday of my beloved child Sarah McGavock! To day she would have been 21 yrs of age! How my heart once exalted in the thought of seeing her grow up to matured woman-hood and discharging all the duties of woman's noble mission in this world! Alas how have my hopes been blighted and vanity stamped on my brightest worldly anticipations! Yet who but He, who gave the life, my beloved one: can tell what might have been thy allotments, had thy span of life been extended? Misfortune & unhappiness might have been thy bitter portion, from which a kind providence has delivered thee! Let me not them murmur at thy early call from earth, but strive daily to become fitter for that holy state to which through the mercy & grace of our Adorable Redeemer I Trust thou hast attained: And do thou o most mer-ciful Father! assist my feeble endeavors by thy grace and Holy Spirit!

Rode to day with Mr. Brother & Mr. Newel to see the Romanish Chapel about four miles distant! It is a beautiful, quiet & peaceful spot—such as one would select for religious meditation and prayers. The clergy who live here are, I understand, devoted to their duties—very assiduous in attending to the needs of the poor & sick, an example which others might well and profitably follow.

July 2. The following touching and beautiful lines commemorate the virtues of Maria wife of Wm. Lygon, an epitaph in the Church at Malvern.

> "Stay, passenger, & from this dusty urne
> Both what I was & what thou must be learn.
> Grace, virtue, beauty, had no privillege
> That everlasting statute to abridge,
> That all must die: then gentle friend, with care
> In life for death & happiness prepare"

When the Priory of Malvern was dissolved it was granted by Henry VIII to Wm. Pynnock & his heirs, who in the same year sold to Jno Knottysford of whom the church was purchased by the inhabitants of Malvern and thus became parochial. The present church is in the form of a cross, as usual, with nave & transept and chapels adjoining—only two of which do I know the names: vis: Jesus Chapel to the North & St.

[264] Godfrey Giffard (1235?-1302) was bishop of Worcester from 1268 to 1302. Prior to that he was chancellor of England.) (**DNB**).

Ann's to the South. The entire length of the building is 171 ft., the breadth 63 [through out?], the height of the nave 63 ft. and of the very imposing & beautiful tower—the upper part of which is occupied by large numbers of nooks is 124 feet. The stained and painted windows in this venerable looking pile, are not surpassed & hardly equalled in nature of coloring by any in the kingdom. Tradition assigns them to Henry VII as a donation. In the north transept of the building, in Jesus Chapel is a large window in which are seen the figure of Henry VII, Elizabeth his queen,[265] Arthur Prince of Wales[266] and Sr. Reginald Bray.[267] If I am not mistaken, Sir R. Bray is the same knight who crowned Henry 7th on the battlefield of Bosworth after the defeat & fall of Richd the 3rd[268] & I think Bray is buried in this church.[269] The figures of Bray & Prince Arthur are yet perfect. In the rear of Bray are Sr Jno. Savage[270] and Sr. Thomas Lovell[271] all kneeling and bearing palm branches.

The west window of the church, in three divisions, has the following subjects beautifully drawn and splendidly colored—Salutation of Elizabeth,[272] Visitation of the Angel to Mary, Nativity, Presentation in the temple, the blind restored to sight, Resurrection of Lazarus, the mutitude following our Saviour and the Last Supper.

The tiles used about the church have many of them very curious inscriptions. Among them is one fixed in the third pillar on the North side of the nave bearing the following in old English character. [sic]

	translation
Thenke man yi liffe	Think man thy life
Mai not eu endure	May not ever endure
Yat you dost yi self	That thou dost thyself
Of yat you art surre	Of that thou art sure
But yat you gevest	But that thou givest
Un to yi sectur cure	To the executors cure

[265] Elizabeth (1465-1503) queen of Henry VII, was the daughter of Edward IV. She was married in 1486. Her death is attributed to grief over the death of her eldest son Arthur. (**DNB**).

[266] Arthur, Prince of Wales (1487-1502) was the elder son of Henry VII and Elizabeth and the first husband of Catherine of Aragon whom he married in 1501. (Katherine of Aragon, **NCE**).

[267] Sir Reginald Bray (d.1503) sided with Henry Tudor at Bosworth. Henry knighted Reginald at the coronation. He was a favorite of Henry whom he flattered. (**DNB**).

[268] After the Battle of Bosworth Thomas Stanley (1435-1504) placed the crown of the fallen Richard III on Henry's head. A year later he was created earl of Derby. ("Derby, Thomas Stanley, 1st earl of," **NCE**).

[269] Neither Bray nor Lovell is buried at Malvern. Bray lies in a chapel at Windsor and Lovell at one in Shoreditch. (**DNB** under each man).

[270] Sir John Savage (d. 1492) was knighted in 1465 and given a Garter in 1488 in recognition of having sided with Henry Tudor at Bosworth. He was slain in France. (**DNB**).

[271] Sir Thomas Lovell (d. 1524) also supported Henry at Bosworth. He was made chancellor of the Exchequer for life and was knighted in 1487. (**DNB**).

[272] Salutation of Elizabeth is the story told in Luke 2 about the meeting of the Virgin Mary and her cousin Elizabeth after the Annunciation.

And eu hit availe ye	And ever it avail thee
Hit is but aventure.	It is but a venture.

Another tile has the sacred symbol of the fish, adopted from a very early period as an emblem of the Saviour. The Greek word ιχθυς (fish) is composed of the initals of the words Iησμς χριστος θεου υιος σωτηρ Jesus Christ, the Son of God the Saviour.

It is an interesting fact that there is extant a letter of old Hugh Latimer written in his own peculiar but forcible style addressed to the Lord Chancellor petitioning that Malvern might remain & be converted to educational purposes and not share the fate of confiscation with the other priories and be suppressed by Henry VIII. **Note.** Mr. [Stallam?] fixes the perior of the Middle Ages from the invasion of France by Clovis[273] to Chs VIII[274] about 1000 years.

Thursday July 3. Nothing worthy of note to-day.

Friday, July 4. Anniversary of American Independence. Rode with Messers. Brother & Newel or Noel to Eastner Castle this morning the seat of Lord Somers.[275] The grounds are very beautiful, the parks are filled with black & fallow deer, the coverts with pheasants, partridges and other game. The castle is a magnificent structure, said to have cost 400,000£. The stone of which it is constructed was transported all the way from the neighborhood of Bristol & of course at an enormous expense. We were shown through the principal apartments by the Housekeeper. The establishment is rather meagerly furnished, by no means in a style corresponding with the external appearance. There are some fine portraits of the Somers & Cocks' families and the library is large & handsomely arranged. There is an artificial pond well replenished with fish in the rear of the castle. After ascending to the top of one of the towers which gives a very extensive and fine view over the country, we drove back to Malvern altogether pleased and gratified over our jaunt & remembrances of the 4th of July 1851.

Saturday July 5. This evening after tea I became increasingly drawn into a discussion of the subject of slavery, as it exists in the U. States. I was amazed at the warmth with which some of the Englishmen enter into debate about a question upon the practical details & merits of which they are exceedingly ignorant. I had resolved not to engage in these discus-

[273] Clovis, king of the Franks from 481 to 511, virtually ended Roman rule in Gaul when he defeated the Roman legions in 486.

[274] Charles VIII, king of France from 1483 to 1498. His involvement in Italian affairs fostered the introduction of the Renaissance into France.

[275] John Somers Somer-Cocks (1788-1852) was Viscount Eastnor, and 2nd Earl Somers. On his death the peerage became extinct. (L.G. Pine, **New Extinct Peerage 1884-1971** [Baltimore, 1973]).

sions. But when flippancy has not enough manners to abstain from making ill natured remarks and ignorance shows it stupidity it is hard to refrain. A Mr. Weymouth was particularly pert on this subject. Yet he has not seen a slave in his life and knows nothing of their condition except from travellers & newspapers. I am again disgusted "ad nauseam" at the arrogance and pride of this people.

Sunday July 6th. I have spent the whole of this day in my room not being allowed by the Doctor to attend church. Wrote to the Bishop of Oxford approving his declaration and protest to the claims of Rome.[276] Last night had a very interesting conversation with [illegible] Crampton of Dublin, upon the subject of Baptism, baptism and regeneration, and kindred topics.

Monday July 7th. Paid Dr. Stummes for board up to this date. Rode with Messers. Brother & Newel to Camp Hill where are vestiges of an ancient fortification which tradition assigns to different people. One account is that it is the place where the Britons made their last stand under Caractacus against the Romans. This can scarecely be true as history places Caractacus[277] in the north and makes him the leader of the Caledonians. Another account assigns the fortification to the Romans. The determination of the question does not present a matter of any great interest. There are the remains of a trench or rather several trenches, carried round the hill in the manner of the ancient ditch & circumvallation, furnishing successive lines of defence one after another until you approach the very summit of the hill which is surrounded by a ditch having outlets on the north and south. The apex presents the finest view I have yet seen from the Malvern Hills. To the Southwest are plainly seen the town of Cheltenham & several small villages near, then further west, the city of Glouchester with the noble tower of its ancient Cathedral— Still further west Bristol Channel distinguishable by the shine of the water. Looking west your eye ranges over the beautiful landscape of Herefordshire, with its highly cultivated farms and until it rests upon the mountains of Wales. The country people seem generally employed in making hay: yet there appears to be no hilarity, no joyousness among them. They plod along as soberly to their work with horses that drag their enormous & heavy ploughs & dead stiff and chilly repose seems to be spread over the whole scene and you look in vain for the stir and activity of human life!

[276] The reestablishment of Roman Catholic bishoprics.
[277] Caractacus or Cardoc fought the Romans from the time of their invasion of Britain in 43 AD to 50 when he was captured and taken to Rome where the Emperor Claudius spared his life. (**NCE**).

Bishop Otey

Dr. Wilson's Water Cure Establishment

CHAPTER II

July 12 Saturday. This day I left London to make a rapid journey through the north of England, Scotland & Ireland and so on, to the south by way of Portsmouth to Paris in France. Take my seat in the first class of cars at the Eastern Counties Station. I set off for Cambridge at 11 A.M. and arrived at 2 P.M. and put up at the Eagle Hotel. After writing letters to Mr. R.W. McGavock[1] and Mr. P. Connelly I went out to seek entrance to the colleges &c. The only letter of introduction which I had was addressed to the Rev. Mr. Carus[2] and he had left Cambridge. I went to a bookstore & made myself known to the owner & asked him whether he could introduce me to the successor of Mr. Carus he promised to do so if he was at home. He soon made inquiry and found that he was at his rooms and dispatched a young man with me to show the way. I entered an apartment in Caisus College & announcing my name was cordially received by Rev. Mr. Clayton the successor of Mr. Carus in Trinity Ch. He very kindly went with me to see some of the public buildings. The first we entered was the Commons' hall or refactory of Caius College. Here are portraits of Irving Taylor,[3] Bp. Cosin,[4] Dr. S. Clark,[5] Baron Alderson[6] & William Harvey[7] who discovered the circulation of the blood. We next went to King's College where the rooms were pointed out to me once occupied by good old Mr. Simeon.[8] We then walked across a beautiful campus to the River Cam spanned by several bridges and its banks adorned with many fine and stately trees. Returning we entered the

---

[1] On July 8th the Tennesseans still in London departed for Paris after waiting a week for the Bishop. According to a footnote in **Pen & Sword**, Otey wrote McGavock on the 7th stating he would come to London. It arrived too late. The letter written from Cambridge reached McGavock in Paris on the 18th and told him that writer was enroute to Scotland and expected to reach Paris in about ten days if his health permitted. (**Ibid**, pp. 214 and 217).

[2] William Carus (1804-91) was an intimate friend of Charles Simeon and successor at Trinity. Later he edited some of Simeon's papers. (**DNB**).

[3] Should be Jeremy Taylor, not Irving. (1613-67) Graduated from Caius and later became a fellow of All Souls, Oxford. He had been a chaplain to Charles I. Charles II made him bishop of Down and Connor, Ireland. He is known for three works, **Holy Living, Holy Dying,** and **Ductor Dubitantium**. (**DNB**).

[4] John Cosin (1594-1672) became bishop of Durham after the Restoration. He was a liturgical scholar whose ideas helped shape the Prayer Book of 1662. (**DNB**).

[5] Dr. Samuel Clarke (1675-1729) started the Trinitarian controversy with his publication in 1712 of **Scripture Doctrine of the Trinity** in which he attacked the traditional doctrine of the church on this subject and was charged with Arianism—i.e., a Fourth Century heresy that Jesus was not of the same substance as God but the best of mortals. (**DNB**).

[6] Baron Alderson probably is Sir Edward Hall Alderson (1787-1857) who as a student at Caius took three prizes. In 1834 he was made a baron of the court of Exchequer. (**DNB**).

[7] William Harvey (1578-1657) in his book **On the Movement of Heart and Blood in Animals** (1628) traced the flow of blood from heart to arteries and veins to heart.

[8] Charles Simeon (1759-1836) despite being an Evangelical who believed in personal salvation resulting from a conversion experience, was appointed through influence to Trinity Church, Cambridge. This shocked many members, some of whom locked their pews and refused to attend. Simeon, however, slowly gained the confidence of most of his critics and became a very powerful person in Cambridge. The Simeon Trust, named for him, controlled several livings which were filled by Evangelicals. (**DNB**).

chapel of King's College—the most imposing structure internally and externally that I have yet seen in England. I stood over the spot on the tesselated [sic] floor where the remains of the celebrated Ch. Simeon are interred. The windows of this building are as superb as can be imagined, representing with their richly colored glass a great variety of Scriptural subjects. From here we proceeded to Pembroke College, the oldest of all in this University. In the Hall are found the portraits of Ridley Bp. of London, Bradford, martyr[9]—good old Bp. Andrews,[10] Spenser[11] the poet & a bust or statue of Wm. Pitt.[12] Bp. Ridley had been Master of this College; and it is said to have had more Bishops among its pupils than any other college. May it never fail to send forth its Ridleys & Bradfords to defend & if need so require to suffer for God's truth!

Sunday July 13th I arose this morning feeling refreshed by a night's rest and thankful to God in my very heart for all his mercies both temporal & spiritual. I dressed and then as some old divines say, endeavored to "dress my soul," by returning thanks to the Father of Mercies for all the blessings of Providence & grace enjoyed through his dear son our Saviour Jesus Christ, by committing myself & all near & dear to me to his merciful guidance & care and by supplicating the assistance of His Holy Spirit to help us all & especially those who have covenanted to pray with me & for me on the morning of this day, rightly to engage in worship and to discharge the duties incumbent upon us. I then walked a considerable distance through this town and got as far as a church called St. Paul's a brick structure bearing the date 1841. The town appears to be kept remarkably neat & clean—to be well supplied with water, streams of which are seen running on both sides of some of the streets, along with gutters as channels. I was especially struck with a fountain in a small square, the building enclosing which appears from the inscription to have been erected at the sole expense of one Hobson a carrier between this town & London. Two other persons have left bequests "in perpetuum," for keeping in repair this fountain, one of them £700. Such donations for the public benefit are very creditable to the founders of such charities and I am happy to remark are of frequent occurrance in England. Returning from my walk I took my breakfast and again about 9 A.M. walked out in the opposite direction passing a very large & magnificent building styled

[9] John Bradford (1510?-55) burned as a heretic at Smithfield. (**DNB**).

[10] Lancelot Andrews (1555-1626) was successively bishop of Chichester, Ely, and Winchester. He was high church and opposed to Puritanism. He is remembered for his **XCVI Sermons**, and his **Private Devotions** which were written originally in Greek and Latin. (**DNB**).

[11] Edmund Spenser (1552?-99), an Elizabethan poet best known for **The Fairie Queen**.

[12] William Pitt (1769-1806) entered Pembroke College, Cambridge at the age of 14. Later he was prime minister from 1783 to 1801 and from 1803 to 1806.

the Pitt Press,[13] in honor of the great statesman who was educated at Pembroke College, and used, I suppose as the Printing Press of the University. Close by and in one of the apartments of Pembroke College I believe, are most of the original manuscripts connected with the Reformation in England—the writings of Peter Martyr[14] and Martin Bucer,[15] & others in autograph. It is from this source that the Parker Society[16] have drawn so largely in their late valuable publications. Nothing can be better adapted it seems to me, to inspire a love of study in the young than the arrangements & accommodations of the various colleges here founded & in operation. They are generally in the form of a hollow sqe. [sic (squared)] the large inner court is usually a beautiful grass plat having paved or gravelled walks running around & through it. Hard by are usually found cool & refreshing shades furnished by aged & venerable looking forest trees—long walks winding along the banks of a quiet stream, kept in perfect order & cleanliness—gardens filled with all kinds of flowering plants & other shrubs capable of enduring this climate and then the vast collection of books &c found in the libraries—the perfect Silence which seems to reign in all apartments, the portraits of distinguished men that adorn the walls—all these things it would seem would naturally inspire a laudable ambition in the young and lead them to improve their opportunities. And doubtless many do. The provision made likewise for the cultivation of religious sentiments is on an ample & liberal scale. All the colleges have connected to them chapels, when in term times the service of the church is celebrated every morning & evening. At 11 A.M. I went to Trinity Church formerly in the pastoral charge of good Mr. Simeon, who was succeeded by Mr. Carus and he recently by Rev. Ch. Clayton the present incumbent. The service was read as with us except that it was introduced with the singing of a hymn—a practice I do not like—and also there was extempore prayer before the sermon which I

[13] Today the Pitt Press building is the symbolic and ceremonial headquarters of the Cambridge University Press which was established in 1584. The structure was built at the suggestion of the university with the surplus money left after the erection of a statue of Wm. Pitt. A few works have appeared as publications of the Pitt Press, (M.H. Black, **Cambridge University Press 1584-1984** [Cambridge: 1984], pp. 130-32).

[14] Peter Martyr Vermigli (1500-62) an Italian Protestant reformer whom Archbishop Laud invited to England making him a Regius Professor at Oxford. When Mary returned the Church of England to the Roman fold, Martyr went back to Strassburg and later Zurich. ("Vermigli, Pietro Martire," **NCE**).

[15] Martin Bucer (1491-1551), a German Protestant theologian who accepted Cranmer's invitation to come to England where he taught at Cambridge. At the request of Edward VI he wrote **De regno Christi**. (**NCE**).

[16] The Parker Society for the Publication of the Works of the Fathers and Early Writers of the Reformed English Church was founded in 1840 and ceased in 1855 with the publication of 53 volumes and a general index. It was named after the Archbishop of Canterbury Matthew Parker (1504-75) who became chancellor of Cambridge in 1545. As Canterbury he maintained a distinctly Anglican position between extreme Protestantism and the church at Rome. He also collected ancient manuscripts which he gave to Corpus Christi College and founded a Society of Antiquaries. ("The Thirteenth and Final Report of the Council of the Parker Society" in **General Index** volume 55, Parker Society [London, 1855 Johnson Reprint]).

do not like. The Rev. Mr. Clayton preached a very plain and practical discourse upon the words of the prophet Malachi, I believe. "Arise ye and
depart hence, for this is not your rest."[17]

After the sermon I walked with Mr. Clayton to several of the
churches—among others **All saints** [sic] where are interred the remains
of **H.K. White**[18] and where is that beautiful mural tablet and an inscription placed there by an American.

On a monumental tablet in All Saints Church, Cambridge, England
erected at the expense of Fr. Booth, Esq. of Boston, Mass; are the following lines composed by Wm. Smith, Esqr. Profr. Mod. Histy, Cambridge

Henry Kirke White
Born March 21st 1785
Died October 10th 1806

Warm with fond hope & learning's sacred flame,
To Granta's bower the youthful poet came;
Unconquer'd power, the immortal mind display'd
But worn with anxious thought the frame decay'd;
Paler o'er his lamp & in his cell retired,
The martyr student faded & expired.
O Genius, Taste & Piety sincere,
Too early lost, midst duties too severe!
Foremost to mourn was generous **Southey** seen
He told the tale & show'd what **White** had been,
Nor told in vain—for o'er the Atlantic wave
A wanderer came & sought the Poet's grave;
On yon lone stone he saw his lonely name,
And raised this fond memorial to his fame.
Unhappy White! while life was in its Spring,
And thy young muse just wav'd her joyous wing,
The spoiler swept that soaring lyre away
Which else had sounded an immortal lay.
Oh! what a noble heart was there undone.
When science 'self destroyed her favorite son!
Yes! she too much indulged thy favorite pursuit,
She sow'd the seeds, but death has reap'd the fruit.
'Twas thine own genius gave the final blow

---

[17] The scripture verse is Micah 2:10: "Arise ye, and depart: for this is not your rest; because it is polluted, it
shall destroy you, even with a sore destruction."

[18] Henry Kirke White (1785-1806), being the son of a butcher, received a sizarship or scholarship reserved
for sons of men with limited means. (**DNB**).

And help'd to plant the wound that laid thee low:
So the struck eagle strech'd upon the plain,
No more through rolling clouds to soar again,
View'd his own feather as the fatal dart,
And wing'd the shaft that quiver'd in his heart
Keen were his pangs, but keener far to feel,
He receiv'd the pinion which impelled the steel
While the same plumage that had warm'd his nest
Drank the last life-drop of his bleeding breast!

Byron[19]

In Trinity Church I saw the mural tablets erected to Henry Martyn,[20] Thomason and their great master Chs. Simeon. I walked through the grounds of Trinity College, the most extensive of all foundations here, having about 500 students. It is celebrated for having produced some of the greatest of men as Dr. Isaac Newton,[21] of whom the Hall contains a fine picture & I think a statue also—and also of the great Bacon. Kirke White was a student of St. John's College. The walks in the rear of Trinity College[22] shaded by magnificent elms & along the banks of the Cam are not surpassed, if indeed equaled by anything that I ever saw.

I attended the University Church this afternoon & heard a sermon from Profr. Schoolfield,[23] [sic] most common & ordinary & civil.

Monday July 14. I have been hurried this day. Soon after breakfasting with Rev. Mr. Clayton, I hurried off to Ely, the seat of a Bishop's see and having one of the finest cathedrals in England. It is now undergoing extensive repairs. The large arched entrance leads into an extensive close as it used to be called on which are situated various buildings belonging to the old Abbey, the cathedral &c. The Abbey seems to be converted into a stable. The Cathedral is a very spacious building, venerable for its antiquity & deeply interesting from historical or rather biographical associations connected with it. The pillars in the interior are richly grouped together and the many arches beautifully formed, seen from different points of view to the beholder a spectacle at once grand, unique and

---

[19] Lord Byron's name is mentioned because the poetic tribute included lines from a short poem the renown poet wrote about White. (**DNB**) The inscription and poem are found in the diary entry for 30 December 1852.

[20] Henry Martyn (1781-1812) was a missionary to India where he translated the New Testament into Sanskrit and Persian. He died of a fever. (**DNB**).

[21] Sir Issac Newton (1642-1727) discovered the law of universal gravity, was a professor at Cambridge from 1669 to 1701, and president of the Royal Society from 1703 to his death. (**DNB**).

[22] The Cambridge colleges mentioned by Otey were founded in: 1347—Pembroke, 1350—Trinity Hall, 1441—King's, 1551—St. John's, and 1558—Caius. Despite what Otey wrote, Pembroke is not the oldest college. Peterhouse or St. Peter was founded in 1284 and Clare in 1326. (**NCE**).

[23] James Scholefield (1789-1853) was a classical scholar at Cambridge. In 1856 a Scholefield prize in theology was established in his honor. (**DNB**).

peculiar. Hugh [erasure], Bp, laid the foundations of this noble building in 1235. It was not completed till 1252. I saw here a monument of Bishop Patrick the Commentator.[24] He died at the age of 81. There is here also a monument to Bp Gunning[25] author of the Lenten fast [sic] and one to Basevi,[26] the unhappy architect who ascended to the upper part of the building with the Dean, and falling through a trap door was instantly killed. One of the most distinguishing features about this Cathedral is what is called the **lantern**—a species of tower like a lantern raised where the main transept crosses the nave. Originally there stood a Norman tower which fell and crushed a part of the building whereupon it was determined to substitute for it the Lantern Tower. The repairs now in progress in painting the glass of the windows as also the ceilings will greatly beautify the interior of the structure. Connected with the Cathedral is what is called the Lady's Chapel, meaning thereby the Chapel of the Virgin M. It is a remarkably beautiful & highly ornamented building and is the part of the Cathedral at present occupied on Sunday for worship.

Leaving Ely a little after 2 P.M. I came to Peterboro which is also the see of a Bishop & of his cathedral. I regret that my limited time allowed me only to walk through this large and magnificent building so imposing in its appearance, & in its history furnishing some incidents of deep & thrilling interest. Like most of the old Cathedrals it has a fine & noble arched gateway or entrance: & then a beautiful plat of ground in front of the main door or vestibule. The nave has noble columns rising from the floor to a very lofty roof, giving to the whole interior an air of grandeur. Within the chancel railing on a slab close to the wall is this inscription Posita sunt ossa—Kynsini[27] - Archiepi, Ebr. A.D. 1059. [Here lie the bones of Kynsini Archbishop of York, A.D. 1059] In one of the side chapels is a slab covering the remains of Catherine of Arragon[28] [sic] the first queen of Henry VIII—1536. There is here also a mural tablet in

---

[24] Simon Patrick (1626-1707) Bishop of Chichester (1689) and of Ely (1691) was one of the five original founders of the Society for the Promotion of Christian Knowledge and a supporter of the Society for the Promulgation of the Gospel in Foreign Parts. He was also a writer of exegetical literature. (**DNB**).

[25] Peter Gunning (1614-84) bishop of Chichester (1669) and of Ely (1675). His "Paschal or Lenten Fast" (1662) was republished (1845). He was also the ancestor of the famous 18th Cent. beauties: Elizabeth who married the Duke of Hamilton and later the Duke of Argyl; Maria was the Countess of Coventry. (**DNB**).

[26] George Basevi (1794-1846) was the architect of the Fitzwilliam Museum in Cambridge. He was inspecting some of the alterations when the accident happened. A plate in the cathedral shows him reading a blue print. (**DNB**).

[27] Kynsige, Kinsius, Kinsi (d. 1060) became archbishop of York. He was buried in Peterborough at his request. His tomb near the high altar was forgotten and rediscovered in the 17th Century. (**DNB**).

[28] Catherine of Aragon (1484-1536) was the daughter of Ferdinand and Isabella. The efforts of Henry VIII to divorce her led to the chain of events that resulted in the English Reformation. In spite of being put aside she remained popular with the English people.

memory of John Hinchcliffe,[29] one of the bishops thro' whom the [apostolic] succession is derived to the Ch: in America. He died Jany. 2 AD 1794 at 62. I saw also a large stone here which once marked the burying places of a large number of people. When the Danes invaded the Eastern part of England in 870, the people took refuge in the Cathedral, the monks then residing closing the gates and refusing the Danes admittance. The place held out three days at the end of which time the besiegers forced an entrance and put all the defenders to the sword & burnt the cathedral. The monks of Crowford Abbey gathered the remains of the unhappy & slaughtered victims & erected over their grave a monument of stone which now occupies a niche in the rear of the Chancel.

After leaving Peterboro I passed Boston where I saw in the distance one of the most beautiful & striking towers I have ever seen. At Tattershall is a very singular structure just in front of a large church & tower. It appears to be a sort of gateway except I could not see any entrance to it or one larger than a window. The towers of which there were four appeared to be very different—two of them like Chinese [?] canopies, the other two dentated battlements. About 8 P.M. I arrive at Lincoln where I resolve to stay all night hoping to see its cathedral in the morning.

Tuesday July 15. I left my bed & room this morning at an early hour and making my way across a bridge, along a street which led up a very steep hill, I presently found myself opposite to a large arched gateway that conducted directly to the Cathedral. The guide's house happened to be very near & by him the gates & doors of the Cathedral were open for my admission. Before I say anything of the interior let me give my impressions of the external appearance. I don't think I have ever seen a building so perfectly proportioned. The towers at the west end or main front of the building are light & airy and yet they strike you as sufficiently strong for all the purposes they were intended to answer. The great central tower erected where the main transept crosses the nave at

---

[29] John Hinchcliffe (1731-94) was bishop of Peterborough (1769-94). During the American Revolution his speeches in the House of Lords first urged coercion but soon favored conciliation. Hinchcliffe was one of the four bishops who consecrated William White, bishop of Pennsylvania, and Samuel Proovost, bishop of New York on 4 February 1787. The other consecraters were John Moore, archbishop of Canterbury (1781-1805); William Markham, archbishop of York (1777-1807); and Charles Moss, bishop of Bath and Wells (1774-1802). White was glad the latter was one of those involved because this bishop initially was concerned over discussion by the Protestant Episcopal Church over whether to keep the phrase "descended into Hell" in the Nicene Creed. His presence assured White that Bath and Wells had resolved his doubts. Before the ceremony in Lambeth Palace both Americans had an audience with George III in which they thanked him for waiving the oath of Supremacy thus making their consecration possible. (William White, **Memoirs of the Protestant Episcopal Church in the USA from its Organization to the Present Day** [New York, 1836, Second Ed.] p. 136). Undoubtedly this consecration had special meaning to Archbishop Moore.. His first wife was the daughter of Robert White, chief justice of the colony of South Carolina (1731-39) and sister of Sir James Wright, Baronet, governor of the colony of Georgia (1761-76 and 1779-82). (**DNB**).

the distance of half or three quarters of a mile rise into the air with all the elegance and beauty of the perfect female form and yet when you close up to the Cathedral you see at once that the tower is of gigantic dimensions.

Nothing that I have seen in church architecture has struck me as more symmetrical & graceful than the towers of Lincoln Cathedral. The first Bishop of Lincoln was said to be Remi or Remigius[30] who accompanied William the Conqueror with an armament of one ship & twenty men to assist him in his wars. He is reputed to have first laid the foundation of a Cathedral at Lincoln. It suffered afterwards by fire & was rebuilt or repaired by one Bishop Alexander. Remigius did not live to see any part of the building consecrated. One Hugh afterwards made Bp. of this see, & canonized founded the present building between 11 & 12 hundred probably near the close of 1200. He was a man of great zeal and piety. After him the principal builder seems to have been one Sutton. Bp. St. Hugh was held in so high esteem that long after his death his remains were transferred to a coffin of beaten gold which was taken possession of by Henry VIII & converted to other purposes than hold a dead body. The great circular window in the South end of the principal transept is remarkably beautiful. It is filled with delicate tracery work in stone, having colored glass and is 27 Feet in diameter. It does not seem to be more than 4 or 5 feet. The carved work in the choir is very rich. Behind the Communion table is a picture of the Annunciation painted by a clergyman (Rev. Mr. Peters). It is a very rich and fine picture but I think it had better be somewhere else. The monuments in the building are numerous—a few only of which I will mention—that of Catherine duchess of Lancester & wife of Jno of Gaunt[31]—one to the memory of Bp. St. Hugh[32] by Bp. Fuller[33]—of Bp. Flemming[34] [sic] in which there is a skeleton represented, placed where he would always see it when he went to his orisons to remind him of his own mortality, his own figure was after-

[30] In 1072 Remigius in accordance with the wishes of William the Conqueror moved the diocese from Dorchester to Lincoln and began the Cathedral in 1086. Alexander the Magnificent added to it during his years 1123-48 as bishop. St. Hugh of Avalon (1135?-1200) rebuilt much of it in his fourteen years as bishop from 1186. Oliver Sutton had the see from 1280-99. At the Reformation the diocese was split between Lincoln, Oxford, and Peterborough. ("Lincoln, Ancient See of" **New Cath Ency**).

[31] John of Gaunt (1340-99), fourth son of Edward III. Catherine Swynford who had been his mistress became his third wife. Her children were known as Beauforts. Through this line the pair became ancestors of Henry VII. (**DNB**).

[32] Hugh of Avalon (d. 1200), bishop of Lincoln (1186) was one of the most saintly prelates of the medieval church. The "Angel Choir" of the cathedral was erected in his honor. (**DNB**).

[33] William Fuller (1608-75) became bishop in 1667. He was a friend of two men who kept diaries, Samuel Pepys and John Evelyn. (**DNB**).

[34] Richard Fleming (d. 1431) received the bishopric in 1420. He was founder of Lincoln College at Oxford and later the Pope named him archbishop of York, an appointment Henry IV refused to confirm. (**DNB**).

wards placed above this. Bp Grostete[35] [sic] memorable for his manly resistance of papal assumptions was interred in this Cathedral. There was a monument here also to a child named Hugh[36] whom tradition mentions as sacrificed [?] by the Jews [?] & about which there is extant a long ballad. I left this magnificent building certainly impressed very deeply with feelings of respect for piety of those whose labors & contributions had been given to its erection.

Taking the R. Road after breakfast I came with a Dr. Gaillard & a Mr. Porcher[37] both of S.C. whom I met accidentally at the Hotel, to the ancient city of York, remarkable for its antiquity dating as far back as the reigns of David & Solomon, so its inhabitants claim for it & no less celebrated for its walls and Minister. **A Mr. Nettleship**, antiquarian and vendor of York relics &c, very soon espied us and acted as our cicerone in pointing out the venerable ruins of Old Hospitable [sic] & abbey which are indeed among the most striking I have seen in England. The view of these ruins mantled with the green ivy creeping about the arches & dressing the grey walls in living green is exceedingly picturesque. Here is the most ample scope given to the imagination. What varied emotions arise in the human bosom when one contemplates these crumbling relics of a former age, yea of ages, and reflects for what purposes these ample courts, lofty pillars, elegant arches were constructed. How many thousands have traversed these grounds, have looked upon these very objects which I have just have been contemplating, and been affected by all the purposes to which it has been devoted were intended to inspire: Here the heart has poured forth its sorrows in remembrances of its guilt, perhaps in the very language of David. "Have mercy upon me, O God! after thy great goodness" &c or given expression to its grief when stricken with affliction. "Bow down thine ear O Lord & hear me for I am poor & in misery"! [sic] Here joy has uttered its voice and the language of praise rung along these vaulted roofs. Dark and malignant thoughts too, like unclean things, have festered here and sent pangs to the soul when it remembered that God was witness to the secret musings of the human

[35] Robert Grosseteste (1175-1253), bishop of London, was one of the most learned men of his times. He was venerated locally as a saint but was never canonized possibly because he attacked Pope Innocent IV for appointing foreigners to rich English benefices. (**DNB**).

[36] Copin, a Jew, crucified St. Hugh of Lincoln (1246-55) after torturing or starving the boy who is buried near Grosseteste. Chaucer and Marlow refer to the story. ("St. Hugh," **DNB**).

[37] In the mid 1850's Charleston has two Drs. Gaillard: Peter Cordes (1815-59) and Edwin Samuel (1827-85). The older graduated in 1837 from the Charleston Medical College which later became part of the University of South Carolina, whereas the younger man was in the class of 1854. Francis Peyre Porcher (1825-95) graduated from the college in 1847. All three were associated with the **Charleston Medical Journal**. Dr. Peter was an associate editor and Dr. Francis became editor in the 1870's about the time that Dr. Edwin who had relocated in Richmond established the **Richmond Medical Journal** and later the **American Medical Weekly**. (**Appleton's Encyclopedia of American Biography** [1900]).

breast, no less than the judge of human conduct. But I must not dwell upon such lucubrations; now they will come up again in future days if life is spared and health regained. Passing from these ruins, in the very heart of a city which claims to be the oldest in the kindom, we were conducted by Mr. Nettleship to his shop of relics &c; & each of us purchased some little trifle by way of remuneration for his attentions. He then pointed out the way to the Minister which we entered, and very soon found a guide to take us through the various parts and relate to us as far as he had learned & remembered his lesson, the history of each portion severally. But how shall I undertake to describe how, a work which has been centuries in the course of its erection and of the various additions made to it from age to age. I was but a few hours in examining its wonders and but one feeling possessed my mind after I had completed the survey as was the case in the morning at Lincoln—unmixed admiration at the grandeur of these structures and a profound feeling of awe & reverence inspired by the objects around me. Upon entering the choirs of both these cathedrals today, I feel drawn involuntarily & almost irresistably to the chancel & there before the high altar I promised myself before the Lord, in my spirit and prayed "Defend O Lord! thy church with thy perpetual mercy &c" and I remembered those whose images are evermore in my heart and prayed that I might rejoin them, in a world of purity, peace & joy in a world where sin and temptation cannot enter & where there is [illegible]

I went into the Cathedral at York and opened the books lying on the communion table, and picking up a block of oak wood lying on the floor of the Chancel I enquired of the guide what was its use. Without answering my question, he said to me "you are transcending your privileges by going into the chancel." "No," said I. "I am not." "Yes but you are." Said I "Sir it is the right of a Bishop to go at all times within the chancel railing." One of my companions I saw whisper to him that I was a Bishop. He looked a little abashed and remarked I was not a Bishop of that Church & no right to go into the chancel on my own. I said to him I was a Bishop in the Church of God & it was the right of Bishops the world over to go into the chancel. Here the conversation on that subject ended. The minster or cathedral of York is built in the form of a cross, and its full length from west to east is 534 feet while the nave's transept is 241 feet. There are two towers at the western end and large tower called a lantern at the point where the main transept crosses the nave. The north transept was built by Bp Grey[38] whose monument is still extent. [?] The

---

[38] Walter Grey (d. 1255) Archbishop of York (1215) was present at the signing of the Magna Carta. His diocese was not enough of a challenge and he became a builder. (**DNB**).

choirhall by Archbishop Roger[39] had previously been taken down. The tomb of Walter Grey is still pointed out to strangers.

The north transept was begun by Jno. Le Romain[40] who also finished it about 1250. Jno. Le Romain,[41] son of the last named, laid the foundation of the nave in 1291. The work was continued after his death by his successors H? Newark,[42] Ths: Corbridge[43] & Wm de Melton[44] who finished [illegible] the entire west end as it now [?] appears. A new choir was built by Archbp Thoresby[45] between 1361 and 1400. In March 1629 the choir was set on fire by one Martin a religious fanatic and came near destroying the entire edifice. The windows are in the "early pointed style" & are very fine particularly the circular window 27 feet in diameter is remarkable for its beauty. I am not sure that I have not given the circular windows to Lincoln Cathedral which belong to York Minister. The windows are full of figure of old [sic] & New testament [sic] saints. Here we see St. Peter & St. Paul and then Abraham, Solomon & Moses. The main tower is at the center as already stated resting on four magnificent arches which rise from the floor to the height of 103 feet. On the organ [?] screen before the choir and the right & left of the entrance thereto are the figures on the north side Wm the Conqueror, Wm Rufus, Henry I, Stephen, Henry II Richard I & Jno: On the South Henry III, Ed I, II, III, Richd II, Henry IV, V & VI. All of them in good state. The lessons in the service are read here as in Lincoln Cathedral from a brazen spread Eagle. Divine service is performed every day at 10 A.M. & 4 P.M. except Sundays. The curved work in the choir over the stalls is very rich. The organ is the finest in the kingdom containing 7500 pipes. The monuments in the different chapels are very numerous & many elaborately adorned. Among them is one to Th. Watson Wentworth[46] by Guelfi[47] &

[39] Roger de Pont l'Eveque (d. 1181) as archbishop revived the claims of supremacy of York over Canterbury and even claimed Scotland. (**DNB**).

[40] John Le Romeyn better known as Romanus because he was an Italian, (d. 1255). He became treasurer of York (1247) and was accused of being rich and avaricious. He built the transept and central tower of the Minster. (**DNB**).

[41] John Le Romeyn was Romanus' son by a servant girl. After receiving a dispensation from his illegitamcy, the younger John ultimately became the archbishop (1285-96). He encouraged his clergy to study theology, rebuilt the nave of the minster, and erected chapter houses elsewhere in the province. (**DNB**).

[42] Henry Newark was consecrated on 15 June 1298 and died 15 August 1299.

[43] Thomas of Corbridge (d. 1304) was archbishop from 1299 to 1304. (The above two are from a list of archbishops of York furnished the editor).

[44] William de Melton (d. 1340) Archbishop of York (1316-40) was treasurer of England (1325-27). Asserted his right to bear his cross in the province of Canterbury. (**DNB**).

[45] John Thoresby (d. 1373) Archbishop of York (1351-73) settled the dispute between York and Canterbury over supremacy with each incumbent allowed to keep his cross erect in the other's province. (**DNB**).

[46] Thomas Wentworth, 1st Marquis of Rockingham (d. 1750). His son the 2nd marquis headed the government in 1765 which repealed the Stamp Act. After the fall of Lord North in 1782 he again headed the minstry but died before the peace settlement with the former American colonies was arranged. ("Rockingham, " **NCE**).

[47] Giovanni Battista Guelfi, an Italian sculptor migrated to England in 1714. His statue of Watson Wentworth is one of his better known works. (E. Benezit, **Dictionnaire des Peintres, Sculpteurs, Dessignateurs et Graveurs** [Paris, 1976]).

the finest in the Church. It consists of a full length figure in a Roman costume and a female in a reclining position. Nearby is the tomb of Archbishop Mathews who died 1626.[48] He was one of my maternal ancestors. Archbishop Sharp[49] who died 1713 has a monument under the East window. To the left of this as you face the east is the monument of Archbishop Scrope[50] who was beheaded June 8 1405 and being the first instance of a Bp suffering death by law in England. Sr. George Savile[51] who had the chief agency in restoring peace between England & America in 1783 has an elegant monument in this part of the church which commemorates his many great & estimable qualities as a man & a stateman. Many of the monuments in this, as I have had occasion to observe in all the cathedrals and churches I have examined, have been despite of their arrogance [?] sadly mutilated by the hands of Parliamentary soldiers during the civil wars. The churches themselves were converted into barracks & stable for the cavalry. The chapter house of an octagonal form adjoining the Cathedral is said to be the most spacious of any in Europe. It has rather a singular inscription over the entrance as follows:

Ut avea phlos phloram   As of flowers the rose is queen
Sic est domus ista dormorum   So of houses this is first

There is one tomb conspicious for its position as much as its richness in the northern part of the main transept which I ought not to omit the mention. It is that of the late Dr Beckwith who left charitable bequests to the amount of £45,000 & among others 50 Thous [?] to the repair of the Cathedral.

In the Vestry rooms of the Cathedral are some very precious relics. Among others is the drinking horn of Ulphus, prince of Deira.[52] This horn

[48] For an account of Archbishop Tobie Matthew (1546-1628) and his sons, Sir Tobie, and Samuel see pp. 159-64.
[49] John Sharp (1645-1714), archbishop of York in 1691, was a commissioner for the reform of the liturgy in 1689 and later a commissioner for the Scottish Union. This group worked out the terms of the act of Union, 1707. (Mackenzie, **Kingdom of Scotland**, Chap. XVIII; **DNB**).
[50] Richard Le Scrope (1350?-1405), became archbishop in 1398. Although he initially supported Henry IV, Richard raised a force against the king. The archbishop was arrested and convicted. His execution which was intended to serve as an example instead made him a popular saint. (**DNB**).
[51] Bishop Otey apparently misinterpreted the influence of Sir George Saville, Bart. (1726-84) on Parliamentary actions regarding the rebellious attitude and the revolt in the American colonies. While voting in 1766 to repeal the Stamp Act, Saville warned the colonists that they might go too far. Eight years later he twice denounced the bill regulating the government of the Massachusetts Bay Colony as a "most extraordinary exertion of the legislative power." The following January he asked that Franklin be heard in support of an address from the American colonists to the king. This was voted down. Shortly thereafter in a debate on the bill for restraining the trade of the New England colonies, he argued that colonial resistance was justified. In 1775 and again in 1784 he moved for the repeal of the Quebec Act. He also supported Burke's bill for composing differences with the colonies. Then in 1781 Saville supported Fox's motion for a committee to take into consideration the state of the American war. The statue that attracted Otey's attention was erected by the citizens of Yorkshire whom he represented in Parliament. (**DNB**).
[52] Diera was the southern part of the Anglo-Saxon Kingdom of Northumbria which in the 6th and 7th centuries stretched from the Humber to the River Tyne. Ulphas is probably Alhfrith whose brother was killed in a battle along the River Trent in 678 that marks the decline of the kingdom. ("Northumbria, kingdom of" **NCE**).

made of ivory is the only title deed which the Cathedral has for valuable lands and property near York. It seems that such an instrument might be used in by gone days as a means or mode of legal indorsement. In this collection of relics is a drinking bowl of the York Cordwainer Company. Next is one of the shoe makers. It seems from the inscription to have been the gift of Archbp Scrope, the same who afterwards lost his head.

Another relic shown was a silver crozier six & a half feet long, the gift originally of Catherine[53] of Portugal queen dowager of Chs: II of England to her Confessor Cardinal Smith.[54] It was seized by Lord Danby[55] in a Romanish procession. Afterwards presented to the Dean and chapter of York. Other relics here deposited are the ring of Archbp Sewall[56] (1258)—a ruby set in gold, Archbp Grenfields[57] the same 1315 & of Archbp Bowet[58] 1425. In the grave of one of the Archbps, Rotherham's[59] who died of the plague & was burnt, was found a wooden head used to represent him for burial in the Minster. Within the chancel rails and on the right of the altar is an old rickety wooden chair, most of whose parts are bound together with pieces of iron, a most uncouth, useless & unsightly piece or article of furniture. Not because it has the reputation of being the old coronation chair and tradition says it was used for that purpose with several of the Saxon kings—no doubt great barbarians—& with Edward IV, Richard III & James I. **Therefore it is honored with a place in the Chancel**. Poof!

There are a great many other objects of interest about York—especially its wall, towers, gates—Clifford Castle & one of the Roman towers. But I had neither the time nor the strength to dwell upon these particulars. Leaving this ancient city so full of objects interest in its churches

[53] Catherine of Braganza (1638-1705) was Charles II's queen. She was unpopular because she was a Roman Catholic. Later Titus Oates accused her of plotting her husband's death. On the accession of William III to the throne she returned to Portugal where in 1704 she was regent for her brother Peter II. (**DNB**).

[54] The incident between Danby and James Smith, D.D., bishop of Calliopolis [Gallipoli] **in partibus infidelium**, occurred in August 1688 shortly after his consecration. He was emboldened by the Declaration of Indulgences which James II issued legalizing the grant of civil and military offices to Roman Catholics. On coming to the city of York Bishop Smith and his priests held an open **te deum** and then a mass in a chapel. Following this they had a procession which seemingly headed toward the Minster. At this point Danby grabbed the crozier. An effort was made in 1700 to name Smith to a cardinalcy and the office of Protector of England. The Duke of Berwick, a son of James and Arabella Churchill, was one of those commissioned from St. Germain, the exile home of James II, to solicit the appointment. ("Danby," **DNB**, and G. Ormsby, **York** [Diocesan Histories, 1882] pp. 302-3).

[55] Thomas Osborne (1631-1712), earl of Danby was a staunch royalist, fervent Anglican and supporter of William and Mary. He was lord president of the council (1690-99) and virtually prime minister (1690-95). For these he became Marquis of Carmarthen (1689) and Duke of Leeds (1694). (**DNB**).

[56] Sewall de Bovill served as archbishop from 1256 to 1258. (From a list of archbishops).

[57] William de Grenefield (d. 1315). His consecration as archbishop was delayed nearly two years by the Interregnum in the Papacy preceding Clement V who held the Papacy from 1305 to 1315. (**DNB**).

[58] Henry Bowet was archbishop from 1407 to 1423. John Kemp who had been bishop of London followed and in 1452 was translated to Canterbury. (From a list of archbishops).

[59] Thomas Rotherham was archbishop from 1480 to 1500. (List of archbishops).

and public buildings, its historic associations ancient & modern, I took the cars and proceded on my way North. It was not long before we came in sight of the city of Durham, situated in a valley, but yet pleasingly distinguishable by the massive proportions of the Cathedral & great towers. The cars did not pass nearer the city than two or three miles and that was the only view I had of the place & its Cathedral was a distant & very imperfect one. We passed Newcastle in the midst of a rain that hid everything but the nearest objects from view. I saw very near to the rail road [sic] and in the midst of the town a rather massive building which I took to be a castle of defense. It was a dark and lofty stone structure, the battlements of which frowns with artillery.[60] Further on the right of the road I saw a singular structure something which I took to be a temple or a mausoleum.[61] It crowned the summit of a hill and consisted of a row of columns [Next line illegible] Afterwards heard a gentleman in the cars say that it was a museum structure erected in honor of James [Jarnes?] distinguished member of the city. I arrived at the town of Berwick about 8 P.M. The Tweed is crossed on a lofty bridge. The passage of the R. Cars is supported by stone pillars [Next two lines illegible] When the work is well proportioned, it always appears with [faded] measurements to the eyes.

I stopped at the King's Arms in Berwick and on the whole was better entertained than supplied. This town is celebrated in history & especially in the wars between the kingdoms of England & Scotland and in the border conflicts of feudal times. At night I felt extremely sad & [lonely?].

Wednesday 16 July. This is a day memorable in my life, not for any remarkable or strange event, but on account of the thoughts & reflections to which the scenes & places I have visited have given rise. Leaving Berwick about 9 A.M. I came by railroad to Ancrum or St. Boswell's station. Here I hired a carriage & boy to drive it & set off to visit those places in the vicinity which the personal history of Sr Walter Scott endow with imperishable interests. Proceding by way of Melton bridge which crosses the Tweed some miles below Melrose I pursued a circuitous route winding among the hills and obtaining picturesque views of distant mountains and undulating surfaces crowned with grass or grain

[60] The rather massive building with battlements probably is the "new castle" which was erected in 1168 by Henry II on the site of an earlier wooden construction put there in 1080 by Robert Curthose, son of Wm the Conqueror.
[61] The temple or mausoleum could be Moat Hall, a Greek revival building designed by John Stokoe. It could be, however, the Penshaw monument constructed in 1844 honoring John L. Lambton (1790-1842), first earl of Durham whose Durham report proposed that Canada be allowed self government within the empire. The document has been called the Magna Carta of the British colonies as its principle has been extended to other colonies. (NCE).

ripe or overripe and ready for the sickle. I at length descended rapidly to some ground rising in a line of terraces and filled with trees. I stopped at a small gate. This was the entrance to the grounds of Dryburgh Abbey.[62] A cottage stood on the opposite side of the road. At this [Illegible] on my guide's instructions. We set forth.—What mound is this to the right of the path? That was the hen houses of the Monks! [Sentence illegible] Passing on we entered through a low door—sheep running before us and horses standing in the grass. On we went. This said my little guide was the kitchen and this the refractory, and this the chapter room. This statue is Dr. Isaac Newton. First I thought standing up and interestedly gazing out. [Sentence illegible] Here we came to the dungeon or keep. This was the church, here was the nave. There the pillars supporting the roof and here was the transept. Poor child! you have been taught your lessons and know as much about naves and transepts as the unlettered child knows the difference [between] Ectasia & Bull's foot.[63] But somethings she did know; leading the way to a part of the old ruin very like an alcove with a gothic arch and pointed roof and with an iron railing she said "here lies Sir Walter and here is his lady." I said to myself in this [world?] of Adam's [faded] "This is the end of Earth" [?] The tombstones appear to be plain slabs of red sandstone no inscription but the name of the tenant below and date of burial, "**Sir Walter Scott**, Sept 26, 1832" And is this all, said I, to mark the burial place of the "**great unknown**"—the mighty "Bard [?] of the north" the man whose genius so long entranced the attention of a world by the pictures which his fancy wove by the flashing of his wit? Here to this humble & lowly spot, to this lonely ruin, this secluded corner the traveller will come to honor by his presence the name & fame to say that "I have stood by his grave!" It is one of the most quiet spots I ever beheld. The very spirit of loneliness seems to hover over the place & to give its impress to everything around. The very sun light appeared to tinge with a melancholy haze the green grass and the leaves of the trees and of the ivy where it crept about the ruined wall and wove its festoons among the broken arches. The grave of Sir Walter in this place seemed to be in mockery of human pride and vanity. In the world of letters he had occupied a position analogous to that of Napoleon in the political world. And here in this setised[?] byecorner of creation, he had come at last to lay down the burden of mortality. Had there been the tombs of other great & illustrious men near at hand to which one

---

[62] Dryburgh Abbey was founded in 1150 and was destroyed in 1322, rebuilt and destroyed again in 1545. Sir Walter was buried here because one time it belonged to his ancestors. (**NCE**).

[63] Ectasia is a swelling or inflammation in a hollow organ. Bullsfoot is also known as coltsfoot, a low perennial herb.

might have turned attention after contemplating Sr W's, the idea of lone-liness had not perhaps pressed so much on the mind. But there was no other monument, no momento of others mortality which might draw away the thoughts. The idea uppermost in my mind was that the great man, had shut out the world, that he had tired of its vanity & emptiness and retired to the loosening shades of these mouldering ruins, the silence of which was broken only by the gentle whisper of the breeze as it sighed through the trees, or by the murmur of the Tweed as its waters flowed peacefully by the consecrated grounds. I found it difficult to analyze my feelings on this occasion. But I found myself inexpressibly sorrowful and it required a great effort to restrain my tears which were ready to flow and yet I knew not why. This I remember too, I thought of those who had been taken away from me—asked myself whether their spirits might not be near me then and thought to myself how deep and pleasant must be the sleep of the grave.

I saw in a part of the grounds a monument to a **Rev Mr. Erskine the youngest of 33 Sons**!

Leaving Dryburg [sic] Abbey I drove by Bemerclyde & up the Leader to Earlstown once the residence of Thomas the Rhymer[64] and returning on the other side of the stream by the Grange & other celebrated resi-dences, the names of which I have now forgotten. I crossed the Tweed & came to Abbotsford. The house &c have been described so often & so fully that I shall say nothing about them except that the collections of rare and curious objects is far more extensive that I had imagined. The servant who met me at the door was very like Mr. Hines[65] of Franklin and with very much of his tone & manner & volubility, gave an account of each room and of the things in it. The second room into which he took me was the one in which Sir Wr. wrote most of his works. **There** was his desk and **there** was his chair, just as he left them. I sat down in his chair, & mused a little while. Then got up & looked at the clothes which the Baronet wore last, previous to his death, and also at his walking cane. Abbotsford is now in the hands of Mr. Hope who married Miss Lockhart[66] Sr W's grand-daughter. He is a Papist & is erecting a chapel

[64] Thomas of Erceldoune also known as Thomas the Rhymer and Thomas Learmont (1220?-97?) a Scottish seer and poet whose sayings reputedly were consulted as late 1715 and 1745. Supposedly he predicted the battle of Bannockburn and the accession of James VI to the English throne. (**NCE**).

[65] C.H. Hines of Franklin, Tennessee is listed in the 1850 census as having been born in North Carolina in 1786 and a farmer. (**1850 Census, Williamson County, Tennessee**. Williamson County Historical Society, 1970).

[66] James Hope Scott and his wife Charlotte Lockhart joined the Roman Catholic Church in 1852. Prior to that they were devout members of the Episcopal Church with leanings toward the Tractarian movement. James had been one of the original founders of Holy Trinity, Glenalmond, a school and college to train clergy. Two of the other initial supporters were William E. Gladstone, thrice British prime minister, and Edward Ramsey, dean of St. John's, Edinburgh. (Lochhead, **Episcopal Scotland in the Nineteenth Century** pp. 79-80, 102).

for Romish worship, in connection with the buildings at Abbotsford. I came away after taking a survey of everything usually submitted to the inspection of strangers & as I left the yard plucked a sprigg opf evergreen as a memento of the place & of my visit. I also wrote my name in a book kept for the autographs of visitors & returned to Melrose. In leaving the place I experienced the same feelings of sadness as in parting with some dear friend. I have been so long familiar with the history & writings of Sr. Walter, that upon entering his house I felt as though I was in the **immediate presence of one** whom I had long & intimately known: and in coming away I could not help turning around at the last point whence the mansion was visible to take a last look and say farewell forever.

That same afternoon I came to Melrose and forthwith sought its abbey—now roofless nearly and in ruins. The view of one of these ancient and now crumbling structures gives one a correct notion of them all. At least they all present the same general features or outlines, the same grand proportions, the same elaborate workmanship and no one of them suggests any idea which has not been produced by the contemplation of the others. I walked around the building on the three parts, two ends & one side, which was accessible and contemplated the whole & each part in detail. It is all impressive and solemn in character & that is all I say. By the 6 o'clock afternoon train I left for Edinboro [sic] where I arrived before dark and put up at the Douglass Hotel.

July 17, Thursday. After breakfasting I proceded to Mrs. Smith's No 4 Bellevue Crescent. Miss Euphemia Smith had called the evening before at the Douglass and left note pressingly inviting me to make her Mother's home my home during my stay in Edinboro. It seemed that I would be considered as conferring an obligation instead of incurring one, by so doing, which made is very pleasant to accept the invitation given me: and indeed my reception and the attention kindly bestowed on me seemed to confirm this notion. For never have I been more comfortably provided for & kindly attended to. Miss S. very soon provided me with a companion to show me Edinboro & its lions, in the person of a Mr. Scott, a young man in the employ of her brother. With him I employed the balance of this day in visiting the different places of interest in the Athens of the North. First we looked at Sr. W. Scott's monument[67] of which an excellent engraving has been made & generally known, it being found an ordinary parlor object in very many families. Its situation is very conspicuous, a statue of Scotland's great son occupies the center. There are niches left for the reception of many figures and when these are placed in

[67] The 200 foot Scott monument was completed in 1846.

position the whole structure will be admirable. Next I went to the gallery of design, a room filled with an immense number of designs in plaster copies, some of these of the master pieces of the great & distinguished sculptors of by gone days—others appeared to be fancy designs of the ancient Greeks & Romans—Socrates, Plato—Cesar [sic], Cicero &c. Went to Heriot's Hospital,[68] an institution founded for the benefit of poor children, in which they are fed, clothed & educated. Heriot was of the times of James I and loaned that monarch money out of which he drew no small profits. I think he is delineated in one of the Waverly Novels. There are several foundations of the same sort with Heriot's in & about Edinburg. [sic] Indeed to become the founder of such institutions is beginning to be in public esteem, a mark of vain glory. From H's hospital I drove round Arthur's seat and returned to Edinboro by what is called the Queen's road, so denominated because Queen Victoria drove along this road & was received upon it by the inhabitants of the city when she visited Scotland some years ago. Arthur's Seat is a high hill which overlooks a great part of the city & is remarkable for nothing more than its exceeding sterility & barrenness. Immediately behind Arthur's Seat is the village of Doddington[69] [sic] celebrated for having a population more addicted to drunkenness than any other place in Scotland. At about the distance of about three miles further in the same direction is Craig Miller Castle,[70] noticeable for having been one of the prisons of Mary Q. of Scotts. [sic] It is now in ruins. I also visited today the Inns or Chambers where the judges sit & who were trying cases—heard one of the advocates pleading in a case and then visited what is called the library of the **writer to the signet**.[71]

July 18 Friday. To-day I was very kindly accompanied in my rambles by the Rev. Mr. Soather[72] [sic] of the Scottish Ep. Ch; and visit first the

[68] George Heriot (1563-1624), a Scot, was appointed goldsmith for life to Anne of Denmark, consort of James I. He became wealthy through his dealings with the Royal family by lending them money. Having no legitimate heirs, he left his money for the education of children of decayed burgesses and freemen of Edinburgh. The "hospital" in which these children were housed was opened in 1659. The £23,625 he left was so judiciously administered that in 1880 the annual income was £24,000. Today the hospital is known as a school. (**DNB**).

[69] Duddington is situated along a small loch. If today's inhabitants have a predilection toward drunkenness, they are loathe to admit it. This editor while on a tour of Edinburgh in 1992 asked the guide who lived in Duddington about the statement. She was surprised to hear it and said perhaps it came from the presence of a very old pub.

[70] Queen Mary chose to go to Craig Miller rather than Holyrood Castle because the latter was associated with the murder of her secretary Ricco. Later when the sick Lord Darnley was brought back to Edinburgh he refused to go to Craig Miller because it was in the hands of an enemy. Instead he opted for Kirk O'Field where he was murdered soon thereafter. (M. Brysson Morrison, **Mary Queen of Scots** [NY, 1960], pp. 137 and 153; See also Antonia Fraser, **Mary Queen of Scots** [NY, 1969]).

[71] Writer of the Signet is a Scottish judicial officer who prepares warrants, writs, etc. Originally he was a clerk in the office of the secretary of state. Scott's father, a lawyer considered himself a writer of the signet. (**Webster's New Twentieth Century Dictionary Unabridged**).

[72] Thomas Suther (1814-83, a Nova Scotian, became a priest in the Episcopal Church of Scotland. His parish was Leith, a suburb of Edinburgh. In 1857 he became bishop of Aberdeen. (Lochhead, **Episcopal Scotland Nineteenth Century**, p. 209).

rooms of the Antiquarian Society.[73] There were may curious things to be seen here & among the most curious was an instrument for beheading people called the Maiden & which must have been the original of the French Guillotine. One of the dukes of Argyle[74] was I believe the last that suffered under the instrument. I saw here also a standard which had been borne by the Covenanters[75] in the Battle of Bothwell Bridge, so fatal to their cause. I next went to the Castle of Edinburg [sic] situated on a most commanding position with heavy artillery mounted on its walls. I walked thro' various apartments & among others that in which James I of England was born & from a window of which he was let down in a basket shortly after his birth & taken possession of by one of the parties which was struggling for political ascendancy.[76] The regalia of Scotland consisting of a crown richly ornamented with jewels, of the sword of state with golden Scabbard, scepters, tiaras, bracelets & a ruby ring worn by Charles I at his execution are carefully guarded & kept in a room fitted up for that purpose in the Castle. For a long time the treasure was lost and no one knew what had become of it. Sr. W. Scott from investigating the matter concluded the Crown jewels were still in the Castle & obtained an order from the government allowing him to search for them. There was a room in the Castle which was entirely walled up & on opening this room an old oaken chest was discovered which on the removal of its lid disclosed the long lost Regalia of Scotland.[77] It was a happy day for Sr. W. & his friends and so entirely had Mrs. Lockhart entered into the feelings of her Father that upon discovering the long lost treasures, it is said that she burst into tears. From the Castle I walked thro' Connongate St. & saw the House in which the famous **Jno. Knox**[78] lived. It is an humble dwelling in appearance & projects far into the street before the

[73] The Anriquarian Society is now the National Museum of Antiquities of Scotland.

[74] Archibald Campbell, 9th Earl of Argyle (1628?-85) was beheaded for treason. In 1681 he was charged with treason and fled to Holland. Later after supporting the unsuccessful rebellion of the Duke of Monmouth. Argyle ws captured and executed. (**DNB**) Otey is in error as the dukedome was not created until 1701. ("Argyle A.C. 1st duke," **NCE**).

[75] Covenanters were Scottish Presbyterians who during the 16th and 17th centuries bound themselves by oath to stay together first in their efforts to make Scotland a Protestant country and then against the efforts of the later Stuarts to impose an episcopacy upon them. The revolt of 1679 was crushed with their defeat at Bothwell Bridge. After the ascension of William and Mary to the throne in 1688 the Presbyterian Church became the established one.

[76] According to the **Blue Guide, Scotland**, edited by L. Russell Muirhead [London, 1967, 5th ed.] this erroneous story is confused with a possible event in the life of James II. Perhaps some contemporaries thought this is what happened because Mary decided about two months after the boy's birth to follow custom and send him to Stirling Castle, the traditional nursery of royal princes. (Fraser, **Mary Queen of Scots** pp. 271-72).

[77] In February 1818 Walter Scott found the Scottish Regalia in the Crown Room of Edinburgh Castle. It had lain unused for so long that many Scottish thought it had been taken to London contrary to the 1707 Act of Union which stipulated that these items were not to be taken from Scotland. (John Buchan, **Sir Walter Scott** [London, 1932] p. 173).

[78] John Knox (1514?-72) Scottish religious reformer who was influenced by John Calvin. This shows in the theology of Presbyterianism.

other houses. Whether this is significant of the character of its original illustrious inmate others must determine. "Non Ego"! Went into the Advocates Library and saw a pennon which had been borne in the fatal battle of Flodden field[79] [sic]. It looked indeed as though it might have been in the heady melee of that desperate fray. I next went to Holy rood [sic] House, the former royal residence of the Kings of Scotland. It has in modern times been occupied by Ch: X, the ex king of France[80] & by other expelled Bourbons. Some parts of the old Chapel connected with the palace are very striking considered as ruins. Several of the Kings were crowned here & among them James VI of Scotland & afterward the first of England.

An old lady acting as cicerone pointed out the bed in which Mary had slept & Charles I & II. Also the room in which David Rizzio[81] was assassinated & the secret doors & stair way by which the conspirators gained access to the Queen's apartments. She also pointed out some dark spots on the floor which she said was Rizzio's blood! Doubtful!! In the afternoon of this day I met at Miss Smith's at Dinner Messers Dr. Alexander[82] an independent minister, Mr Campbell, advocate, Rev Suther, Drs. Gaillard & Duncan and Mrs Alexander & spent a very agreeable afternoon. At night [met] Mr. Robinson, Mrs Lare & daughter. My stay in Edinboro has been very pleasant and I greatly regret that circumstances do not permit me to remain longer. I received last evening a note from Mrs Terrot wife of Bp. Terrot,[83] inviting me to breakfast or to take lunch with the family saying likewise that the Bp was from home. I accepted the invitation & went this morning to breakfast and had a very interesting time with the family. I met Rev Mr. Malcolm son in law of the Bp at breakfast. Mrs Terrot asked me to conduct family prayers which I did, with much satisfaction to myself & I trust not without a good impression upon those present; for Mrs Terrot wrote me a note tonight thanking me for praying with & for them & especially that I had recognized the Communion of Saints as embracing those who had departed this life in the

[79] Flodden Field was the site of a battle in which the English in 1513 under the Duke of Norfolk defeated the Scottish army led by James IV who was killed.

[80] Charles X (1756-1836), youngest brother of Louis XVI, was the last Bourbon king of France (1824-30). He abdicated during the Revolt of 1830 and returned to England where he had lived as an emigré from the French Revolution and Napoleon. Later he moved to Prague.

[81] David Rizzio (1533?-66), an Italian who was Mary's secretary for French affairs. Her husband, Lord Darnley was led to believe that Rizzio was Mary's lover. For this reason the Italian was murdered. (Frazer, **Mary Q.**).

[82] Dr. William Lindsay Alexander (1808-94), was a theologian in the Scottish Congregational church. He wrote articles for the **Encyclopedia Britannica**, and edited the 3rd edition of Kitto's **Biblical Cyclopaedia**. (**DNB**).

[83] Charles Hughes Terrot (1790-1872) was of Hugenot ancestry and born in India. Educated at Cambridge, he was ordained in 1814. Later he went to Edinburgh where in 1841 he was consecrated bishop, becoming primus in 1857. He was twice married. He and his first wife who was so gracious to Otey had fourteen children. Their eldest daughter served as nurse with Florence Nightengale in Crimea. (**DNB**).

true faith & fear of God's holy name!

Saturday July 19. Early in the morning & before I had an opportunity of seeing & thanking my kind hostess Miss Smith for her hospitality I went to the R.R. Station to take my passage for Stirling. We were very soon on the way and as soon passing by objects of great interest to the Traveller. This **Niddry** Castle where Q. Mary is said first to have slept after her escape from Loch Leven Castle.[84] **Uphall Village** in a church here lie buried the celebrated H. Erskine[85] & his Bro. the chancellor. **Linlithgow**, remarkable for the birthplace of Mary Queen, & for the Church in which James IV[86] was warned by an apparition of his fate at Flodden field. Next place worthy of note is Falkirk celebrated for its battles. Here Wallace[87] was defeated by Edward I in 1298 & again Genl Hawley commanding the English forces [was defeated] by the Highlanders under Charles Edward 1746.[88] **Bannockburn** a short distance from Falkirk between it and Stirling is famous for a victory achieved by Bruce[89] over the forces of Edward II June 24, 1314. The stream or burn is insignificant in size & could oppose no formidable impediment to the operations of armies. The place or field where the battle was fought lies to the left of the road as you approach Stirling and just behind a hill called to this day, the Gillies Hill from the following circumstances. Gilly is the Scotch word for servant. Bruce had disposed the servants of the army and the luggage behind this hill in his rear. In the heat of the action they made their appearance upon the summit of the hill & the English thinking that they were fresh reinforcements coming into action instantly turned to flight. The Gillies rushed down the hill to join in the pursuit & to plunder and ever since that day this hill has been denominated the Gillies hill.

Stirling is a very old town once the residence of the Scottish kings. It is chiefly remarkable for its Castle which is strong by nature and indeed

---

[84] Loch Leven Castle, now in ruins, was on Castle Island, where Queen Mary was imprisoned in 1567-68. It is pictured in Frazer, **Mary Q.**, opposite p. 368.

[85] Henry Erskine (1746-1817) was a Scottish lord advocate whereas his younger brother Thomas, first Baron Erskine (1750-1823), became Lord Chancellor of England. They were sons of Henry D. Erskine, Tenth Earl of Buchan. (Both are included in **DNB**. The first under Erskine and the second under his title.)

[86] James IV (1488-1513) declared war on England in 1513, invaded and was defeated at Flodden Field where he along with twelve earls, fourteen lords, the archbishop of St. Andrews and two bishops were killed. (Mackenzie, **Kingdom of Scotland** p. 145).

[87] Sir William Wallace (1272?-1305) led his army to victory over the English in the battle of Stirling Bridge in 1297. The following July Edward I defeated the Scot. In 1305 the latter was captured, taken to London and executed.

[88] Charles Edward Stuart (1720-88) was the Young Pretender and "Bonnie Prince Charlie," the Jacobite claimant to the throne of Great Britain.

[89] Robert Bruce, Robert I was king of Scotland from 1274 to 1329 and one of Scotland's heroes. He defeated the English at Bannockburn in June 1314. In 1328 the English recognized the independence of Scotland and Robert's claim to the throne. According to a well known story he was inspired to continue the long and seemingly futile struggle against the English by watching a spider spin its web despite many setbacks. The field of battle is closer to St. Ninians than the village of Bannockburn. (**Blue Guide**, pp. 217-18).

almost impregnable by art. The palace was built by James V.[90] One of the apartments is pointed out as the one in which Wm Stu[?] earl of Douglas was assassinated by James II[91] & that after the Royal word had been given for his safety. The walls of the castle are high & thick and huge guns point downs from their dizzy eminence. At an angle in the wall is pointed at the spot where Queen Victoria and Prince Albert stood together on their visit to the castle & whence they took a survey of the surrounding country, and further on is the place where Queen Mary sat and looked through an opening in the wall at the tournament in the plains below. The height from this point is very fearful to contemplate. From Stirling Castle may be seen the scenes of many famous battles & murderous conflicts. Among them the contest between the notorious Cressingham & Sr. Wm Wallace Sepr. 1297.[92] The forces of the Scottish Chieftain were concealed in part by Abbey Craig until the English general had crossed the Forth with a large part of his army. Wallace then fell upon him with his whole force, and obtained a decisive victory. The appearance of the country around Stirling as seen from the lofty battlements of the Castle is exceedingly picturesque. The Forth pursues its serpentine course amid well cultivated fields, its banks adorned with villages and private edifices till it is lost in the wide frith or firth that spreads out its waters before the city of Edinburgh [sic] which is clearly discernible from Stirling Castle in a fair day. After a full survey of the town and its objects of interest & after partaking a refreshment at the house of Rev. Mr. Henderson Ep. clergyman of the place, I left in the cars for Aberdeen and on the way passed the city of Perth well known in Scottish history and chiefly remarkable for its church called St John & from which the city was sometimes denominated Johnstowne.[93] About two miles from Perth & at the junction of the Almond & the Tay is the palace of Scone[94] now the property of Lord Mansfield[95] but once cele-

[90] James IV made Edingurgh his regular seat. At the same time he began building the palace at Stirling which was finished by James V. ("Edinburgh," NCE).

[91] James II was king from 1437 to 1460. In 1452 he invited William Douglas, eighth Earl of Douglas to Stirling where the king attempted to gain the loyalty of the powerful earl. When the effort failed, James charged the earl with treason and slew him. Agnes M. Mackenzie thinks Douglas was the one who broke the safe conduct by repudiating it (Kingdom of Scotland, p. 125).

[92] In 1297 Hugh Cressingham, the English treasurer, was slain in a fight with Wallace at Cambuskenneth or Stirling Bridge. The field is across the river from Stirling. After the battle the Scots stripped Cressingham's skin from the body and used it as a belt on which to hang their swords. (DNB, W.P. Hall and R.G. Albion, A History of England and the British Empire [Boston, 1937], p. 166).

[93] Until the 17th Century Perth was known as St Johnstoun and was the capital of Scotland from the 11th to mid 15th Century. (NCE).

[94] Scone was the site of Scottish coronations from the time of Kenneth (k. 843-60) to Charles I (k. 1625-49). The famous tea cake, the scone, is the Scottish contraction of the Middle Dutch word schoonbrot, meaning fine bread.

[95] In 1851 the earl of Mansfield was William David Murray (1806-90), the fourth titleholder. (Burke's Peerage).

brated for the residence of the kings of Scotland & for the famous **stone** which is placed in the coronation chair of the English monarchs now kept in Westminster Abbey.[96] The road passes in sight of Montrose situated close to the sea & connected with many interesting events in the history of Scotland. It was from this place that one of the Douglases[97] embarked for the Holy Land taking with him the heart of Rob: Bruce: and here also the great Marquis of Montrose was born.[98] I strained my eyes to catch a glimpse in passing the village of Lawrencekirk [Laurencekirk]—the birth place of Dr. Beattie[99] author of the Minstrel and the scene of Ruddiman's[100] labors as a Teacher & who was the author of the **Latin Grammar**. Shortly after leaving the place we saw the residence of Lord Monboddo[101] celebrated for his peculiar and fantastic views in relation to Philosophy &c. I arrived Aberdeen about 7½ P.M. and stopped at the Union Hotel.

Aberdeen Makes Otey a New Man

Sunday July 20. Mr Cox came late last night & about 11 we set off for St. Andrews Church where we heard that Bp. Skinner[102] would officiate. The service was read by Mr Ryde assistant in the parish to Bp Skinner who read the antecommunion. Rev. Mr Ryde preached a very good sermon. We had been in the vestryroom where we were cordially received by Bp. Skinner who now invited us to dine with him at 4 P.M. We accepted his invitation. Rev Mr. Coxe walked to see the brig of **Balgownie**,[103] and I walked with the Bishop through part of the Town. I should have mentioned that after the sermon the Bp. walked with Rev. Mr Coxe & myself to the place where **Bp. Seabury of Connecticut**[104]

[96] Edward I in 1297 took the Stone of Scone back to England and had a chair built for it about 1307 which has since been the seat on which English monarchs have been crowned. In 1950 Scottish Nationalists took it back to Scotland. It was returned to Westminster Abbey. As Edward also took the regalia with him, he might have done this to show the Scots that he was their feudal overlord. Some of this is from **Steinberg's Dictionary of British History, Second Edition** (NY, 1971).

[97] Sir James de Douglas, lord of the Douglas, (1286-1330), started for the Holy Land with the heard of Robert I. However, he was killed fighting the Moors in Spain. According to tradition the heart was ultimately returned to Scotland and was buried in Melrose Abbey. ("Robert I" **NCE**).

[98] James Graham, 5th Earl of and First Marquis of Montrose (1612-50), gained fame in the Civil War by leading a force of Highland clansmen against the Lowland Presbyterians and defeating them. In turn he was defeated, fled and on his return captured and hanged. (**NCE**).

[99] James Beattie (1735-1803) was a Scottish poet. His work "The Minstrel" (1771-74), which was autobiographical, placed emphasis on the effect nature and influenced Byron. (**NCE**).

[100] Thomas Ruddiman (1674-1757) was a philologist who wrote and published **Rudiments of the Latin Tongue**. Its fifteen editions during his lifetime surpassed other books of this type. (**DNB**).

[101] James Burnett (1714-99) was Lord Monboddo, a Scottish judicial title assumed when he became a lord of ordinary session. Bishop Otey's derisive comment probably refers to his lordship's contention in his six volume work **Of the Origin and Progress of Language** that the orangutang is a class of human species which accidentally lacked a language. He was a friend of George III who received him with special favor. (**DNB**).

[102] William Skinner (1778-1857) was the son of a priest whose imprisonment he shared. Ordained at 19, he became bishop coadjutor of Aberdeen and in 1819 the diocesan. (**Mod. Eng. Bios.**, VI).

[103] Brig o' Balgownie which spans the river Don was built about 1320. (**Blue Guide**, p. 307).

[104] Bishop Samuel Seabury see: p. 11.

was consecrated 1784 by **Bps Kilgore, Skinner** & **Petrie**. The house **no longer** remains: its site being occupied by a chapel which was afterwards sold to the Methodists, to whom it still belongs. The house in an upper room of which Bp. Seabury was consecrated was the residence of the first Bp. Skinner and his son the present Bp was born in it. It is an interesting fact that an old man named Grubb still survives who remembers to have heard Bp Seabury preach in the afternoon of the day when he was consecrated. I saw this old gentleman myself.

We went to dine with Bp. S. according to appointment and spent several hours very pleasantly with him & family. He gave us some interesting reminiscences of his father in the form of pamphlets containing the Scottish Ep. Com: Service. We also saw at the Bp's a fine model bust or statue of his Father by Chantry[105] and a piece of embroidery wrought by the hands of Mary queen of Scots while in prison. We also became acquainted with a very warm hearted & pleasant gentle man named **Cheves**—a devoted friend of the Church!

Monday July 21. Got up at 5 A.M. and walked with Mr. Coxe to the Sea-shore and for the first time in my life, I bathed in the Ocean. It was very cold but on the whole pleasant and refreshing.[106] We returned and took our seats in the Post Coach for Inverness. The weather was cold and rain; but the company on the whole was pleasant and one or two gentlemen manifested a great readiness to point out many objects of interest to a stranger. The first place of note which we passed was Forres near to which are seen the ruins of the Abbey of Kinloss.[107] Just before entering Forres I saw a large stone of an obelisk shape, perhaps 20 or 25 feet high—set upright in a field, near the road—marked with many hieroglyphicks [sic] very like the Roman characters.[108] Some say it was to mark the limits to which the Romans had carried their arms. Others that it was erected by the Danes. Near Forres, Macbeth is represented by Shakespeare to have met the witches and we saw some old women today, near the place, which it would hardly require the genius of Shake-

---

[105] Sir Frances Legatt Chantrey (1781-1841) was an English sculptor whose work includes the statue of George Washington in the Statehouse at Boston. (**DNB**).

[106] Although Otey does not mention the impact of the swim, it made a new man of him as becomes evident in the course of the next few days. The later Bishop Coxe described the event. "In the morning he was ready, at the hour appointed, and we had a most refreshing bath in the wild surf coming in from the Baltic. [Coxe's geography is slightly mixed because he called the North Sea the German Ocean.] We walked back to our hotel, and he cheered me by confessing a genial glow. From that day he grew better, and frequently he said to me that he owed his recovery to his bath at Aberdeen. 'Not the first time,' I remarked, 'that our Episcopate had been recruited from Aberdeenshire'." (Coxe, "A Letter," in Green, **Memoir**, p. 354).

[107] Kinloss Abbey was founded in 1151. After the Reformation it served as quarry, thus little remains. (**Blue Guide**, pp. 327-28).

[108] Swemo's Stone is 23 ft. high and carved with figures, knots, and animals. It is thought to represent the victory of Sweym, son of Harold in 1008, over Malcolm. (**Ibid.**, p. 328).

speare to transform into witches![109]

I should have stated that shortly after leaving Aberdeen a gentleman pointed out the battlefield of Harlaw[110] in 1411 between the Highlanders & the English. In this battle Earl Leslie and all his sons but one were slain and their graves are still pointed out in a field near the road, marked by upright stones, on passing. We soon came in sight of Fort George,[111] regular built fortification, said to be the only one in Great Britain. To the right of the road is seen Castle Stuart in ruins (and said to have been the place where Ch: Edward slept the night previous to the battle of Culloden.) This action so fatal to the hopes of Ch: Edward was fought on Culloden Muir about 5 miles from Inverness. It was **Culloden House**[112] at which Prince Chs. slept instead of Stuart Castle as stated above and into which mistake I was led by the information of the coachman. Elgin on the road from Aberdeen to Inverness is very old looking town and chiefly remarkable for the remains of the Abbey[113] which on the right of the road still presents an attractive assemblage of broken walls and ruined arches to the eyes of the passing traveller. Inverness is itself one of the most beautiful places I have seen in all my rambles. Situated at the mouth of the Ness and at the head of the Caledonia Canal: abounding in picturesque views of the surrounding hills adorned with many beautiful buildings and ornamented with a variety of walks shaded with trees and kept clean and neat, it is just such a place as the tourist would not expect to find in this remote corner of the world; but which having found, he is struck with an agreeable surprise at the discovery. Macbeth once owned a castle near Inverness. It has long since been demolished and but for vestiges of its existence, none remain.

Tuesday July 22. Before 6 A.M. this morning we were on our way to the steamer which plies between Inverness & Oban[114] by way of the Cale-

[109] A second stone is nearby. It is granite and marks the spot where witches were burned. (**Ibid**).

[110] The route up the Urie River Valley through Inverurie brought the travellers near the field where the Battle of Harlaw was fought. It was between two Scottish forces over the claim to the earldom of Ross with the loser Donald MacDonald (d. 1420?) surrendering his claim. Had he won, this along with his position as Lord of the Isles would have made him a powerful and dangerous noble. Reputedly the battle determined the ultimate triumph of the Lowlanders over the Highlanders in Scottish affairs. (**Blue Guide**, 321; "McDonald, Donald" **DNB**; Mackenzie, **Kingdom of Scotland**, p. 107).

[111] Fort George was constructed from 1748-60 and housed the Seaforth Highlanders until 1958 (**Blue Guide**, p. 330).

[112] The present Culloden House was built in 1772-83 on the site of the one where Prince Charles stayed. (**Ibid**, p. 380).

[113] The abbey at Elgin was once a cathedral and one of the finest churches in Scotland. Construction began in 1224 and was completed in 1270. Decay began in the last third of the sixteenth century. (**Ibid**, pp. 325-26).

[114] Today passenger boats no longer travel between Inverness and Oban as the twenty-nine locks on the canals linking the various lochs of the celebrated Caledonian Canal have a small capacity. These have not been altered because trawlers have the power to make the voyage around the northern tip of Scotland. Construction began in 1803 and the canal was opened for traffic in 1822 and finally finished in 1833 at a cost of £1,256,000. In summer excursion boats make the twenty-two mile round trip from Inverness to Castle Urquhart. **Ibid**, (pp. 366-67).

donian Canal & the Lochs or Lakes which form the greater part of this inland communication. The most remarkable object to attract attention upon first leaving the landing was a huge earthen mound, so large as to create a doubt whether it could be the work of art, and yet as regular in its structure as to forbid the idea of its being anything more than the work of man's hands. It is in the form of a boat or the keel of a vessel turned upside down. It is called Tom-na-heurich, or hill of the fairies. Proceeding on the Canal from Inverness we presently entered a small lake called Loch Dochfour on the margin of which & amidst a grove of beautiful trees rises a splendid Italian villa, the property of the late Mr. Baillie. Immediately after passing this we enter Loch Ness & on the right in the distance discover a craggy point which juts into the Lake the ruins of **Urquhart Castle**. It was originally a place of much strength as one would naturally conclude from its advantageous position, and is said to have been the last of the Scottish strongholds that surrendered to Edward I. Just before coming to Urquhart Castle now in ruins, the beautiful dale called Glen Urquhart opens on the right and is said to contain several fine mansions. **Mealfourvonie**[115] raises his lofty & frowning brows on the same side and seems to look down in haughty pride upon the world below as it is engaged in the busy pursuits which impart activity to human life. On the left is seen very soon, mist or spray rising out of the woods which come down to the margin of the Loch, and on inquiry you learn that that mist indicates the spot where are seen the Falls of Foyers.[116] Further on on the same side and perched on the lofty sides of the hills that tower upwards is seen a mansion called Boleskin where Prince Charles is said to have sought & found concealment after the unfortunate battle of Culloden. On the right side are seen Invermoriston House and Glen Moriston beautiful in situation & shortly after we approached Fort Augustus at the head of Loch Ness. The fort is kept by a small number of soldiers whose chief employment is I presume to keep the premises neat & clean, thus preventing their decay, and to wait upon an officer or two, who probably lives in this spot upon the bounty of government—the reward of past service. This fort was built to keep down the Highlanders & dates back as far as 1715. By locks at Ft Augustus we rose to the level of Lock Oich which is the summit level of the Caledonian Canal. Near the mouth of the Garry in Glengarry are the ruins of Invergarry Castle on the right side of Loch Oich where the Clan of the Macdonnels had their gathering place. Leaving Loch Oich we next pass

[115] Mealfouruonie which is at the edge of the Ness rises to an altitude of 2,284 ft.
[116] Apparently the two Falls of Foyers do not have the volume they did in Otey's day. (**Ibid**, p. 371).

into Loch Lochy on the northern shore of which & near its termination is Achnacany the residence of Cameron of Locheil chief of his clan & who still maintains among his people the customs of his ancestors, in dress &c. From Loch Lochy the boat passes along the canal leading into Locheil. On the right there is a fine Inn established called Bannavie at the place called Neptune's Staircase from the number of locks there constructed, and further on on the left are the ruins of Torcastle which I think finds mention somewhere in Ossian.[117] To the left as we approached Ft. William are seen very plain on the low grounds the ruins of Inverlochy Castle[118] near to which the Earl of Montrose surprised and slaughtered 1500 of Argyle's[119] men with the loss of only three of his own. In passing a house in Edinburg [sic] I remember that a balcony was pointed out to me in which the Duchess of Argyle sat and spit upon or at the unfortunate Montrose as he passed along to the place of execution. Those were the times when the fierce passions of men were but little under restraints which a better system of laws regulated by Christian teaching has introduced into social life in our age & country. From our entrance into Loch Lochy & perhaps before we had a full view of the celebrated Ben Nevis on our left. It assumed a great variety of aspects as our position changed in the progress of the boat along the canal & locks. It is an "exceedingly high mountain" rising 4500 ft. nearly above the level of the sea and until lately conceded the highest mountain in Scotland. That distinction is now claimed, though not without being disputed, for Ben. The hollows of Ben Ness about its summit we could very clearly see were filled with snow. At Corpach where the canal enters Loch Eli I made a sketch or an outline of Ben Nevis[120] with one end of a rainbow resting on its cloud capped summit. We passed Ft. William built by Genl Monk[121] on our left and left the steamer at Coran ferry to procede to Ballachulish. From this point we walked after crossing the ferry to the Inn called Ballachulish which we found exceedingly pleasant & neat as a resting place for the night. Mr

[117] Ossian reputedly was a legendary Gaelic poet who recited tales and poems about deeds of valor performed in the Third Century A.D. The name is best known through translations which James Macpherson (1736-96) claimed Ossian wrote. Actually they are a combination of traditional Gaelic poems and original verses by Macpherson. (**NCE**).

[118] Montrose's victory appears to have influenced Charles I to break off negotiations at Uxbridge. This decision ultimately cost the king his life.

[119] Archibald Campbell, 8th Earl of and 1st Marquis of Argyle (1607-61) was the leader of the Covenanter Army against Montrose, supported Cromwell, then in 1651 crowned Charles II in Scotland and later submitted to the Lord Protector of the Commonwealth. His execution after the Restoration for treason was long before the creation of the Argyle dukedom. (**DNB**).

[120] Ben Nevis at 4,406 ft. is the highest point in Scotland.

[121] In 1654 when General George Monk (1608-70) built Fort William, the site was known as Inverlochy. Its garrison was a peacekeeping force in this part of Scotland. By 1690 it was in ruins and was rebuilt by General Mackay who named it after William of William and Mary. Today the fort is gone. As a result of General Monk's significant role in restoring Charles II to the throne, the grateful sovereign created him Duke of Albemarle. (**Blue Guide**, p. 367, "Monck, George 1st duke of Albemarle," **NCE**).

Coxe & myself were alone, we carried our luggage on our backs. The distance was a little over four miles—and we thought not at all of the weariness of the way, so much was our fatigue beguiled by the varied and pleasant discourses in which we engaged. We talked of the poets & poetry & of those near & dear to us now far distant & of those deceased to me who had passed to that silent & distant bower whence no traveller returns. This was an evening long to be remembered and I am sure it will be recollected by me while life & sense & feeling have any being or a holy thought that aspires after a better world shall find a place in this bosom.

Wednesday July 23. Up early this morning and bathing in the salt loch or creek that makes up from Loch Eil to Ballachulish toward Glencoe. About 7 A.M. the post coach came along from Ft. William and we took our seats to Oban to pass through the wild defile of Glencoe & by way of Loch Awe. We very soon came to the celebrated slate quarries of Ballachulish at which 500 workmen find employment & entered the pass of Glencoe not less remarkable for its wild & savage appearance than memorable for the cold blooded murder or massacre of the Macdonalds perpetuated by order of King William III[122] & which no matter what, policy of the state, may plead must forever fix a dark spot of infamy on his character. His myrmidens [sic] were sent here to gain the confidence of the inhabitants of this district by becoming their guests & enjoying their hospitality: and when every suspicion was lulled and each soldier had no doubt singled out his victim and was prepared for the onslaught, early one morning a signal gun was discharged from a rock which was pointed out to me in the center of the valley, and the work of death was begun and ended in the utter destruction of the Macdonalds or Macdonnels. The Chieftain himself after a desperate combat was overpowered and shared the merciless fate of his unhappy but brave clansmen. The people of this glen speak of this atrocious transaction to this day, with a spirit that flashes from the eye in glances of fiery indignation. The road winds up the vale between rugged & jagged mountains—the sides washed into ravines of various sizes by the rains untill [sic] the burns or sides of the hills look as if icicles were depending [sic] from them while the summits are so rifted & torn as if they had been split by thunderbolts. A small

[122] King William offered an amnesty to the Highland Scots who would take the oath of allegiance to him by New Years Day 1692. This some were reluctant to do until James II released them from their oath to him which he did in time for them to comply. As MacDonald of Glencoe was six days late, William on the advice of Lord Carmarthen decided to make an example and carry out the threat to use fire and sword. Although regular troops were to help, they were late in arriving. This did not deter Campbell of Glenlyn who early in the morning of 13 February carried out the orders. A few escaped. (**Blue Guide**, p. 365).

stream issues from a little lake or tarn called Triochatan about half way up the pass, which itself is fed by rills that trickle from deposits of snow which at this season even, are seen whitening the higher hollows of the mountains. This stream enlarging as it descends through the defile towards the Loch is the Cona of Ossian & far up on the sides of Glencoe is pointed out a cave called Ossians Cave. At the extremity of the pass on the left is a rough hill called the Devil's stair-case across which a road leads to Ft. William. On the right hand or opposite side is the rugged mountain called Buchaille [Herdsman] Etive. As we journeyed the top of the mountain became capped with a dark looking cloud, while the ravines made down its sides by the washing of the winter rains exposing the ashy colored or sandy looking earth presented an appearance which it required us great effort of the imagination to picture in the mind's eye as streams of fire. It is just such a sketch as I have often seen in books of Mt. Sinai at the delivery of the law. I pointed it out to the Rev Mr Coxe and he was forcibly struck with the fancied resemblance. Clearing the pass we came to what is called the King'shouse Inn;[123] so denominated from a tradition that one of the Scottish kings built the house in the midst of this moor for a summer residence. Why, it would take a fool or a very wise man to assign a reason. The road then leads over this Black Mount—a barren & desolate moor—to Inverary on the banks of Loch Tulla, a new hunting box containing sixty bed rooms, of the Marquis of Breadalbane.[124] Away we went after a glimpse of his Lordship's stag hounds apparently more than I could count in an hour, across the Orchy & a little distance along the vale of Glenorchy to Tyndrum. Near this place the ground is pointed out which was the scene of desparate conflict between Robert Bruce & his party and the Lord of Lorne & his men.[125] The great personal strength of Bruce enabled him to escape from the hands of his enemies far superior in numbers, but with the loss of his brooch which it is said fell into the hands of Lorne's[126] men and in 1842 was worn by an officer of the R.N. who steered the barge on which her

[123] The inn at Kingshouse has been enlarged and serves a ski resort. (**Blue Guide**, pp. 347-48).

[124] John Campbell (1796-1862), Marquis of Breadalbane, was one of the biggest landowners in Scotland. Victoria's visit in 1842 to Taymouth, one of his estates, was the first of such visits in Scotland by the Queen. (**DNB**).

[125] In the Summer of 1308 Robert Bruce, Robert I, defeated both Alexander McDougal, Lord of Lorne, and Alexander MacDonald, Lord of the Isles. The two chieftains were allied with the English under Edward II. Robert gave the chieftainship to Angus MacDonald who henceforth followed him. (Mackenzie, **Kingdom of Scotland**, p. 89).

[126] During the battle in 1308 between Bruce and John MacDougall of Lorne one of the latter's men, even though mortally wounded, grabbed such a hold on Bruce's mantel with its brooch that the king was forced to leave it. Now the jewel is known as the "brooch of Lorn." (**Blue Guide**, pp. 342 and 351).

Majesty queen V. [sic] was seated in her visit to Taymouth Castle. At Tyndrum today I met unexpectedly with Rev. Dr. Breckenridge[127] on his way to Inverness. Two miles from Tyndrum is St. Fillan's Ch:[128] and close at hand is a pool in which it has been the custom as late as 1844 to dip or immerse lunatics for their cure. The method was to bind the patient hand & foot, immerse him in the pool and then place him in St. Fillan's Ch: yard where he remained all night. I should call this Hydropathy! most certainly!! From this place we passed along the borders of Loch Awe with its beautiful scenery. The road leads down the Orchy to Dalmally, passes by the old church of Glenorchy & about two miles further crosses the Strae a short distance from the point where both streams enter into Loch Awe. On the point of land at the head of the Loch stands the celebrated **Kilchurn** Castle[129] now in ruins—once the lordly residence of the bold chieftains of the Magregors. Closeby is the lofty Ben Cruachan rising to the height of 3,400 feet[130] and with its bald and weatherbeaten summits looking down frowningly on the peaceful waters of Loch Awe. The contrast presented everywhere between the rough & savage aspect of the bare, rocky & sterile mountains of Scotland and its calm and quiet lakes, the smooth surfaces of which are scarecely dimpled by a ripple, is very striking and remarkable. Lock Awe discharges its waters by the river Awe into Loch Etive. The river is forced into a narrow vale by the mountains encroaching at their bases upon the waters of the Loch as they emerge & dash forward with impetuousity roaring & foaming over the rocks as if to escape the threatening pressures on both sides and makes its way at last into Loch Etive. At a narrow pass before it reaches this point was fought the great battle between Bruce & Lorn [sic] in which nearly all of the McDougals were slain.[131] The cairns where these fierce warriors were buried after their last battle was fought are still plainly visible in the little places which skirt the bank of the river. We pass next by the Inn of Taynuilt and pursuing our road down the shores

[127] After the meeting with Dr. Breckenridge Coxe assumed that the Dr. must be happy to be among fellow disciples of John Knox. Not so, Otey replied. "He was telling me how much he preferred the Prebyterians of Kentucky: he says they all drink toddy here, and he never saw so much whiskey before among Christians." (Coxe, "Letter" in Green, **Memoir**, p. 356.)

[128] St. Fillan, Foilan, or Felan (d. 777?) was an Irish missionary to Scotland. One of his relics is a bell weighing 8 lbs, 14 oz. It was long preserved in a churchyard at Strathfillan, Pertshire and was regarded as having great curative powers, esp. for insanity. How the cures were effected was not explained in the **Dictionary of National Biography** account. According to the **Oxford Dictionary of Saints**, those suspected of insanity were dipped in a pool, then tied and left in corner of the ruined chapel. If the suspects were found loose, they were judged cured.

[129] Kilchurn Castle, built in 1441 was the home of the Campbells until 1740. Six years later Royal troops were garrisoned there. (**Blue Guide**, p. 343).

[130] Three thousand six hundred eighty-nine feet high Ben Cruachian is one of the most visible mountains in the Highlands.

[131] The battle in which the forces of Lorne were nearly destroyed was fought in the narrow Pass of Brander through which the River Awe rushes.

of Lock Etive see many places full of traditional interest till we come in
sight of Dunstaffnage Castle[132] at the entrance of Loch Etive. It is a fine
looking ruin; formerly it belonged to the McDougals who lost it upon
their defeat at the pass of the Awe by Bruce in 1408. From this castle the
Stone of Scone, as it is called, was taken—which being carried to England by Edward I is now found in the coronation chair of the English
Monarchs in Westminster Abbey. Near to this is the village of **Oban**[133]
which is the concluding point of this days journey. On a rocky promontory just above the town towards Dunstaffnage are seen the ruins of
Dunolly Castle[134] which was also once inhabited by the McDougals. Stop
at the Angus.

Wednesday July 24. Arose early and bathed in the bay of Oban before
breakfast. A little before 7 A.M. went aboard the steamer to make the
excursion to Iona[135] and Staffa. I was amazed on embarking to find
aboard my friends Mrs Peter from Phila: and her daughter-in-law Mrs
Thos King of Cini: I. [sic] It was gratifying as it was unexpected to meet
these friends at such a time & place. Mrs K is in deep mourning for her
husband not many months deceased. Our steamer with a pleasant party &
favorable day soon passed the rough little island of Kerrera interesting
only from the tradition connected with it as the landing place of Haco
[Haaken][136] king of Norway—his interview with the neighboring chieftains to engage their assistance in his expedition against Scotland, & the
ruins of the old Danish fort. Instead of passing through the Sound of
Mull, the usual course, our boat took the way around the southern point
of Mull so as to approach Iona first. This island about 3 miles long by
about 1½ in breadth is only remarkable for the ruins of its church and
religious house founded by Columba[137] about the year 565. All ecclesiastical history as far as it speaks upon the subject goes to show that this
establishment continued for a long time to teach the pure doctrine of the
Gospel, that the practice of the monks & nuns who inhabited the spot
was in conformity with the precepts of Christianity & that, in the darkness of a barbarian age, the true light of divine truth here shed forth its

[132] Flora McDonald who helped "Bonnie" Prince Charlie escape after the defeat at Culloden Moor was temporarily imprisoned in Dunstaffnage Castle during 1746. (**Blue Guide**, p. 352).

[133] According to Fodor's **Great Britain** Oban is a popular part of the country in Summer. ([NY, 1974], p. 194).

[134] The "Brooch of the Lorn" is kept in Dunollie House next to the castle. It was out of the possession of the
McDougals from 1645 to 1826. (**Ibid**, p. 351).

[135] According to the **Blue Guide** travel on an excursion boat is not the best way to see Iona. One should spend
a night there. (p. 354).

[136] Haakob Haakonson, Haakon IV or Haco (1204-63) became king of Norway in 1217. Under his rule the
country reached its Medieval zenith. He campaigned in Scotland entering it via the Firth of Clyde. His men raided
inland as far as Stirling. He gave up the attack against Alexander III. On the way home he died in Kirkwall,
Orkeney Islands which were part of his domain. (**NCE**).

[137] St. Columba or Columcille (521-97), a prince of the O'Donnells of Donegal, landed on Iona in 563. Reputedly he is buried in Downpatrick, Ireland, the final resting place of Sts. Patrick and Bridget. (**NCE**).

bright beams, and enlightened & blessed the neighboring countries. There are a great many interesting relics in the form of crosses—the significant symbol of the Christian faith—set up in this island. By order of the Synod of Argyle 1500, nearly all of them were broken and cast into the sea. A few of them still remain and the carving on them certainly attests no inconsiderable skill in the art of cutting stone. The church is roofless—not a piece of wood is to be found in any part of it. The walls are gradually crumbling under the heavy pressure of the hand of time and for this same cause many of the arches of the doors and windows are falling in and the stone mullions are visibly mouldering and decaying. Many are the graves which have been made in an around the precincts of this sacred fane, and curious the emblems and figures engraved or carved upon the grave stones. Some of them have inscriptions in Latin elaborately and ornately cut in the stone and a few of them are legible. There are kings, bishops and missioners[?] and monks & nuns all buried here. In some of the tombs which have been opened by accident or design not a bone has been found and hardly a little black dust to denote that a human body has mouldered there. The burial ground has for ages been regarded with great veneration and many of the noble families in the highlands have asked in their last hours that their remains might be transported to the consecrated grounds of Iona and there allowed to rest in the hope of resurrection. The scenery of this island with its interesting remains of antiquity has been described by the masterly pen of Wilson and I should be treading on forbidden grounds to follow a tract over which he has trod. Having gathered a few flowers within the walls of the church and purchased some shells and pebbles of the poor ragged & squalid children who crowd about visitors & offer such things for sale & indeed importunities are raised to annoyances, we again boarded the steamer & started for Staffa.[138] We arrived in a short time and were presently seated in the boats to visit the caves of world wide celebrity which are here found. On Iona we contemplated the work of man, sacred by its association but still in ruins—here in Staffa we looked upon the work of God's hand and there was no mark of decay here—there was no marked & perceptable hastening of endurance and with an air of grandeur thrown over the whole that at once made the soul feel solemn, and acknowledge that **God Only is Great**! The officer who conducted the movements of the boat in which I was seated stated that we enjoyed a rare concurrence of good fortune today—the water was calm—the tide

---

[138] Staffa was virtually unknown to the outside world until 1772 when Sir Joseph Banks (1743-1820) accidentally visited the island on a voyage to Iceland. (**Blue Guide**, p. 361).

was favorable and the wind fair—so that our boat was enabled to enter all the caves that are ever visited and this he said he had never known to happen before in an experience of 14 years. The accompanying boat today was enabled to enter only two out of the three caves which are the great objects of interest to visitors. I shall undertake no descriptions here of the glory and magnificence of this stupendous scenery. Profr. Wilson and Sr: W Scott have already appropriated it as their own and I may not add anything which might appear to denigrate from their right or from the merited beauty & interest of their respective delineations. When we had got into the first cave—called the cormorant cave,[139] from the circumstances of that bird's building its nest there—someone proposed that we should all raise a loud shout in order to hear the reverberation of many voices along the pillared sides and vaulted roofs of the cavern. I felt that such an act would be like an act of desecration. I arose to my feet and said I propose that we sing the 100th Psalm of David to the tune of Old Hundred. It was instantly assented to and I gave out the lines of the first verse which we all joined our voices to sing. We next entered what is called the boat cave[140] just wide enough to admit one boat and this cave our companion boat did not enter. We then entered the largest and deepest cave of all called Fingal's Cave;[141] and landed on the rocky sides. Here once more I got out the lines of Old Hundred beginning with the 2d verse, and we all sang it—the "anthem pealing nave" furnishing the base to our voices with fine effect. Certainly I never heard that Psalm sung with such effect in church or in the deep & aged forest where all things would conspire to give it impressive solemnity. From Fingal's cave we walked around the rocky shore of the island where the basaltic columns seemed to be bent by the superior cumbent weight, past a small island called the herdsman, where the columns are disposed in every possible position from the horizontal to the vertical, til we came to what is called Clam or Shallop Cave. Here we ascended the rocky & precipitous brow of Staffa and reached the summit. There is nothing specially

[139] The Cormant's Cave is also known as Scart's. It is 48 ft. by 50 ft. and is 220 ft. long. (**Ibid**).

[140] Boat Cave is smaller being but 12 ft. by 16 ft. and 150 ft. long and is the usual landing place. (**Ibid**).

[141] Fingal's Cave is 227 ft. long, and rises 66 ft. above the water level. It has about the same depth of water. (**Ibid**). Apparently the Bishop was unaware that Felix Mendelsohn-Bartholdy had expressed a musical reaction in "The Hebrides Overture or Fingals Cave" (1830-1832). If he had known of the composition, surely Dr. Otey, who was a violinist, would have mentioned it as part of his emotional involvement. Coxe later wrote: "But I never saw him [Otey] so excited as when we entered the cave at Staffa, rowed by stout fisherman, and accompanied by nearly a dozen other tourists. I said, 'It is a natural church amid the waters.' He caught at the idea; and, as we stepped on a ledge of rocks that served as a chancel, he said, with a commanding air, 'Let us all sing the doxology, **Praise God from whom all blessings flow**.' And so we did. I don't know who started it but those walls and rocky vaults resounded with Ken's sublime **Gloria Patria**, to which the echoing waves seemed to respond **Amen**, as they surged into the cavern, and at times lashed its walls. The floods **clapped their hands** indeed, and seemed to worship with us. I wonder if such a worship was ever offered there before, with a Bishop and a Presbyter to make it liturgical and catholic!" (Coxe, "Letter," Green **Memoir**, p. 355).

remarkable in its appearance. On the eastern side we saw the remains of a stone house which was begun with the intention of using it as an Inn, but which idea was subsequently abandoned and the structure never completed. Having surveyed everything of interest we returned to our steamer thankful to a kind Providence that not the slightest accident of mishap had occured to mar the pleasure of our trip and that we had enjoyed the rare felicity of a favorable tide & wind and a calm sea for our visit. We returned to Oban through the Sound of Mull passing in our route what was pointed out to us as the Ladyrock—a rock which at the rising of the tide is covered with water. To this rock one of the Highland Chieftains chained his wife at low water, thinking that she would perish at the rising of the tides. In the meantime she was discovered & released by some of her Father's people who in turn avenged the insult that was offered to their countrywoman by slaying her husband whose name was Maclean. On shore of Mull are seen the ruins of Duart Castle formerly the residence of the Chieftains of the powerful clan of the Macleans. On the left is the island of Lismore, in ancient times the residence of the Bishops of Argyle. On the same side in approaching Oban are seen Dunstaffnage Castle & Dunnolly already mentioned. All along these coasts at every natural strong position nearly may be seen the ruins of old castles where the fierce men of these northern climes fortified themselves during the middle ages and lived by depredations upon their neighbors & levied contributions upon such as fortunately fell into their hands without any other pretension of justification but such as superior might gave![142]

Friday July 25 After rising early, taking a seabath & getting breakfast, we took our seats in the coach for the Trosachs, Just as we were about to leave, we saw the exqueen of France,[143] the widow of Louis Phillipe[144] & several members of the family, as Prince de Joinville,[145] Duchess of Saxe Coburg. The duke of Saxe Coburg[146] & family were on a visit to the

[142] Otey accurately assesses the impact of the almost continual warring among the Scottish clans. They suffered from it. In a day when a similar state of affairs frequently appeared elsewhere, the Scots were regarded as barbarians. Merchants learned to their cost that travel among these people could be hazardous. The traveller faced the very likely prospect of being robbed and the strong possibility of losing his life.

[143] The ex-queen of France was Marie Amelie (1786-1866), daughter of Ferdinand I, king of the Two Sicilies, and of Maria Carolina of Austria, a sister of Marie Antoinette. Marie Amelie and Louis Philippe were married in 1809.

[144] Louis Philippe (1771-1850) king of the French (1830-1848) as Duc d'Orleans spent part of his exile in the United States. His tour of 1797 brought him and his two brothers to Tennessee via Abingdon. They stopped in Rogersville, Knoxville and Maryville where they visited Cherokees. From there they went to Nashville and on to Bardstown, KY. Later Louis Philippe donated some oil paintings to the cathedral (now proto) at Bardstown. (Louis Philippe, king of the French, Diary of My Travels in America [NY, 1977]).

[145] Francois, Prince de Joinville (1818-1900) was the third son of Louis and Marie. During the Civil War he was with the Union Forces.

[146] Augustus of Saxe-Coburg-Gotha (1818-81) was a prince of that house but not the reigning duke as Otey implies. In 1843 he married Clementine (1817-1907), the youngest of Louis and Marie's three daughters. She became the mother of Ferdinand (1861-1948) who through her political manueverings became ruling prince of Bulgaria and later tsar of the country. (Ghislain de Diesbach, Secrets of the Gotha [NY, 1968], pp. 90-92).

Queen of France who was spending a few days at Oban and they were now leaving by coach; and it was thus we had the opportunity of seeing them. The whole bearing of the familiy & their friends, dignified & becoming their rank & position. I was particularly struck with the propriety of behaviour which marked the deportment of the Duke of Saxe Cob: on our journey. Instant attention to his wife & family & again, a lady with us Mrs Peters cannot bear the smell of tobacco. Upon mentioning this to the duke he instantly threw away the cigar which he had lighted although in the open air, outside the coach and manifested the utmost readiness to sacrifice his personal gratification to the comfort of another. Our route until we came to Tyndrum was the same as from that place to Oban by Loch Awe & already described July 23. At 9 Mr Coxe and myself struck off for Crianlauch or rather at Crianlarich we went off by Post thinking of going to Taymouth [mouth of Loch Tay], Aberfeldy, &. but upon reflection we concluded to stop at a place called Leek's & walk through Glen Ogle to Lochearnhead. And this we did. Our walk through this place along a good road bounded on either side by wild hills & mountains was very pleasant to us. We reached Lochearnhead in good time carrying our luggage ourselves—stopped at Walker's, a comfortable & cleanly Inn, got refreshments and then hired a drosky to convey us to Callendar. On our way we passed Balguhidder the burial place of Rob Roy[147]—also along the Loch Lubnaig in the waters of which Helen McGregor had the exciseman drowned according to Sir Walter Scott's account in RobRoy [sic]. We saw the point which is made the scene of this incident & it is by no means striking in its appearance. Indeed I could not divine a satisfactory reason why such a spot should have been selected as the scene of such a tragedy. It is by no means so suitable a place for dispatching a man by drowning as the pass of Leny where the waters rage & roar & dash along amidst wild rocks & overhanding trees forming now & then dark & deep pools most frightful in appearance. We had a fine view of the Ben Ledi which towers above Loch Lubnaig and arrived at Callendar in good time to get our tea and prepare for early rest after our tramp[148] through Glen Ogle & in anticipation of another to the Trossachs in the morning.

July 26, Saturday. Arose between 4 & 5 A.M. and hired a drosky to convey us on our way 6 miles towards the Trossachs, &c. The first place

[147] Rob Roy (1671-1734), Born Robert McGregor, a Scotish freebooter made famous by Sir Walter Scott's novel, **Rob Roy**. Loss of his estates forced him to raid cattle and sell "protection," During the Jacobite uprising of 1715, he continued plundering. He was jailed and sentenced to be transported but was pardoned. (**NCE**).

[148] This tramp as Otey called it indicates the change in his physical well being which Bishop Coxe attributed to the swim in the brisk waters of the North Sea at Aberdeen. Some of the improvement might also come from Otey's relaxed state of mind.

of classical interest we passed was Coilantogle ford—the scene of Conflict between Fitz-James & Rhoderick Dhu. Next comes Loch Vennachar & then Loch Achray. Just on the north side of Vennachar is a small plot of level ground which is reputed to be the mustering place of Clan Alpin. Dismissing our drosky near this place we pursued our journey onto the brig of Turk's Inn having a singularity unpronounceable Scotch name where we breakfasted. Then we came to the Brig itself. Here Fitz-James horse either fell or died. It is in the midst of the Trossachs,[149] nothing more nor less than some conical shaped hills or knobs, not half so immense nor picturesque as can be seen at many places on the Holston in East Tenn. We passed this famous ground and came to Loch Katrine. No great thing after all that has been said & written about it. But after being made the scene of one of Sr: Walter Scott's most popular poem, every body seems to feel under some sort of an obligation to praise Loch Katrine. It is a small dark looking lake, surrounded by bleak & barren hills—very few trees clothed the sides or shores of the Lake & these are of stunted growth. The guide books, it is true, speak of enchanting scenes—of magnificent views—of glens adorned with many forest trees—of caves the residence of fairies & goblins; but it requires a vigorous fancy, indeed, to form these pictures from the realities here displayed to view. The Steamboat which piles on this Loch is about as contemptible an affair to be dignified with such an appellation as I have ever seen afloat. Ellen's island, on which some lady, in a fine fit of enthusiasm revelling, undertood a few years ago to erect a house, is passed close on our right as we sail or steam on the Loch and at best is a very common sort of looking island. No vestige of building is seen on it now, nor are there any traces that I could discover of care or cultivation. Various localities are pointed out as we proceed to the boat house for Loch Lomond—Ben Lomond[150]— the Arrochar Alps[151] in the distance, Leanderine, &c &c. Arriving at the Boat House travellers may have their choice of conveyance across the country 5 miles to Inversnaid mill on Loch Lomond, of the three following modes—First a species of waggon [sic] provided with seats—2nd a sort of Donkey on which to ride astraddle or lastly on your own reliable bail your feet. Five others & myself chose the latter method and shouldering our luggage set off with hearty good will to make the distance in time for the boat. There were at least four different

[149] The Trossachs means bristly country. A tour of the region is one of the most popular in Scotland. As the tour includes travelling by boat as Otey and Coxe did, it can not be completed by automobile. (**Blue Guide**, pp. 220-21).

[150] Ben Lomond is 3,192 ft. high.

[151] What Otey calls the Arrochar Alps probably are the three mountains, Ben Arthur or the Cobbler, Ben Narnian, and A'Chrois. They are west of Loch Lomond.

races of people represented in our party Americans, English, Scotch and French. I was gratified to find that we Americans (Coxe & myself) led the way the whole distance across. It was said that Rob Roy's gun was to be found at a cottage on the roadside. On enquiring at the only cottage near the road which we passed we learned that the supposed weapon of this redoubtable chief had been transferred to one of the steamers on Loch Lomond.[152] We saw close to the road the ruins of Inversnaid fort, reported to have been once occupied by the celebrated Genl: Wolfe.[153] It was built to keep the Macgregors in fear. We reached Loch Lomond just as the boat going to the head of the Loch pushed off from the landing. Had the officers been possessed of ordinary accommodation, they might have waited a moment till we could have boarded the boat & made the trip to the head of the Lake which we wished to do. And moreover it would have afforded me the pleasure of seeing some friends that I afterwards learned were on board. But Jno: Bull is always wilful!! We remained at the Hotel till the steamer came down the lake at 2 P.M. when we went aboard and proceeded down the Lake. There is a beautiful little waterfall into the Loch at Inversnaid Mill. The Hotel is very neat. The views on Lock Lomond are much the same as in all lakes among the hills or mountains, occasionally had some [?] glens open on either side which are occupied by beautiful houses &c. Then the mountains descend with their bold sides to the very waters edge: Here you see a wooded island & there a cultivated field. In one place the ruins of some old feudal castle, in another modern structures & ornamented grounds of the present proprietors. A village is occasionally passed with some notice stuck up at an inn or hotel to accommodate visitors. We arrived at Balloch the fort of the Loch about 4 P.M. Here we took the rail-cars for Bolin[154]—enroute Alexandria & Dumbarton with its frowning castle the Gibralter of Scotland: an immense & craggy rock rising out of the Clyde on the little plain which skirts the banks of the river & the waters of which here wash the walls of the castle. The fortress appears to be divided into two parts by a sort of tunnel or cleft that penetrates the hill from side to side. The natural defences of the place appear to be strengthened by high & massive stone walls carried all around where an enemy might possibly gain a

---

[152] Loch Lomond is the largest lake in Scotland being 23 miles long and from 1 to 5 miles wide.

[153] James Wolfe (1727-59), a British general. During the French and Indian War he captured Louisbourg, the French North American naval base. Then he laid siege to the city of Quebec. This ended with his victory over the French on the Plains of Abraham outside the city. During the battle he was mortally wounded and Montcalm, the French general, was killed.

[154] Bolin is the way the bishop heard Bowling (boulin) pronounced. The village is about half way between Clydebank and Dumbarton and was the western terminus of the Forth Clyde Canal. (Material from the British Library of Information).

foothold by climbing up the rock.[155] The place is especially famous in the wars waged by Sr: Wm: Wallace. At Bolin Mr Coxe proceeded on by boat to Glasgow & I to Greenock to see Mrs Noble an old acquaintance, whom I had not met since I was a child. I found her after some painstaking when I reached Greenock, living on the outskirts of the city; had a pleasant chat of half an hour saw one of her sons & five of her daughters & then returned by the 7½ clock train of Rail Cars to Glascow and stopped at Camick's Hotel where Mr Coxe had already secured lodgings for me.

Sunday July 27. This is always a day of sad remembrance to me no matter where I may be or how employed. This day 21 years ago I first tasted the bitterness of death in the decease of my precious little boy Reginald Heber! This day has therefore been chiefly given to meditation upon death—to the thoughts of those dear ones whom I have loved perhaps too intensely and devotedly and whom it is my daily & fervent prayer I may meet in a holier, purer world! With Rev Coxe I walked to the church at which Bp. Trower usually officiates[156] & found in the vestry two clergymen, as they said from England, engaged to officiate today. We made ourselves known to them, but they had not the good manners to ask either of us to take any part in the services of the day! As for myself I should not have accepted any invitation to assist, so that they might have saved their manners as well as their labor if they loved it by asking: & I am very sure Coxe cared nothing about reading prayers or preaching. One of the clergymen read prayers and the other preached a very plain, practical sermon which any man might have listened to with profitable attention & interest. In the afternoon Mr Coxe did not call for me as I expected and consequently did not go out to ch: as it had been my intention to do. At night I was waited upon by Mr I Donaldson of Baltimore by whom I was informed that Mr Gwaltney & family were there at Queen's Hotel. I went to see them and very soon found myself in the company of friends from Richmond, Va. It was a high pleasure and spent a very agreeable evening together.

Monday July 28. Immediately after breakfast I called on Mr P. Smith 33 Blackfriars St. He was not in. I wrote him a note and sent the parcel for Mrs Mcleod to Mr. S to be forwarded to my apt in London. I then in

---

[155] In 1571 supporters of Queen Mary scaled the rock with ladders and ropes and captured the castle. John Hamilton, archbishop of Glasgow, was apprehended. Four days later at Stirling he was hanged for complicity in the murders of Darnely and regent Moray. (**Blue Guide**, p. 140).

[156] As Bishop Trower did not appear at his church, Otey was unable to act upon Trower's invitation made on 31 May in London—i.e, visit him at his home.

company with Mr. Coxe visited the Crypts of Glasgow Cathedral[157]—the most celebrated things of the kind in Europe. They are not at all used for the purposes of their original construction since they fell into the hands of the Presbyterians. We walked through the various apartments of this magnificent cathedral. The occupation of the chancel with pews struck me as very outré & strange. I saw at a distance the necropolis & Jno: Knox's statue standing in it.[158] Returning to the Hotel I called on Messers Mitchell 76 Von [?] Street. Not in. I then hurried off to the R.way station and took a seat for Ayr, the scene of Rob: Burn's early adventures &c. We arrived after a pleasant jaunt thru a well cultivated country and put up at the King's Arm's Hotel. Very soon we engaged a carriage & in company with Mr Coxe, Donaldson of Md and Humes of D C started for Burns' [sic] Monument, birthplace &c. We soon arrived at "the ford where in the snow the Chapman was smoor'd", the little stream is now crossed by a good bridge & no ford remains to tell the accuracy of Burns' [sic] statement. Next we stopped at the "vera hoose" in which Burns was born.[159] The walls are black with the names of visitors and the tables are all carved over thick with letters indicating the names of those who have come here to seek this species of immortality. I bought some pictures as mementos of the spot and went out to see Riva Alloway.[160] There stands the naked stone walls of the old kirk roofless, now converted into a burying place. It did not come up to my expectations at all. It was not so large & so high by one half as my fancy had depicted it. I pulled some flowers as mementos and went to look at Burns' [sic] monument. The bust of the Poet is a poor affair: but the statues of Senter Johnny & Tam O'Shanter[161] are as good as anything I have ever seen. Next I went to the brig that crosses the Doon where Tam's [?] mare Meg lost her tail—robbed of it by Cutty Sark. I pulled some Ivy from the "auld brig", and came back to the Hotel to watch the eclipse.[162] When it occurred and the dim light was present to shed a mellow & softened radiance over the scene, I thought long and sorrowfully of my darling little Fanny and repeated the touching lines of Burns [sic] "The gloomy night

[157] The best known feature of St. Mungo's Cathedral is its high vaulted crypt. The church was named after St. Mungo who reputedly founded the city in the latter part of the 6th Century A.D. (**NCE**).

[158] The Necropolis is the old Fir Park of the bishop's. One of its features is a Doric column erected to the Reformers and crowned with a statue of John Knox. (**Blue Guide**, p. 122).

[159] The cottage in which Robert Burns was born was called Alloway.

[160] One time the roofless old church was known as Alloway Kirk.

[161] James Thom (d. 1850) sculptured the statues of Senter Johnny and Tam O'Shanter. Sometime afterward he went to New York where he worked in Trinity Church. (**DNB**).

[162] In England 82 per cent of the sun was blocked. According to the report in the **Times** of the 29th: "It was a very dull afternoon for July and at 3 o'clock one could flatter oneself into the belief that the sky was more than commonly overcast." The last total eclipse seen in London occurred in April 1715. The next would be on the morning of August 19, 1887.

is gathering fast" the last the dear creature ever learned. This was enough. I cared nothing more for the eclipse, for the world or for anything therein! Returning we called on Mrs Bagg [sic] the sister of Burns.[163] She seemed much pleased at the compliment paid her by four Americans calling upon her. After a few minutes conversation & compliments paid and returned we took our leave & returned to Ayr. This day has somehow or other conjoined a number of sad reminiscences. First it is the day on which I buried my precious Heber—2dly [sic] it is the day of the month on which my beloved Sarah died & lastly—by reminding me of the last piece of poetry ever learned by my darling Fanny, it has brought her vividly to mind!—At the Hotel saw a book with R. W. McGavock's name on it.[164] I wished to take it but the lady of the hotel said it had been left as a specimen copy by the agent of a publishing house at Glasgow. So, I had to leave it. Came with Mr. Coxe to Ardrossan whence we set-off by steamer at 8 P.M. for Belfast.

Tuesday July 29. Arrived at Belfast early this morning—went ashore to the Imperial Hotel & called for breakfast. After a long time it was brought & that being dispatched we took seats in the rail cars for Dublin. We passed Armagh—saw the Cathedral at a distance—travelled through an undulating and well-cultivated country. I saw many old castles on the route especially one at Drogheda[165] and arrived in Dublin between 3 & 4 P.M. & stopped at the Imperial Hotel. Letter from H.S. Fogg to whom I wrote as also to Mercer—to Mr. Miller & Mr. Jackson—and then retired to bed having sent out my notes of introduction.

Wednesday July 30. After breakfast went with Mr Coxe and Mr Wilson to St. Patrick's Church.[166] Dean Swift[167] was connected with this church—saw his monument also Stella's—a Mrs. Johnson—attended service here. Went to Christ Church.[168] Mr Debutts a clergyman joined us here—rapped him pretty hard about Mr Gorham's book & baptismal regeneration &c. Visited the Bank of Ireland—library—Hall—refractory &c. The Dublin Academy of Antiquaries—the national School—The

[163] Isabella Burns Begg (1771-1858), the youngest of seven children, was the source of some information on the activities of her elder brother, Robert Burns. ("Burns, Robert," **DNB**).

[164] Randall W. MacGavock had been in Ayr on 26 June enroute to Burns's birthplace. No mention is made in his journal of any hotel in the vicinity.

[165] Although Otey made no historical reference to Drogheda, the city and its environs were the scene of two battles in the 17th Century. In 1649 Cromwell's forces stormed the city and massacred the defenders as the general brought Ireland under Parliamentary control. Forty-one years later the battle on the banks of the Boyne River ended the military attempts of James II to regain the lost throne of England. He was defeated by his son-in-law William of William and Mary.

[166] St Patrick's is the national seat of the Episcopal Church in Ireland.

[167] Jonathan Swift (1667-1745), author of **Gulliver's Travels**, was dean of St. Patrick's from 1713 to his death. "Stella" was Esther Johnson with whom he had a life long attachment and is buried alongside her. Whether they ever formalized their relationship is not clear. (**DNB**).

[168] Christ Church is the oldest in Dublin having been built in 1038.

Botanical gardens which contain a vast number of rare & valuable plants and then return to my Hotel with Mr Coxe & dine. In to-day's visitations have been accompanied by Mr Thos Christian & by Rev Mr Debutts. And then I have brought up my journal once more to date.

Among the interesting things seen to day may be mentioned as worthy of remembrance, a manuscript copy of the Gospels written by St Columba. It is most beautifully executed in old English black letter. (I may call it perhaps) & illuminated. It is in Latin and on parchment and well preserved. How highly valued must the sacred writings have been in ancient times when we see copies of them written out with a degree of labor, care & elegance which it would seem to us, must have employed a man's whole life and nearly all the hours of that life. The collections in the Dublin Academy of Antiquaries present many very curious specimens for contemplation—among them a richly ornamented & jewelled cross to which there is a curious history attached—as that it belonged to some Bp on whose death it fell into the hands of a Priest that tried to make himself Bp's successor & then into a woman's hands who concealed it for a long time: but at length in extremis was compelled in confession to reveal the secret, &c.

Thursday July 31 Came [?] after breakfast & taking leave of my dear companion in travel Mr. Coxe, to Kingston to embark for Hollyhead. In the cars met an Irishman who learning that I was an American seized my hand & shook it saying he loved all Americans as his brothers. The passage to Hollyhead was boisterous and made nearly all the passengers sick.[169] I remained on deck engaged in reading & protecting myself in the best way I could till we arrived at our destination. Here I drank a glass of Porter & ate a hard biscuit, & having booked for Chester was very soon again on my way at the heels of the fire-horse. In passing, I had an imperfect view of the celebrated tubular iron bridge over the Menais[170] [sic] Straits. The tubes are supported on an immense stone pillars and what advantage the tubes possess over the arch I cannot imagine. The whole must have been a work of immense labor and expense. At a place called **Conway**, [Conwy] I observed an immense Castle or fortification[171] situated close upon the sea. It is the most extensive work of this kind which I have seen in England. I do not remember ever to have seen any mention made of this place in English history. It was probably con-

[169] MacGavock wrote in his account that when he made this crossing nearly everyone was sick and that the trip is reputed worse than an ocean voyage because it is shorter. (**Pen**, p. 204).

[170] Menai Strait is fourteen miles long and varies in width between 200 yds and two miles. The tubular bridge was built in 1850 by Robert Stephenson for rail traffic. (**NCE**).

[171] Conway, a picturesque town, has a high wall built in the 13th Cent.

structed in early times to repress the incursions of the Welsh. There are many private residences along the line of this road & facing the sea, of vast size & dimensions and the construction of which must have cost the owners large sums of money.

At Chester I stopped over one train with a view to gain a sight of the Cathedral[172] and the walls, &c of this singular old town. My curiosity was amply gratified. The Cathedral looks as though it might be as old as the Exodus, built of a species of red sandstone that is evidently crumbling away in the lapse of time under the corroding effect of the atmosphere and the rains. The choir with its carved work, stalls &c is very beautiful—so are the windows of stained glass both ancient & modern—while the monuments which crowd the walls and the numberless inscriptions under your feet send to you impressively the lesson of man's mortality and make you feel very solemn. The cloisters, chapter house, lady chapel &c are but slight variations in some things from what is seen in all Cathedral churches, vast spaces for no practical uses. The walls of Chester no doubt originally constructed by the Romans[173] and the Rows[174] or covered ways along the streets, the results simply of the **vestibula** of the Roman houses, are curious things. Not having the time or space to devote to their minute description I bought a little book containing an historical account of the city & cathedral; and took the evening train for Shrewsbury.

Friday Aug: 1st I find myself in this ancient city this morning walking by 5 A.M. along silent streets and viewing its venerable ecclesiastical structures—one called St. Mary's Church[175] & the principal one I take it, having an exceedingly lofty & beautiful spire. The walls are blackened with age. The church originally cruciform, but now having double transepts & other additions like private chapels. The stained glass windows I take to be very fine. I had no opportunity of seeing the interior. Then there is St. Julier's [?] Ch: and another I could not understand from my informant accurately the name. Lastly the remains of a church now converted I was told into a school having on the gable end the following inscription.

In this sacred enclose

[172] The Chester Cathedral began in the 10th Century as a church which in 1092 Hugh Lupus made into an abbey. It became a Cathedral when a bishopric was established there under Henry VIII. The north aisle of the present structure has part of the 12th Century church. (**New Cath. Ency.**).

[173] Originally Chester was a Roman camp, some of whose walls are part of the present ones or the modern ones are built where the Roman ones were.

[174] In the Rows some of the walkways are the roofs of the shops.

[175] The stone spire of St. Mary's is one of the three tallest in England and its stained glass windows are considered to be the finest in Shropshire. (**Shell Guide England**, p. 695).

Stood the ancient church of Saint Chad
which was founded A.D. DCCLXXX
Being the first Saxon Church in Shrewsbury.
Another Collegiate Church
Spacious & cruciform
Was erected on the same site A.D. MCCCXCIII 1393
It fell July IX A.D. MDCCLXXXVIII 1788
This usually called the Bishop's Chapel

Being the only portion extant Shrewsbury[176] gives name to a battle between the forces of Cromwell & Charles 1st.

The castle near the station of the R.R. is in a state of good preservation and is the inhabited by a private family. It is now the property of Lord Liverpool.[177] Towers flank the walls which are pierced with windows and the whole structure situated in the midst of trees and upon an eminence combines many advantages in itself to make it comfortable as a dwelling. A little out of the town I observed a curious looking building with a great tower which I took to be a church and not very far off another with many small towers & buttresses, all of brick which I suppose may serve for an infirmary, College or a hospital. In the town & near to St. Mary's there is a large fine looking building which I was told was an infirmary—for what class I heard not. At Shifnall [sic] on the right as the Train passed, I had a view of a very fine looking old church[178]—cruciform with tower in the center with transepts, &c. Arriving at Wolverhampton I was struck with the number of furnaces & manufacturies in operation. It is a large town & engaged most extensively in the hardware trade. Wellington celebrated for its locks & **Walsall** for Saddlery. Arrived at Birmingham I had to tarry more than an hour for the train that proceded south to Gloucester. The time was rather pleasantly passed in conversation with a gentleman whom I met with in the cars & who was very attentive to me & especially after he learned who I was & whence I came. We exchanged cards. His address is Cornilius Bennett, organist &c at Shifnall [sic]. I take him to be a worthy & deserving man. From Birmingham I came by cars to Gloucester. Here I learned to my disappointment that I could not reach either Southampton or Dover to

---

[176] Otey must have confused one of the battles at Newbury (1643 and 1644) with Shrewsbury. The battle associated with the latter community occurred in 1403 when Henry IV defeated the force commanded by Henry Percy "Hotspur," whose head was displayed in the town after the battle. Young Prince Henry, later the V, commanded the Royal army at the battle.

[177] When Otey penned this account, Charles Cecil Jenkinson (1784-1851) was the 3rd earl of Liverpool, but that October his lordship died suddenly bringing the peerage to an end as he had only daughters. In 1905 it was revived in favor of a son of the second daughter. (Burke's **Peerage**).

[178] A fire in 1591 destroyed all of Shifnall except for the largely Norman church of St. Andrew and the timber framed Idsall House. (**Shell Guide England**, p. 694).

night. The R.R. managers have arraigned matters in such a way that passengers are at their mercy and the **tender mercies** of their subordinates to a traveller's purse are the extremest manifestations of cruelty! Finding that I should be delayed here again more than an hour I embraced the opportunity to survey the ancient city of Glouchester—where the cruel Gardiner[179] was once Bishop, and a much better & historic[?] man after him [sic]—together with its famous Cathedral.[180] The streets are in many places very narrow and crooked, laid off—apparently without any regard to convenience or beauty. The Cathedral is a very fine old building among the most imposing and impressive of all that I have seen. I now regret that I did not when stopping so long near it at Malvern avail myself of the opportunity of making a thorough examination or inspection of it. I had not the time or the opportunity to day to enter this old pile. I could only gaze upon its grand outlines & admire its external grandeur & imagine what its inner decorations &c must be. A part of the outer walls is undergoing repair, a thing I was glad to see. I saw some of the cloisters as they were once used by the monks—looked at St John's Church & some others & returned to the R.R. depot and now I am seated here at Reading in my chamber at the Hotel: all alone not a living soul do I know here. I did think when I stopped, of taking a gig & riding 25 miles to pass the night with poor Connelly & his children.[181] How glad I should have been to do so. But that distance was to great & I was weak & feeble. Darkness has closed in and no one in this world can imagine how sad, how very sad I feel!! or how my heart yearns after those living & dead who are absent from me in body but who are always present in my thoughts. But let me strive to keep up my spirits for their sake if not for my own and as they have urged me to this weary pilgrimage so far from the scenes that are dearest to my heart in the hope that I may be restored to them in health, let me use every proper effort not to disappoint their hopes. Above all let me indulge in no thought that may seem to dishonor God, doubt the love of my Saviour or do discredit to my Christian pro-

[179] Stephen Gardiner (1493?-1555) became bishop of Winchester in 1531 and is thought to have been author of the Six Articles reaffirming support for the medieval church. On the ascension of Edward VI Gardner lost his diocese which Mary restored and then made him lord high chancellor. He was active in purging clergy who resisted the return to Rome. (**DNB**).

[180] The cathedral at Glouchester "is the chief glory of the town" according to the **Shell Guide to England**. Initially it was Norman in architecture. Edward II is buried here. The church became a cathedral when Henry VIII created a new diocese.

[181] When the Connellys took the vows of perpetual celibacy and Pierce was ordained as a priest in the Roman Catholic Church, the children remained with their mother. She then achieved her desire of founding a religious order, the Holy Childhood of Jesus. When Pierce renounced his vows as a priest and returned to the Protestant Episcopal Church taking the children with him, Cornellia was placed in difficulty and almost lost control of the group she had founded. Its initial Motherhouse was in Derby, England. A chapter was established in the United States in 1862. In 1986 the society had 362 members in the USA. "Connelly, Cornelia," **New Cath. Ency.** and **Official Catholic Directory Anno Domini 1986** [Wilmette, IL] p. 1132).

fession. To-morrow I expect once more to encounter the perils of the sea. If it please God to recall the life which he had given & has so long continued to me, I pray besides his mercy, which I implore, that my frail body may by kind hands, be at last placed by the side of my beloved Sarah & darling Fanny.

Saturday Aug 2. Got up early this morning and walked through the streets of Reading. It is an old town, but the situation being healthy, the country fruitful and also near to London, it has become the residence of many wealthy people who have likewise erected good houses in the modern style of building. It is a place which one seeking a quiet home would be apt to choose for a residence. There is a good looking parish church, here a Romish chapel built from an old Abbey the remains of which are very extensive and just by their ruins a very ornate building which on inquiring I learned was the county prison. In the market I saw some very fine fruits, plums, cherries, &c. I bought a few cents worth of the plums more for the purpose of getting the seed than for the eating which I nevertheless found very delicious. I returned liesurely to the Hotel, ordered breakfast and sat down composedly to read the newspaper when the Englishman with whom I had travelled the preceding day came in & remarked that it might be well for us to be at the depot as the train would leave at 7½ A.M. I had thought it was advertised for 10¾. I at once rose to depart and called for my bill, which was forthwith presented containing a charge of 2 p[ence] for breakfast—breakfast which was not ever set & was of course untasted. The cloth was not spread nor was the tea made & yet the landlady wished to get money from me because I had ordered breakfast. I appealed to the Englishman, my fellow traveller. He said he had never heard of such a thing. After some chaffering this lady agreed to deduct the 2 p from the bill which I then paid and so took my departure. The agent of the R. road managed to book us to Reigate in the Express train from Reading; charging us of course nearly double the common rate and we very soon were on the way to Reigate whence we proceeded to Folkstone & terrace above where we took passage for Calais. The country thro' which I have passed to-day has been rather barren & sterile, & as we approached the sea shore, became evidently sandy & less productive. The line of sea coast I perceived, so soon as it came in sight, was defended by towers or castles placed at short intervals from each other and served in the French War, when no doubt they were erected as posts where a lookout was kept up, and also as fortresses of defence against an invading force. Upon arriving at Dover we passed under what is Shakespeare's Cliff, and under the walls of a frowning fortress full of loop holes, and the parapets bristling with great guns, and very soon were at the Steamboat with an immense crowd pressing on board, most of them being on the way to the great fete given by the City of Paris, next week, to the Lord Mayor of London. I deposited my luggage, consisting of a light carpet bag and Scotch plaid near the center of mast of the boat—procured a stool to sit on and made myself as easy & as comfortable as I could in the midst of an immense crowd & under the burning rays of a bright & cloudless sun. The steamer moved slowly out of the dock and in two or three minutes we were under full weigh crossing the Strait to Calais. The sea is always troubled in this arduous [?] passage even in the most calm and settled weather: and when the wind is only a little fresh against the tide the waves rise to a fearful height—the sea is thrown into a violent commotion and the passage across in either direction is very unpleasant. Calm and undisturbed as the sea was to-day the motion of the steamer was notwithstanding so great, that a great many persons were made very sick. They were lying about the deck [faded] wretching or heaving over the gunnels [Illegible] In the course of two hours, I caught a glimpse of the low coast of France as it trailed away to the S. West. I said to myself "And is that indeed La Belle France of which I have read so much from the days of my early childhood even to the years when time has silvered my locks?" From the days of Julius Caesar who crossed into Britain at no great distance from this place, to the time of Napoleon, France has been the object of contention among the great conquerors of the world, and often indeed the theater upon which have been enacted some of the most thrilling scenes that have marked the history of Mankind. Land of La Fayette, of Fenelon,[182] of Barthelemy[183] all hail! Land of Napoleon! of Ney![184] Of Lannes![185] I greet you! I have at last put my foot upon the soil of France. I have at length breathed the air of a country whose deeds in arms have astonished the world and whose contributions to science & art have surrounded her sons with a halo of glory that will never lose its lustre. Here then I bring of this volume to an end. I must now open a new book for new records and express here my grateful sense of the divine goodness which has so far followed me!—

[182] Fenelon, Francis de Salignac de la Mothe (1651-1715) was a French theologian, leader of the Quietism heresy and archbishop of Cambrai. (**NCE**).

[183] Barthelemy—probably Auguste Marseille (1796-1867) who was a French poet and satirist. (**Ibid**).

[184] Ney, Michel (1769-1815) was probably the best known of Napoleon's marshals. He was nicknamed "The Bravest of the Brave." (**Ibid**).

[185] Lannes, Jean (1769-1809) Napoleon regarded him as one of his best generals. He was killed in the battle of Essling. (**Ibid**).

EPILOGUE

James Hervey Otey did not record his experiences during the continental portion of his trip to the Old World. Most of his itinerary, however, is known through other accounts. These lack his candid impressions of the French, Belgians, Germans and Swiss. His diary for 1852 does give a few glimpses of the two months on the continent.

He arrived in the French capital along with an influx of English. Despite the crowd he seems to have known where to contact his fellow Tennesseans and secure lodgings. The English, particularly Londoners, were drawn to Paris by the invitation extended the Lord Mayor to attend a fete honoring the Great Exhibition. Prince Louis Napoleon, the French president, had suggested the idea as a counterpart to the London success. Later in 1867, as Napoleon III, he used the completion of the design by Baron Georges Haussmann (1809-91) to rebuild Paris as the excuse for an exhibition. Then in 1889 a second exposition was held. This one is remembered for the Eiffel Tower which still dominates the Parisian skyline whereas the Crystal Palace was relocated after the close of the London affair, damaged in 1936 and demolished in 1941.

Initially Victoria and Albert had been invited. When the Royal couple declined, the Lord Mayor of London was invited along with the commissioners of the Great Exhibition who were led by the Earl of Granville, the vice chairman. Thus Sir John Musgrove was the first lord mayor to visit Paris officially. This fact was emphasized at the banquet honoring him at the end of his year in office and it explains the baronetcy given him by Victoria. Prior to the mayor's arrival the Parisians were curious about his official status. Somehow they thought he ranked next to the sovereign, and the aldermen a type of bodyguard.[1]

The visiting English scarcely had time to put their bags down on 2 August before they were off to a banquet for 500 at the Hotel de Ville, the city hall. Their host, the prefect of the Seine, was the highest local official of the department in which Paris is situated. Next morning on the 3rd an estimated crowd of a hundred thousand journeyed out to Versailles for a display of the palace's water fountains. Randolph McGavock was one of the mass. The following day he, Bishop Otey and Maria Bass drove to St. Cloud, the presidential residence.[2] Tickets for the event were provided by Colonel Henry Sanford,[3] secretary of the American Lega-

---

[1] **Times**, 4 August 1851, 11 November 1851.
[2] The palace at St. Cloud was destroyed during the siege of Paris in 1870.
[3] Henry Shelton Sanford (1823-91) from 1847 to 1890 was virtually a professional diplomat at a time when the United States did not have such a group. In 1871 during a period when he was not serving, he founded Sanford, Florida. (**DAB**).

tion. On the 5th a Great Ball was held in the Hotel de Ville. According to McGavock it was without a doubt one of the most brilliant events ever given in Paris. He was there with Misses Pennington and Bass along with his aunt, Mrs Eakin. All of them were accompanied by Col. W.P. Bryan who claimed to be a Tennessean.[4] The feature the next day was a mock battle between several large French units. Troops on the Champs-de-Mars side of the Seine (the left bank) were attacked by an equal number on the other side who captured the bridges and crossed over. Then the two groups united and were reviewed by the president and the lord mayor. An opera that evening ended the affair. McGavock missed the final event being too tired to attend.[5]

A day later the American Minister to Russia and Mrs Neill S. Brown came to Paris. On the 12th the group went to Brussels by train. Here they hired carriages for a tour of the field at Waterloo where they purchased souvenirs and climbed the commemorative mound erected by the Dutch. A little "forget-me-not" stimulated the bishop's poetic impulses and he composed:

"On Seeing the '**Forget-me-not**' Blooming on the **Field of Waterloo**"

There is a flower whose opening bloom,
Beams softly o'er the Hero's grave;
Whose trembling leaf & sweet perfume,
Denote the dwelling of the brave.

No urn is there; that little flower,
Alone remains their woes to tell,
How oft they bled in battle's hour,
How valour fought & prudence fell.

Sweet child of Spring thy modest head
Was born to grace some happier spot
And wilt thou bloom among the dead
And only say "forget me not!"

I would not leave this place of rest
For brighter skies & milder climes;
Here I repose on honor's breast,
Unmov'd by fear; unstain'd by crimes.

At midnight oft the orphan steals,
O'er me to pour the sacred tear

---

[4] Neither a W.P. Bryan or a W.P. Bryant appears in the 1850 census list for Tennessee.
[5] McGavock, **Pen and Sword**, pp. 221-23: **Times** 5-8 August 1851.

And while his heart a throbbing feels,
He knows his parent's grave is here.

And shall I leave the Hero's tomb
Or mock the orphan's tender woe?
No! stranger! I was born to bloom
Where streams of widow'd sorrow flow.

Guard of the midnight hour farewell!
Still o'er the slumb'ring warrior wave;
Be mine the sacred task to tell
The charm that smiles on Glory's grave!

Tuesday, December 1852
(undoubtedly composed earlier.)

The following morning the party broke into two groups with Mac-Gavock and William Johnstone of South Carolina, whom he met in Paris, leaving for Antwerp and Amsterdam. For the next year the two travelled together in Europe, Africa, and Asia. Meanwhile Otey, Mrs. Eakins and Miss Bass along with the Browns headed for Aix-le-Chapelle and onto Cologne where they left on the 19th for Coblentz. MacGavock missed them as he arrived that night.

During the short stay in Cologne Otey saw the relics of St. Ursula and the thousand virgins. Here he scoffed at the priest in attendance when the latter showed the veil of Virgin Mary and the water pots from Cana. Through his interpreter he asked. "**On what evidence** do you assert this?" When pressed for evidence the priest held out the veil and pointed to water pots as he shrugged his shoulders implying: Here they are, what more evidence do you want?[6]

The Rev. Mr. Coxe joined Otey about the time he entered Switzerland where they travelled together. Near Lucerne they climbed the Rigi on foot and enjoyed the view from the Rigi Kulm watching the sun set over the Lake of the Four Cantons as its last flames tipped the snowy peaks of the Oberland. Then they rode mules over the Kaiserstuhl from Sarnen enroute to Interlachen. Here they climbed to Lauterbrunnen and its nearby falls, the Staubbach with a 930 ft. drop.[7] A heavy rain at Wengen kept them from going up the Wengren Alp where at 6,145 ft. level the view of the Jungfrau and the Mönch is unparalled.[8] Disappointed they turned toward Thun, Berne, and Fribourg. At the latter city they took an

---

[6] Coxe, "Letter," in Green, **A Memoir**, p. 357.
[7] Staubbach means a falls with a long drop.
[8] "Wengren," **NCE** and Vivian H. Green, **The Swiss Alps** (London, 1961), p. 93.

over night post chaise to Chillon and Lausanne. In Geneva Otey was reunited with the female members of the party and the two Henrys, Maney and Fogg, who had come over from France. Coxe who was going to Italy formed a partnership with Samuel Wilburforce, bishop of Oxford, who was also headed that way. Before they parted on their separate itineraries Otey and Wilburforce had several conversations. Afterward the latter expressed his admiration for Otey's "warm and generous affection, his fidelity to the Church, his missionary spirit, his Apostolic earnestness, and, with all, his child-like simplicity and unworldliness, his real dignity and elevation of spirit."[9]

As tourist's in John Calvin's city Otey's group visited Cappet, the home of Jacques Necker, twice minister of finance for Louis XVI, and of his daughter Madame de Stael. Some of her fame came from being an enemy of Napoleon who ordered the destruction of her influential book, **De L'Allemagne**. They also went to Chamonix for a better view of the snow crowned mountain they could see in the distance, Mount Blanc, the highest peak in the Alps. The Mer de Glace, an ice field was another attraction. Before leaving for Berlin Maney wrote his parents that he had met Bishop Otey and found him looking well and feeling himself a new man.[10]

Retracing some of their steps the party headed for Lausanne and Vevey along the northern shore of Lake Geneva with the aid of a privately hired Vetturino who provided a four wheel carriage. Sometimes a contract with these men included meals and lodging. As the castle of Chillon was near Vevey they visited it, their interest having been aroused by Lord Byron's poem, "The Prisoner of Chillon." After examining the pillar where Francois de Bonnivard had been chained in that cold cellar-like dungeon, they looked at the upper chambers. In one of these when the guide was not looking, Maney using the bishop's knife "did feloniously cut away one of the numerous little knobs of carving on the post of the bed used by the duke of Savoy."[11]

Next day outside of Bulle while headed north they passed McGavock and Johnstone who were enroute to Geneva. Randolph became so engrossed in conversing with his friends that the public conveyance drove off without him. Ultimately with the aid of a farmer's buggy he reached Vevey.[12] At Fribourg the travellers crossed over the Saane River

[9] Coxe, "Letter," Green, **Memoir**, pp. 357-58.
[10] Crabb, ed. "Letters Over the Water," **Tenn. Hist. Quarterly XVI**, p. 265.
[11] H. Maney, **Memories Over the Water**, pp. 86-87.
[12] McGavock, **Pen and Sword**, p. 237.

on the 941 foot long bridge suspended 180 feet above the stream. From here they moved on to Interlaken where they made a side trip by horseback to Grindlewald and the Wengren Alp.There they did what Otey earlied had failed to do—enjoy the view of the Jungfrau. Some years afterward when Otey and Coxe met in the United States, the Tennessean teased the bishop of Western New York with: "I have the advantage of you, for I made that passage of the Wengren, after all; saw the avalanches, and came down to the Lutschine again, sorry to think of how much my friend, Cleveland Coxe, had missed by going into Italy in such hot haste to see Rome and the Pope." Coxe wrote that Otey triumphed over him but salved it all with a quote from Horace, "Nil ego contulerim jucundo sanus amico."[13] (Nothing will be pleasureable without an amicable friend. Trans. W.D. Burgess) From Interlaken Otey and Maney went by boat on Lake Brienz to a village of that name at the head of the lake where the bishop bought souvenirs.

Leaving here the two walked up the Brunig Pass. On the way down the other side they encountered a party coming up. As they met, the Americans gave a "Yankee hurrah" while the other travellers raised their hats. After a stop at Lungern they took a carriage to Alpnach Stad and from there a boat on the Lake of the Four Cantons. In Lucerne the reunited group worshiped in one of the chapels erected to serve the many English attracted by the mountains of Switzerland. The Alps cast their spell on Otey. Months later a refreshing balmy breeze at Tellico in East Tennessee with its mountains reminded him of the invigorating airs of the Swiss mountains. He also idealized his impressions on a dreary December day in Memphis when the weather was disagreeably cold and threatened snow all compounded by a tooth ache:[14]

> I have often thought that the long winter nights in Scotland, Switzerland and other northern countries must have in their employments something very attractive to the inhabitants of those regions. The contrast presented by the dreary aspects of snow-clad fields and forests without and the comfort of cheerful fires blazing on the hearth within, is in itself agreeable to the human mind. And then social feeling enlivened by tales and legends in which these people are universally found to delight must contribute greatly to relieve the otherwise gloomy nights of much of their dreariness and discomfort.

While in Lucerne the bishop bought several wooden items that were

[13] Coxe, "Letter," in Green, **Memoir**, p. 358.
[14] Otey, Diary, 26 June and 21 December 1852.

severly damaged when they arrived fifteen months later in Memphis. Their arrival had been delayed because a shipping agent had attempted to add specifically excluded extra charges.[15]

At Arth which lies between Lucerne and Zug the group visited the William Tell Chapel which was built after the death of Gessler who forced the Swiss hero to shoot an apple off the top of his own son's head. Later in Zug, a Catholic canton, the Americans visited the cathedral. Some of them became excited on hearing the news that Cuban authorities had executed General Narsico Lopez and some of his followers as a consequence of a failed attempt to free the island from the Spanish.[16] Maney who mentioned the incident did not offer an explanation for the reaction. In Zurich the Tennesseans were attracted by the city's commercial vitality. From here they journeyed to the 64 ft. high Falls of the Rhine[17] and crossed a wooden bridge to Eglisau where the coachman fed the horse bread especially baked for it.

From Schaffshausen they went up the Rhine by boat to the German city of Constance. As this was the place where John Hus and Jerome of Prague were burnt at the stake as heretics, the sedan that bore John to his execution was of special interest. The most shocking thing, however, was the sight of two bearded men hugging and kissing each other.[18]

Next they crossed Lake Constance or the Bodensee to the Württemburg city of Friedrichshafen and thence to Ulm by rail. The stay in Augsburg was long enough for a transfer to a stage coach for an all night ride to Munich. With Lola Montez and her activities very much in the news the past three years, her cottage in the Bavarian capital was a must. Her interference in domestic affairs led to an uprising by "an infuriated mob of students." The resulting revolt forced Lola's "protector" to abdicate.[19] From her abode the group moved on to the Royal Residenz and to the Pinacotheque, an art gallery,[20] where the porter, according to Maney, "was a huge lantern-jawed, big fisted, raw boned, slab sided Porphyrion

[15] **Ibid**, 8 December 1852. In view of the purchases in Brienz perhaps the bishop mistakenly thought the items had been bought in Lucerne.

[16] Lopez made three attempts to liberate Cuba. His last one was in August 1851 when his force of about 400 men was defeated and captured. Many of the prisoners including the general were executed. Much of the American support came from Southerners who wanted to preserve slavery on the island by annexing it. (Julius W. Pratt, **A History of American Foreign Policy**, [New York, 1955], p. 29).

[17] McGavock who had seen Niagara Falls was disappointed and felt that no American should visit the Falls of the Rhine as these are inferior to many in America. (**Pen & Sword**, p. 233).

[18] On witnessing a similar scene McGavock wrote: "looked very queer to me although it is the custom in Germany." (**Ibid**, p. 232).

[19] Lola Montez (1818?-61) was of Irish parentage. She was a mediocre dancer whose beauty drew men. In 1846 she became the mistress of Ludwig I of Bavaria. The revolt in 1848 caused Ludwig to abdicate and Lola to flee. In the Fall of 1851 she came to the United States on the same ship that brought Louis Kossuth, the Hungarian freedom fighter. She resumed dancing and travelled over much of the country. In 1855 she went back to Europe and later returned to America where she died in Brooklyn. She is a woman about whom there is a lot of myth.

[20] Construction on the Pinakothek began in 1826 and finished in 1836,

by whose side our portly Bishop dwindled into corporeal insignificance."[21]

At Hof, near the Saxon border, a lit cigar again led to an incident. As the drifting smoke annoyed Mrs Eakins who was eating breakfast, the bishop strode across the room, looked the smoker in the face and with sign language asked the man to put down the cigar by pointing to the lady. Slowly, the astonished man removed it and the bishop returned to the table without a word being spoken. This filled Maney with greater admiration for the clergyman.

In Berlin, the Prussian capital, carriages were needed for visits to places like the Charlottenburg Palace which then was three miles from the city, today it is part of it. They also saw the tomb of Louisa (1776-1810), consort of Frederick William III (1797-1840). She had won the admiration of the Prussians for her futile efforts to get Napoleon to lighten the terms of the Treaty of Tilsit (1807).

As Otey wanted to meet Baron Alexander von Humboldt, the famous explorer, he secured a letter of introduction from Daniel D. Barnard,[22] the American minister to Berlin. Thus armed the bishop and Maney journeyed out to Potsdam where the Baron received them. In their conversation Humboldt referred to rising American astronomers and philosophers and was particularly complementary of Lieutenant Matthew Maury for the latter's wind and ocean current charts. The German was critical of America's war with Mexico, to him it was unjust and proved that Americans were more rapacious than they should be. Before leaving Otey requested and received an autograph: "Baron von Humboldt, 82 years old" written with a bold and steady hand. Prior to returning to Berlin the bishop and his young companion inspected the palace of Sans Souci, but did not see the king who was reviewing troops.

On 23 September members of the group went to the opera in hopes of seeing the king and queen. They were disappointed. Afterwards they visited a room in the royal palace where some of Frederick the Great's possessions were kept. One of these was his flute which Otey took up and played a few notes. As they were leaving, King Frederick William IV (reigned 1840-61) arrived.

The following day Maney and Fogg set out for Vienna and Florence. From the latter city they accompanied McGavock and others to Rome and Naples. The same day Bishop Otey, Mrs Eakin, Miss Bass and little Willie

---

[21] Maney, **Memories**, p. 125. The Porphyrion is a bird with a strong beak and long legs that is found in the Eastern Hemisphere.

[22] Daniel D. Barnard (1797-1861) was American minister in Berlin from 1850 to 1853. His stay in Europe have him an opportunity to study the results of the Revolutions of 1848 just as an earlier sojourn permitted him to study the revolts of 1830. Both sets appeared in **Political Aspects and Prospects in Europe** (1854). (**DAB**).

left for Paris and home. When Mrs Eakin[23] decided that her daughter's health might improve back in Tennessee, the bishop agreed to go with them and forego the trip to the Holy Land.[24]

Mrs. Lizinka Campbell Brown, wife of the former governor, returned with them on the **S.S. Atlantic** as her husband resumed the post of American Minister at St. Petersburg, Russia. The ship sailed from Liverpool on October 1st and arrived in New York on the 15th. It was delayed forty-nine hours by an engine breakdown. In the **New York Times** report of passengers aboard the bishop is listed on page 3 as Bishop Oter and on page 4 as Bishop Otis.[25] Thus if the American paper did not spell his name correctly, the mix-up at the Lord Mayor's banquet and the omission or confusion of the name in the (London) **Times** is understandable.

After Otey landed in New York, his travels for the remainder of the year are uncertain as he did not return home immediately. Apparently no diary was kept until 1 January 1852 when he arrived in New Orleans with his youngest son, Mercer, and was met by his wife. From there they slowly moved up the Mississippi River with visits both in the state of Mississippi and Arkansas where an older son, Paul, lived. After a brief stop in Memphis Mrs Otey and Mercer went overland to Columbia, Tennessee while James Hervey went to Nashville by boat. He arrived there on 23 March, 1852, fifty-three weeks after leaving. Six days later he was back in Columbia "after an absence of more than twelve months."

Bishop Otey began 1852 with a summary of his travels in 1851:

> By the providence of God, I am brought to the beginning of a Newyear [sic]. The past has been a remarkable one for me, in that I have been permitted to cross the Atlantic Ocean and visit many foreign countries, see many objects of art & nature of great interest, form the acquaintance of many distinguished men and lastly to experience the restoration of my health. For the protection and blessing God vouchsafed me during the past year I desire to record here my sense of gratitude and humbly and heartily pray to God our Heavenly Father, through His blessed Son our Saviour J. Christ that he will by His Holy Spirit grant me grace to live this year in a way answerable to the great favors I have received and to mercy and

---

[23] Sometime after returning to Nashville Felicia Grundy Eakins married Robert Massengill Porter (1818-56). He attended Harvard Law, graduated from Princeton Theological Department, and the Medical Department of the University of Pennsylvania. For the next two years 1845-47 he studied medicine in Paris. His death came as a result of an infection which developed from an anatomical demonstration. (**Pen & Sword**, p. 326, footnote).

[24] Maney, **Memories**, pp. 72-133 has been the source for the account of Otey's travels from Geneva to Berlin.

[25] New York **Times**, 16 Oct. 1851. On the 16th the packet ship **Waterloo** began its first eastward crossing since the one in the Spring. On the westward trip in August it had carried 352 passengers (**Ibid**, 30 Sept. 1851 and 17 Oct. 1851).

grace yet vouchsafed to me that if this year shall close my earthly career, I may also be found prepared for death & for the enjoyment of life eternal.

Before the following new year (1853) the water brash returned and James Hervey Otey had moved to Memphis.

The European trip which brought contact with the universities of Oxford and Cambridge seems to have intensified Otey's desire to establish a college. Finally in July 1857 several bishops and others from the South who were interested in having an institution of higher learning with direct connections to the Protestant Episcopal Church met at Lookout Mountain, Tennessee. Here the first steps were taken. Sewanee, Tennessee was chosen as the site of the school because 10,000 acres of land had been donated and the site was accessible by rail. Bishop Otey having been elected the first chancellor wrote various European universities asking for guideline that would be helpful in establishing policies. Funds were raised and so were buildings. The first class gathered in 1859, that same year the University of North Carolina gave both Otey and President James Buchanan an honorary L.L.D. The Civil War disrupted the development of the fledgling school which had to be rebuilt in the post war period.

The war posed problems for Otey. He favored Tennessee going with the Confederacy but opposed removing the diocese from its union with the Protestant Episcopal dioceses of the North. To him the break in the political union had no effect on the religious unity of the denomination. Furthermore in the early stage of the conflict he addressed a telegram to Secretary of State Wm. H. Seward, urging the Federal government to moderation. These two factors probably explain why General William Sherman, when he was in charge of Memphis after the Union forces occupied it, showed his respect for the bishop and sometimes attended the latter's church.

In 1861 Eliza P. Otey died exhausted from bearing nine children and caring for the family during her husband's long absences such as in 1851 and 52. That year he arrived home from Europe in March and was gone again from mid May to September. Worn out, he died in 1863 and was buried in Memphis until the end of the war when he was reburied at St. John's, Ashwood, Tennessee.

Whether or not his will was ever carried out is uncertain, for in 1957 it was found in box amid the rubble of a Memphis water front building which was being demolished. After disposing of his property in Memphis, Chattanooga, Arkansas, and North Carolina, he urged his children to read and study the Bibles and Prayerbook that were found along with the five page had written document. Lastly they were not to sell the six slaves who were to be allowed "the blessings of Christian worship and fellowship."[26]

Genealogy

James Hervey Otey traced his ancestry back to Archbishop Tobe or Tobias Matthew through his mother Elizabeth Mathews (1767-1855).

Elizabeth Mathews was the daughter of William (d. 1772) and Frances Crowe Mathews.

William Mathews was the son of John and Anne Archer Mathews.

John who moved to Augusta County, VA about 1734 was the son of Samuel and his first wife, a Miss Braxton;

Samuel Mathews (d. 1718) was the son of John Mathews and Elizabeth Tavenor:

John Mathews was the son of Samuel Mathews, mother not named.

Samuel Mathews was the elder son of Governor Samuel Mathews and daughter of Sir Thomas Hinton.

Samuel Matthews (1592-1660) was the son of Archbishop Tobe Matthew and Frances Barlow.[27]

The Archbishop

Archbishop Tobie (Tobias) Matthew (1546-1628), a maternal ancestor of James Hervey, was the son of John Matthew and Eleanor Crofton. After a boyhood spent in Bristol, England he entered Oxford, graduating in February 1563-64 [O.S.][28] from University College. Two years later he received the M.A. from Christ Church and was ordained. When Queen Elizabeth visited the University that year, the reverend participated in a debate by arguing for an elective monarchy instead of a hereditary one. His handsome presence and ready wit made an impression on the queen that lasted her lifetime. In 1572 he became one of her actual chaplains and was also elected the fifth president of St. Johns College. On being chosen dean of Christ Church Tobie resigned the post at St. Johns. Later the earl of Leicester, the chancellor, named Dr. Matthew the university vice chancellor. In a sermon before the university the new official defended the Reformation by citing the teachings of Christ and primitive Christianity without quoting or defending Martin Luther.

[26] Rodgers, **Romance of the Episcopal**, p. 212.
[27] **Ibid**, p. 211. The **Dictionary of National Biography** lists the Archbishop as Matthew as does the list of archbishops furnished by the archdiocese.
[28] O.S. refers to the Old Style or Julian calendar in which January, February and part of March were at the end of the year rather than the beginning as they were after the adoption of the Gregorian calendar. The British did not make the change until 1752.

After his installation as dean of Durham, England in 1584 Tobie resigned the deanship at Christ Church. In the new assignment the dean who was a political agent for the government vigorously pursued recusants—i.e., those who refused to recognize the authority of the Church of England. Meanwhile his services as a preacher were sought to such an extent that he betook himself "to his bed for refreshment." That he was popular is attested by his record. As dean of Durham he preached 721 times, as bishop 550 times and as archbishop another 721 sermons.

In 1595 he became bishop of the diocese, no easy task for this northern region was hard hit; land was deserted and poverty was abroad. According to one remedial proposal the bishop could help by insisting that incumbents be residents of the parish and preach instead of permitting the practice of having "mean curates"—i.e., poorly said. Slowly improvements were brought about.

Tobias was elevated to the archbishopric of York in 1606 following the death of Dr. Matthew Hutton whom he had succeeded as bishop of Durham. For the first several years in his new position the archbishop continued his political activities. They lessened as he grew older and by 1624 his infirmities kept him from attending Parliament. Ill health must have plagued him shortly after becoming archbishop, for from 1607 on rumors of his death circulated almost yearly. One comment on the rumors gives an insight into Tobie's devotional life. "I doubt not but in the Apostle's sense he died daily in his mortifying meditations."

He married Frances Barlow, daughter of a bishop of Chichester and widow of Matthew Parker, second son of the archbishop. Of her it can be said she had bishop as a father, an archbishop as a father-in-law, four bishops as brothers and an archbishop as a husband. Their union produced three sons, the famous Sir Tobie, John and Samuel and two daughters.

Obviously the archbishop was a man whom Elizabeth and James in turn felt could be relied upon to watch and guard the northern districts. He was a statesman and prelate. As both he and James Hervey shared many characteristics, the archbishop surely would have been proud of the distant grandson.[1]

The Knight

Although Sir Tobie Matthew's father was an archbishop, the activities of this son are either better recorded or of more interest for the account of the priest and courtier in the **Dictionary of National Biography** is twice

[1] DNB.

as long as that of the elder. At the time of the son's birth in 1577 at Salisbury, the father was dean of Christ Church, Oxford. Tobie was twelve years when he entered his father's college graduating in 1594. Three years later he had an M.A. Then he entered Gray's Inn for study to be a lawyer. During these years his extravagance and debts caused friction between the parents and the lad. Later political enemies charged him with alleged libertinism in this period. As a result of the debts the archbishop willed his son merely a piece of silver worth 20 marks having spent £14,000 on him.

In 1601 young Tobie was chosen Parliamentary representative from Newport, Cornwall. [Today it is a suburb of Launceton.] When Parliament was called in 1604, Tobie took over St. Albans, a seat formerly held by his life long friend Sir Francis Bacon (1561-1626), later Viscount St Albans, who now sat for Ipswich. Toward the end of the year during a parliamentary recess Tobie went to Italy despite having promised his parents he would not go there because the mother, a staunch Puritan, suspected her son might succumb to approaches from Roman Catholics. Reputedly when older he regretted having lied to his parents because he wanted to go in order to become proficient in Italian. Contacts, however, with Catholics such as Fr. Robert Persons, a Jesuit, had their impact, for he joined that church in 1606. Sometime after his return to England Tobie was imprisoned when the archbishop of Canterbury could not persuade him to renounce his new faith.

After being released through the efforts of his father and Bacon, Tobie was permitted to go back to the continent where apparently he headed for Madrid and developed a circle of friends and acquaintances. From there he returned to Rome, studied for the priesthood and was ordained in 1614 by Cardinal, later Saint, Robert Bellarmine (1542-1621), a Jesuit.

Three years later Tobie was allowed to reenter England. This time his difficulties arose out a refusal to take the oath of allegiance, a defiance that offended James who sent him into another exile. However when the duke of Buckingham and Prince Charles began the fruitless negotiations for the hand of a Spanish infanta, Tobie was asked to use his contacts. These efforts won him a knighthood in 1623. They also gained him Charles's favor after the prince became king. For the next few years he spent his time as a courtier. Meanwhile the archbishop of York continued efforts to bring the son and heir back to the Anglican fold. Then in 1633 Viscount Thomas Wentworth (1593-1641), later earl of Strafford, was appointed lord deputy of Ireland and chose Sir Tobie as his secretary. The stay was short and on returning to court he gained the ear of the Catholic queen consort Henrietta Marie (1609-1669).

Sometimes the courtier played the fool such as once after offering to make the queen a cup of chocolate, a new drink, he "absent-mindly" drank it himself. According to the French ambassador Sir Tobie worked solely for the advancement of Catholics. His influence roused the ire of Puritans. Despite efforts to hide his priestly status slowly the secret became apparent as shown through the denouncement made in 1640 by Andreas Habernfeld and Boswell's "Particular Discover of the Plot against King, Kingdom and Protestant Religion." It charged that Sir Tobie Matthew was a "Jesuited priest and dangerous man in the pay of Cardinal Barberini" (1597-1679). The accusation led to a Parliamentary petition and ultimately banishment from court leading to acceptance of the offer from the earl of Worcester to be chaplain at Raglan Castle. On the outbreak of the Civil War the priest retired to Ghent where he lived with the Jesuits until his death in 1655.

His relationship with the order is unclear but there is no question about his strong affinity for this famous religious organization. Nearly all his activities in the Roman Catholic Church involve the Society. On one occasion he was a definite advocate for the Jesuit position. About the time when the Spanish marriage was under consideration efforts were made to reestablish a Roman episcopacy in England. As the Jesuits were against it, Sir Tobie used their sophistry with King James by exaggerating Papal intentions. These arguments angered James who saw the plan as an infringement on royal perogative. Then the opponents gave Gregory XV a distorted account of the English king's attitude thereby scuttling the plan.

The Reverend Sir Tobie Matthew (S.J.?), who was no Pietist, had an open mind on matters other than religion, for he was selected one of the eighty-four "Essentials" who would form the basis for a Royal Academy which came to fruition years later. As a friend of Bacon he translated the latter's essays into Italian (1618). Bacon then honored Tobie with as essay on "Friendship." Later Tobie Matthew's translation of the "Confessions of the Incomparable Doctore S. Augustine" appeared in a little book. His "A True Historical Relation of the Conversion of Sir Tobie Matthews to the Holie Catholic Fayth, with the Antecedents and Consequences thereof," a 140 page manuscript account was not published until the Twentieth Century. After the Restoration Dr. John Donne, son of the poet, edited Tobie's letters.[2]

Apparently Otey had little knowledge about the activities of either his ancestor or distant uncle, for surely some comment would have appeared in the journal.

[2] (**DNB**; **Catholic Encyclopedia** (1913), X, 66; **Bibliographical Dictionary of English Catholics**, IV, 531-33; C.V. Wedgewood, **The King's Peace**, p. 13)

The Governor

Samuel Matthews (1597-1660) was the third son of Archbishop Tobie and Frances Mathew and a younger brother of Sir Tobie. In 1622 he came to Virginia. Like other younger sons he went there seeking his fortune probably because his father appears to have had an interest in the area. Samuel was soon involved in local affairs and led a force against the Pamunkey Indians. This resulted in his being elected to the Assembly in which he served intermittently henceforth. In 1624 the Privy Council named him one of four commissioners to investigate conditions in the colony. Five years later he wed the twice widowed Frances, daughter of Sir Thomas Hinton. Her first husband had been Captain Nathaniel West, a younger brother of Lord de la Ware. After his death in 1624 she married Abraham Piersey, then the wealthiest man in the young colony. His wealth came from having been Cape Merchant, i.e., a combination supercargo and factor as he accompanied a magazine ship to the colony and then dispensed its cargo. Samuel as a result of the marriage and his own efforts accumulated an estate of about 9,000 acres. Some of this wealth was used to protect the area from Indian raids when he and William Claiborne built a stockade between the James and York Rivers. Later, angered by the usurpations of the governor, Samuel persuaded the governor's council to depose Sir John Harvey who appealed to Charles I. The king was angered by the effrontery to his royal appointee and ordered the leaders be sent to England. Through influential friends these men escaped punishment. Meanwhile Sir John took revenge on his former friend by ransacking Samuel's property and confiscating it for his private use. The Privy Council ordered the governor to return it.

Mathews was restored to the council in 1642. He became a Puritan and was sympathetic to the Commonwealth. From 1652 to 1657 he was the colony's agent in England to bring about the restoration of Maryland to Virginia. When this aim proved impossible, he signed an agreement with Lord Baltimore settling the difference between the two colonies.

Within a month after the Assembly elected him governor in March 1658, Samuel and that body quarreled. Exalted ideas of his station caused the Assembly to break custom by excluding both the governor and his council from sitting with the burgesses. Thereupon he dissolved the Assembly but the members of that body declared themselves still in session. Then Mathews offered concessions which the Assembly not only rejected but deposed Samuel and his council. When the latter two agreed to recognize the authority of the Assembly, it reelected the governor and the council. During the Commonwealth period the House of Burgess choose both the governor and the council. The remainder of his administration was uneventful and terminated with his death in January 1660 [1659 old style]. This left the colony without a leader at the same time as Richard Cromwell stepped down in England as Lord Protector and Charles II mounted the throne. As a result of this transformation Samuel Mathews was the third and last governor of the colony under the Commonwealth.

Obviously Mathews was a highly regarded and capable individual who contributed to the colony's success with his political ability and his economic leadership as a trader and planter. He welded a large estate which provided work for weavers, tanners and other laborers. Mathews had one son, Samuel through whom Bishop Otey traced his ancestry. Whether the T.M. who wrote the account of Bacon's Rebellion, and who usually is thought to be Thomas Mathews was son of the second Samuel is unclear. Reputedly the senior Samuel married a second time taking for wife the widow of Sir Sebastian Harvey, a lord mayor of London.

Archbishop Mathews is said to have quipped that he had one son with wit and no grace, probably Sir Tobie, another with grace and no wit, and a third with neither. Surely Samuel, although the youngest did not fit the last characterization. Of course the Archbishop had no way of knowing that he and two of his sons would be among those in future lists of notable personages.[1]

The Physician

Bishop Otey's eldest son, Paul was educated at Kenyon College, Gambier, Ohio, an Episcopalian school where the President of the United States in 1878, Rutherford B. Hayes was a classmate. Instead of taking theological training Paul studied medicine and was a highly regarded doctor both in the army of the Confederacy and in Memphis in post war days. He defended vigorously his medical views which did not always agree with current practice. One instance where his passionate arguments prevailed was at the beginning of the Yellow Fever epidemic in 1878. He urged that camps be set up outside of the city for the poor from the districts where the fever was most virilent. This counteraction was consistent with some of the current thinking about the disease because the real cause had not yet been identified. Yellow Fever was thought to be spread by filthy conditions of which there were plenty in the city. One visitor insisted Cairo, Egypt was a

[1] Compiled from accounts in the **Dictionary of American Biography**, the **National Encyclopedia**, vol 13, **Virginia Magazine of History and Geneology** vol 2, pp. 91-92; Philip A. Bruce, **Economic History of Virginia in the Seventeenth Century, an Inquiry into the Material Conditions of the People, Based upon Original and Contemporaneous Records** (N.Y., 1935) Vol. II.

cleaner place. To reduce the chance of infection disinfectants were used and people were warned not to go out at night. Thus the camps which were intially built with the thousand tents furnished by the army and some wooden structures were models of cleanliness. Here the death roll was low even in the one set up for the Colored who in previous infestations suffered little but this time their immunity was gone. Somewhere, Paul became infected and died on 28 September. Seemingly he was worn out from overwork.

The **Memphis Appeal** in its tribute to him said, "genial, kind, tender and true his memory will live in the hearts of those of his friends who survive him." **The Memphis Daily Appeal** declared: "...the public quick to overlook eccentricities of habit, thought or conviction, will forget whatever of these cropped out in him and hold him in affectionate remembrance as a physician who never wearied of well doing."[1]

* * * * * *

Confusion exists regarding James Hervey Otey's academic degrees. According to Moultrie Guerry, author of **Men Who Made Sewanee**, the future bishop graduated from the University of North Carolina with a degree in Belles Lettres, "a distinction hitherto unknown to the institution."[2] It must have been unique because today the schools credits him with an AB. In 1823 he acquired an MA which was neither earned nor was it honorary. Instead the MA was bestowed during the period before 1875 when alumni who requested the degree were usually granted it. Since then it is considered a special degree and is marked with an asterick(*). The DD was given the Bishop by Columbia College when he visited New York shortly after being consecrated in 1834. Guerry lists this as an STD which was awarded in 1833. Bishop Green, however, in titling his **Memoir** of Otey put an DD after his friend's name. There is no dispute about the LLD from North Carolina.[3]

[1] Compiled from the **Memphis Avalanche** and **The Memphis Daily Appeal** for August and September 1878 and P. Robbins, "Alas Memphis" [1878]. **American History Illustrated** Vol 16, Jan. '82, pp. 38-46.
[2] pp. 2 and 10.
[3] "Honorary Degrees—More than 600 Have Been Given by the University," **University Alumni Review** [North Carolina] March 1970 pp. 6-7ff.

Selected BIBLIOGRAPHY

The following sources were consulted:

Manuscript

James Hervey Otey, Diary 1852. This manuscript is in the Southern Historical Collection, Wilson Library, Univerity of North Carolina at Chapel Hill.

Printed Sources

Coxe, Arthur C., **Impressions of England: or Sketches of English Scenery and Society**, 5th ed., Philadelphia, 1863. Unfortunately this account is limited to England and says nothing about his joint travels with Otey in Scotland and Ireland.

Crabbe, Alfred Leland, ed., "Letters Over the Water," **Tennessee Historical Quarterly**, XVI (Sept. 1957).

Green, Rt. Rev. William Mercer, D.D., Bishop of Mississippi, **Memoir of Rt. James Hervey Otey D.D., L.L.D., the First Bishop of Tennessee**, New York, 1885.

Journal of the Proceedings of the twenty-fourth Annual Convention of the Clergy and Laity of the Protestant Episcopal Church in the Diocese of Tennessee.... 5, 6, 7, & 8 May 1852.

Journal of .... the 25th Annual Convention 1853.

Journal of .... the 30th Annual Convention 1858.

Maney, Henry, **Memories Over the Waters or Stray Thoughts on a Long Stroll** with an introduction by the Honorable Edwin H. Ewing, Nashville, 1854.

McGavock, Randal W., **A Tennessean Abroad, Letters from Europe, Africa, and Asia**. New York 1854.

Pen and Sword, The Life and Journals of Randal W. McGavock, Colonel C.S.A., Edited by Herschel Gower and Jack Allen, Nashville, 1959.

White, William, **Memoirs of the Protestant Episcopal Church in the USA from Its Organization to the Present Day**. 2nd. ed., New York, 1836.

Without the information provided by these encyclopedias and dictionaries much of the biographical material in the footnotes would not have been available to the researcher here in Upper East Tennessee.

The many volumned **Dictionary of National Biography** founded by

George Smith and later edited by others was in most instances the first source consulted for facts on English personages.

For Americans it was the **Dictionary of American Biography**, initially edited by Allen Johnson.

Boase, Frederick, **Modern English Biographies.** London, 1897, Reprint 1965. These short accounts are more on the order of Who's Who. Apparently many of the people listed are not included in the **Dictionary of National Biography.**

Burke's Peerage and Baronetage was a useful tool in identifying those nobility not significant enough to be in the **Dictionary of National Biography**.

The **National Cyclopedia of American Biography** supplied material on a few Americans not in the other series.

The **New Catholic Encyclopedia**, 1967 edition, is more in the tradition of this style reference work.

Gillow, Joseph, **A Literary and Biographical History of Bibliographical Dictionary of English Catholics From the Breach with Rome in 1534 to the Present Time**, New York, 1884 is what the title describes.

London Encyclopedia, edited by Ben Weinreb is place oriented associating people with various streets, buildings and sections of the greater city.

Oxford Dictionary of the Christian Religion is more theme or topic oriented than person.

Shell Guide to England, edited by John Hadfield. NY: 1970. A book filled with information about most English communities.

These printed works supply a background:

Albright, Raymond W., **A History of the Protestant Episcopal Church**. New York: 1964.

Armentrout, Donald Smith, **James Hervey Otey, First Episcopal Bishop of Tennessee**, Published by the Episcopal Diocese of Tennessee, 1984.

Bowen, Desmond, **The Idea of the Victorian Church, a Study of the Church of England 1833-1889**. Toronto, 1968.

Briggs, Asa, **Victorian People, A Reassessment of Persons and Themes, 1851-67**. Chicago: 1970.

The Anglican Episcopate in Connecticut (1784-1899), A Sheaf of Biographical and Institutional Studies for Churchmen and Historians with early Ecclesiastical Documents, Edited by Kenneth Walter Cameron. Hartford, CT.: 1970.

Crowther, M.A., **Church Embattled: Religious Controversy in Mid**

Victorian England., Newton Abbott, Devon and Hamden, Ct.: 1970.

Davies-Rodgers, Ellen, **The Romance of the Episcopal Church in West Tennessee 1832-1964.** Memphis: n.d.

Guerry, Moultrie, **Men Who Made Sewanee, For Makers of Sewanee Today.** Second edition, revised. Sewanee, TN, 1944.

Kellogg, John Harvey, **Rational Hydrotherapy, a manual of Physiological and Therapeutic Effects of Hydriatic Procedures and the Technique of Their Application in the Treatment of Disease.** Battle Creek, MI, 1923.

Lochhead, Marion, **Episcopal Scotland in the Nineteenth Century,** London, 1966.

Mackenzie, Agnes Mure, **The Kingdom of Scotland, a Short History.** Edinburgh: 1948, reprint.

Price, Robin, "Hydropathy in England 1840-70," **Medical History** Vol. 25 (1981) pp. 269-280.

Priestly, J.B., **Victoria's Heyday,** London: 1972.

Purple Sewanee, A Reprint of "Sewanee" by permission of the copyright owner, Charles E. Thomas and surviving editors Charles Gailor and Sarah Hodgson renamed to conform to common usuage. Supplement and Index added. Sewanee: Copyright 1961.

Solway R.A.,, **Prelates and People, Ecclesiatical Thought in England 1788-1852.** London: 1969.